What Is English?

Peter Elbow

The Modern Language Association of America
New York, New York

The National Council of Teachers of English
Urbana, Illinois

Library of Congress Cataloging-in-Publication Data

Elbow, Peter.
    What Is English? / Peter Elbow.
      p. cm.
    Includes bibliographical references.
    ISBN 0-87352-381-4 (cloth) ISBN 0-87352-382-2 (paper)
    1. English Coalition Conference (1987 : Wye Plantation)
    2. English philology—Study and teaching—United States.
    3. Language arts—United States. I. Title.
    PE1068.U5E47   1990
    420′.7′073—dc20   90-44931

Third printing 1995

Published by
The Modern Language Association of America
10 Astor Place, New York, New York 10003-6981

The National Council of Teachers of English
1111 Kenyon Road, Urbana, Illinois 61801

Contents

Preface

W hat is English?" The title is not intended as a question I can answer with my book, not a slow lob that I can try to hit for a home run. The title *is* my answer, my summing up, my picture of the profession. This book is trying to paint a picture of a profession that cannot define what it is. I don't mean this as scandal, and I don't take our not knowing as the most important news from the English Coalition Conference (if it was news). Yes, it might be more comfortable and convenient if we knew just what English studies is, but this very absence of comfort and convenience in the profession is probably a good thing. English is percolating at various levels, and I don't think anyone can know where it's going to end up. On good days I even say, "It's about time we finally don't know what we are."

I've been nervous about this book from the beginning—a long time ago. I accepted the invitation of the MLA Executive Council to write a book about the 1987 English Coalition Conference, but only when it was made clear to me that I was being invited to write exploratory and subjective reflections rather than a full or official reporting. What I have written, then, is a series of professional and personal ruminations on the conference and, in doing so, sometimes on the profession of English itself.

The official report, *The English Coalition Conference: Democracy through Language*, was edited by Richard Lloyd-Jones and Andrea A. Lunsford. (Conference participants are listed in appendix A and are also identified by level—elementary, secondary, or college—in the appendix and in the interludes that appear between my chapters. The distinctions between levels are not always neat, however, since many members of the ele-

v

mentary and secondary groups are both school teachers and university faculty members and three of the college faculty members, Wayne Booth, Bob Denham, and Richard Lloyd-Jones, were members of the secondary section at the conference.) In addition, members of the elementary section at the conference have published a book about the conference: *Stories to Grow On: Demonstrations of Language Learning in K–8 Classrooms*, edited by Julie Jensen. That book contains the full report of the elementary members of the conference but consists principally of helpful, extended stories of what their recommendations for teaching and learning actually look like in the classroom.

My nervousness has made me clarify for myself my goals for the book. First, I hope that what I write about the conference will be "fair" in the limited sense that people who were there will say, "Yes, that's the conference I was at; he hasn't really distorted things or given a twisted picture. He's left out a lot, and he's imbued it with his own preoccupations and biases, but he's been open about showing what those preoccupations and biases are." I'll be disappointed if participants say, "But that's not really how we talked or felt about it"—though it's hard to imagine I can succeed at this goal. For example, I have permitted myself at numerous points to write phrases like "participants said" or "participants argued." This is obviously problematic. It is my shorthand for "I had a sense that most people tended to feel"—and I acknowledge that it does violence to the wide divergence of views at any moment. I probably have a weakness for trying to find commonality of view.

Second, I hope that what I say can help all of us in the profession to think about important current issues. That is, though I have tried to evoke some of the details and flavor of what it was like being at the conference (I have started each chapter with an epigraph more or less copied from my notes about a particular moment or event or detail from the three weeks at Wye), I hope that people who weren't at the conference will be able to say something like this: "He isn't just trying to memorialize a long-past local gathering. He's used his account of the conference and his reflections on issues implicit at the conference to throw useful light on important matters for English." In my reflections I am exploring some of the tensions that I sense were present in the conference, tensions I find in myself and ultimately, I think, tensions that are in the profession.

I have tried to be a reliable narrator, but that's even more hubristic than trying to speak about a whole profession. It would be nice if my deviations were always in the direction of Huck or Gawain—or the Chaucer of the *Tales*. But I've been warned that I tend to drift more toward two other heroes of mine, Alice and Gulliver.

A note about the structure of the book: The earlier chapters, though not by any means designed as careful reporting, are somewhat more directly focused on the conference than the later chapters are. That is, in the earlier chapters I am trying to summarize what was said at Wye or figure out what it meant. In the later chapters I permit my focus to drift further from the conference in order to explore and reflect on important issues that were emergent or even latent at the conference. (Two exceptions to this structure: I put the chapter "Goals and Testing" late in the book because of the nature of the topic—but in that chapter I explore how the conference handled these issues; similarly, I put my second theory chapter (ch. 5) early in the book so as to link it to the first theory chapter, but I use it as an occasion for examinations that some might call distant from the conference.) I have relegated to the appendix section two short essays that, though they relate to conference issues, propose a couple of particular and concrete educational changes. As proposals for change, they are liable to raise a different kind of response or even controversy, and I hope that their location as appendixes will keep any such reactions from clouding responses to the main body of the book.

The genre of the book I have written is somewhat blurred. There's a bit of narrative and description of what happened at the conference, a bit of summary of participants' views. But mostly I am writing my own reflections long after the conference—reflections as I read over my notes and write out thoughts and feelings, look at what I write, invite others to read it, and finally write and revise more.

But there is also lots here that I didn't write. I have sought a way to get the voices of many of the conference participants into the book. Between each of my chapters I have put a selection of short pieces written by those participants. The pieces tell of their perceptions and experiences as teachers and learners: stories, verbal snapshots, reflections on experience, accounts of the teaching or cultural situation. Most of these interludes were written during the conference, though some were written beforehand in position papers and a few afterward. Even more important, these interludes illustrate a main theme of the conference: the importance of stories as a form of knowledge—not necessarily polished, literary stories but the everyday stories we tell each other in passing. Since everything that was concluded at the conference and everything I conclude in these pages derive ultimately from experience, I see the stories and my chapters functioning to some degree as corrective to one another. If something I say doesn't fit the stories, that's probably a sign that what I say is wrong. Also, most of the pieces were written by members of the elementary and secondary sections and so will serve somewhat to counterbalance my writing from the point of view of a member of the college section.

But I didn't write the book to fit the interludes. I'd read them either during or right after the conference and was immediately sure I would use them between my chapters. I put them aside, however, for what turned out to be more than two years while I was struggling with my book and thinking, "Well at least I don't have to look at the stories— they're already done—I'll just throw them in where they fit." But they don't always fit neatly into the themes of the chapters. In the end, I intend them to be frankly interruptive—I like a broken structure, a relief, a polyvocal collage effect. (More about stories in chapter 10, "Questioning Two Assumptions.")

About my quotations of what was said at the conference: I don't go as far as Thucydides did and put in people's mouths what they "ought to have said," but I have been working from notes and do not claim exactness. For this reason I use quotations sparingly. But as I was taking notes at the conference, I tried to capture key words and phrases, not just gists, so my quotations are attempts not just to summarize but to get some of the flavor of how people made points. Occasionally, more or less in passing, I use unattributed quotations. (It's not becuase I can't remember who said it: when I can't, I say so.) In these cases I am trying to make audible what I feel was a major idea or feeling—something that was prominently in the air and that probably was said by more than one person. I also include short passages from my notes (often as epigraphs to chapters). These are fairly faithful transcriptions from the ongoing stream of notes I took, but I have slightly clarified, cleaned up, and expanded them to make them understandable.

I have sometimes used notes to add passages that might illustrate or give a counter view to the story I am telling. These are sometimes passages from reports of individual sessions and sometimes excerpts from responses by people who read earlier drafts of my chapters.

This book has taken a long time. I've had a chance for second and third thoughts, and I've been lucky to get many helpful responses to earlier drafts from participants and nonparticipants at the conference. I am enormously grateful for the much needed help and support I got from the following people who gave me thoughtful and extensive comments: Paul Armstrong, Carol Avery, Pat Belanoff, Marie Buncombe, Paul Connolly, Angela Dorenkamp, Sidney Feshbach, Joan Hartman, Shirley Brice Heath, Anne Herrington, Betsy Hilbert, Richard Johnson, Richard Larson, David Laurence, Andrea Lunsford, Kathleen McCormick, Nancy McHugh, George Moberg, Helene Moglen, Charles Moran, Joseph Moxley, Twyla Papay, Susan Stires, Eleanor Tignor, Elizabeth Wallace, and Art Young. My grateful thanks go also to the thoughtful editors at MLA: Joe Hollander, Alicia Mahaney, Elizabeth Holland, and Rebecca Lanning—and to the anonymous MLA reviewers.

From a Letter to Wayne Booth

Nellie McKay
(college section)

HERE ARE MY reflections on the conference. You may do with them as you wish while you contemplate your book. . . .

The evening before I left for the conference, I had dinner with friends. . . . They were skeptical of what would come out of such a gathering, noting that these meetings are generally gatherings of the "stars" in the profession, and the people who do the work in the "trenches" are usually left out. From Wye Woods I sent a postcard to my friends, gleefully noting that the "stars" were few in number at this meeting and that the majority of the participants were indeed the people in the trenches. Frankly, I was impressed by the makeup of the group and learned a great deal from listening to those who are more in the trenches than I am—not only elementary and secondary school teachers but especially from those who teach in community colleges. . . .

In the last several years I have given only minimal time to what we were talking about as "the teaching of reading, writing, speaking, and listening" or to prime issues in the way students learn, although I consider myself a "good" teacher. Part of the blame for that comes from the pressures that those of us who have recently entered the university feel in terms of the artificial split between research and teaching.

In the struggle to achieve tenure, we are encouraged to concentrate, not on how best to help students to learn, but on individual research and publishing. Thus, by the time we have achieved that goal (and six years is a long time for such socialization), we have almost forgotten that the reason we were attracted to the profession in the first place was a love of literature and the wish to bring young people to love it too. The seduction of seeing one's name in print has by then taken over.

The conference was especially good for me as a reminder that at least a half of my business ought to be about students—how they learn and

1

how I facilitate that. By the end of the first week I began to think of them in different ways than I had done in years. . . .

Since I do not teach composition as such, I now suspect that most of my teaching over the last few years has been content-oriented, in a manner in which I do not hold myself responsible for how students read and write, listen and speak. On the other hand, I am outraged when they cannot perform these functions to my satisfaction. This is the first time I have had to question my pedagogy. In the large introductory courses that we teach in a university as large as Madison (and here I think of courses with several hundred students in "English" and even the smaller intro-ductory courses in Afro-American literature, where the numbers usually hover around a hundred), there are few opportunities to interact with individual students. However, in smaller classes, say of forty-five or less, there is a lot of room for close attention to students, if one makes the effort. The trouble, as I see it, for many younger faculty members in institutions where the rewards are given almost solely for research is the lack of incentive to be concerned about students as learners at the risk of career advancement. Our system seems intent on proving Darwin's theory in terms of both students and younger faculty members, who teach the large courses and are expected to produce quantities of scholarship that may have small relationship to anything they teach.

Thus I suspect that part of my reaction to the conference is a kind of pessimism regarding how much impact those of us who were there can have on the overall system. Personally I can make some adjustments in my own thinking in respect to students whom I see in small classes, but I am not hopeful many of my colleagues, with their research orientation, will change very much, even after more information on the conference becomes widespread public knowledge. Still the conference was a very good thing to do, and many of us who were there will be nourished by it for a long time. . . . [McKay goes on to talk of things she wants to try in her teaching, such as small groups.]

So the conference gave me ideas for teaching that I might implement immediately. For the last few years I've been more concerned with my own "work" and nonclassroom professional activities: with finding a place for myself in the large "Profession." It was quite refreshing to be with a group of teachers who cared about teaching/learning and students for a change. I would like to think there is room in the profession to do both—good teaching and important research. . . .

1 | Introduction: About the English Coalition Conference

*S*omeone reads his summary report on a college section meeting to the entire plenary group. It's rambling and much too long; people get visibly irritated. Then Bill Teale reports for the elementary group, and he is crisp, clear, helpful. He took the time to figure out what happened—to make a meaning out of their meeting—whereas the college reporter did not. (Or was the elementary meeting itself more focused?) Teale is complimented on the report. He smiles and says, "We elementary teachers do what we're told." A deft zinger. In effect, "Notice how we are always getting told what to do—especially by university people. But notice too, by the way, how we often do a better job than the people giving us orders." But wholly tacit and gracious. A pointed moment; the tensions between levels.

THE IMPULSE behind the English Coalition Conference of 1987 was to have a kind of twenty-year follow-up to the Dartmouth Conference of 1966 (on that conference, see Dixon; Muller). When I first read about the Dartmouth Conference, I felt a mixture of things: "Oh gee, if only they'd invited me; it sounds so interesting; they seem to know so much." But also, "What do those supposedly learned authorities know? If they want to talk about reading and writing and the learning process, I could tell them more from my experience than all their fancy scholarship and research." Now, as I finish writing this book, I imagine readers feeling the same things (and I hear knives sharpening) about the sixty of us put up for three weeks in Maryland and invited to think deep thoughts about "the profession."

In 1987 we were larger and more representative of the whole profession than the group at Dartmouth. They were forty-six to our sixty; they had no school teachers, only six women, and a higher proportion of senior eminent people (though they had participants from England and Canada, not just from the United States). I think their group had a heavier representation of people interested in learning and learning theory; ours had a heavier representation of people interested in literary studies. Another interesting difference was the presence of five community college teachers at our conference. Community colleges were already a significant presence in higher education in 1966 but were not represented at Dartmouth. Now, of course, they can be said to rival four-year institutions in importance, if not in prestige. And it sounds to me that they had a more learned, scholarly time of it—more paper reading—though this may be a trick of perspective: to freshmen, seniors look so glamorous and wise—but when we get to be seniors, it looks like we're just mucking along as we've always done.

The "coalition" in the title of our 1987 conference was a coalition of the eight major professional organizations in English: the Association of Departments of English (ADE), the College English Association (CEA), the Conference on English Education (CEE), the College Language Association (CLA), the Conference on College Composition and Communication (CCCC), the Modern Language Association (MLA), the Conference of Secondary School English Department Chairs (CSSEDC), and the National Council of Teachers of English (NCTE). The planning had gone on for a couple of years and in a sense can be traced back to 1982, when a small group of officers of most of those organizations started meeting at the major conferences in the profession (the annual MLA, NCTE, and CCCC conferences). But these ongoing and informal meetings did not have a stable membership: they were attended by whichever officers happened to be at a given conference, especially since officers tend to change from year to year. People joked that a floating crap game planned the conference so it would be hard to finger the guilty parties if the conference flopped. But the two executive directors, Phyllis Franklin of the MLA and Jack Maxwell of NCTE, were there most of the time and repeatedly stuck their necks out to make the conference finally happen.

Our sixty participants came from three levels—elementary, secondary, and college/university, the last group being the largest of the three. Participants were chosen by the eight organizations, but there was relatively little sense at the conference of people "representing" an organization. Participants chosen by the MLA were named by the Executive Council, the body that appoints members of most MLA committees. I'm not sure how it worked with other organizations. No matter what the process, there were inevitably some misgivings and resentment about who was invited. Nevertheless, as Nellie McKay points out in her letter, which precedes this introduction, it wasn't all "stars" and no "troops in the trenches." There were gray heads and gray beards, but we were a relatively young and lively bunch. That is, though many participants were well known and well published in the profession, probably only Wayne Booth, Janet Emig, Richard Lloyd-Jones, and Robert Scholes count as venerable sages.

The spirit at the conference reflected a bit more commitment to teaching than to scholarship. It's not that we *lacked* any commitment to scholarship, but I sensed a tacit premise that teaching was in more danger than scholarship. That is, the collective concern was more for the future of our institutions as teaching institutions and for the future of our students than for the future of scholarship. In addition, of course, well over half of us were K–12 teachers not defined as scholars or publishers or given much time and encouragement in that direction—though plenty of the schoolteachers among us had in fact published significant work. In short, one could say (and it was said) that we didn't have as heavy a representation of lustrous senior figures who identified themselves primarily as scholars or researchers.[1]

Funding for the conference came mostly from the Andrew W. Mellon and Rockefeller foundations, with additional support from the Exxon Education Foundation and the National Endowment for the Humanities (not to mention considerable support from the coalition organizations themselves). What was in it for the foundations? one may well ask. I haven't worked at uncovering hidden agendas—taking at face value their acceptance of the planners' stated goals:

> to reach across levels of schooling in a constructive way; to see if a consensus about the teaching of English could be achieved; and to identify solutions to the problems that teachers of English have been encountering as a result of changes in the student population, in institutional and community circumstances, and in the field itself. (Franklin 2)

The planning committee required all participants to write short position papers *before* the conference (on topics laid out by the planners). These were reproduced and distributed beforehand or on the opening day. This arrangement had beneficial results: we couldn't just arrive in a passive mood—sitting back and waiting to see what others would say. We had all been required to "put out" in advance—to reveal not only a piece of our views but also a piece of ourselves, as one inevitably does in a position paper (and few participants settled for reticent essays). We had to do all this writing and reading before getting a chance to meet or listen to others. As a result, there was little time spent in that familiar process of everyone defensively sniffing everyone else—trying to keep one's own views under wraps till one can see what other people think.

The published schedule was daunting: full work days every day—including both Saturdays and one Sunday. As it happened, the troops revolted a bit, and we ended up with a schedule that was merely heavy—not compulsive. We typically met all morning and much of the afternoon and some evenings—and this went on for three weeks. Even with our revolt, we didn't get out of those two Saturdays and one Sunday.

During the three weeks of the conference, everyone met daily in both "A-strand" and "B-strand" groups. The A-strand groups represented primary affiliations: elementary, high school, and college. The B-strand groups were mixed gatherings that each contained members from all three levels. To make for even more cross-fertilization, the populations of these B-strand groups were shuffled each week. Thus, by the end, everyone had been in a small group with a majority of the other sixty participants.

This weekly shuffling of membership in B-strand groups may have heightened the sense of the A-strand group as "primary"; nevertheless —and this is a manifestation of perhaps the main fact about the process of the whole conference—numerous people remarked that discussion was more fruitful and rewarding in the heterogeneous B strands than in the stratified A strands. Somehow, from the beginning, people seemed to feel the need to learn from, listen to, and find a way to talk to one another across educational levels—rather than huddle: not only for the sake of the conference but for the sake of the profession.

In short, it might be that the biggest news from the English Coalition Conference was that an unwieldy, oversized group of well-respected English teachers and scholars from kindergarten through graduate school can work together productively: with mutual respect and pleasure; without that edginess, defensiveness, hyperpoliteness, and condescension that so often characterize these attempts. Most participants said they'd never seen school and college people work together so well —an observation echoed by numerous visitors.[2]

Why this productive interaction? Was it that the planning committee and participating organizations had the sense to choose *us* rather than our impossible colleagues? Or that we were all tired out from a year of behaving badly and decided to take a break and behave well for three weeks? It helped enormously that we all had to write position papers first and that we were immediately plunged into both stratified and mixed groups. Perhaps most of all we knew we were stuck with one another for three weeks in weather that was unmercifully hot and meeting rooms that were inhumanely cool. We're in the same boat; we better learn to get along; we have work to do.

Work to do. In fact, this was an interesting perplexity. For in truth we did *not* have an explicit task. That is, at the start we were told that there were not to be final reports. The plan was—to put it crudely—to sit around and discuss. Yes, there was an agenda of topics for each day, and we had to take minutes and publish a report on each session, and (as I learned after the fact) the planners had hopes that a consensus would emerge. But we weren't asked to agree on conclusions. There would be no final report, just a "Record of the Conference" drawn from all those minutes. (For the first week, much meeting time was devoted to hearing summaries of discussions in other meetings—for the sake of maximum dialogue and overhearing. We all protested and had this feature cut back, but we kept up written reporting—putting a strain on photocopying facilities that was finally too much for them.)

You might say that this plan represented a fierce commitment to process rather than product. The planning committee told us that they had adopted the arrangement because of their experience with previous conferences that became bogged down by everyone having to agree on conclusions and especially on the exact wordings of resolutions; that this forced consensus led to interminable bickering and parliamentary maneuvering; and most of all that documents were continually watered down and made opaque or meaningless because of the problem of having to meet everyone's objection.

At first I was dismayed when I heard the plan. I like discussion, but three weeks? Yet I was also intrigued. In a sense it was an attempt to invite more discord and disagreement, more risk taking, more adventure, by keeping people from being handcuffed to that final report that they kept imagining their colleagues back home reading. This was the planning committee setting an example of risk taking to try to persuade participants to talk turkey, to come to grips with what they really thought—perhaps even to change their thinking—instead of having to be wary and political and always play it safe.

This arrangement didn't lead to unrelieved disagreement. Gerald Graff, when he visited for a day and a half, accused us of not fighting enough, but I saw no fear of disagreement or lack of honesty. What happened, I think, was that by the time the conference was half done, we all felt a strong urge to struggle toward some genuine agreement. We couldn't stand the idea of this much good discussion and thinking not coming to some solid results. This urge, of course, grew from a foundation of sensing, even from the position papers, that there was a lot of *potential* consensus to be had—much more than any of us had expected. We couldn't bear not to record some of it. (Or was it just the normal perversity of academics: "If they're trying to tell us not to agree, we'll fix *their* wagons!") In short, we fairly soon came to an impelling sense that things need to be done for the health of the profession. Therefore we needed to see if we could hammer out some agreement.

I was enormously grateful for one striking legacy of that original no-closure plan. When it came to making our final reports in the last week, there was remarkably little political maneuvering about wording: wrestling, haggling, watering down, sabotaging. The rule of thumb was this: "No fair quarreling about wording; there will be a subcommittee after the conference to edit these reports and create a small pamphlet by way of redaction, and they will take care of wording." This principle was often invoked whenever discussion fetched up on a snag about wording, and it is a remarkable testimony to the people involved and the spirit of trust that had emerged by the third week that we were willing to go along with this trust-oriented plan of operation. Remarkably, this final editorial group (Lloyd-Jones and Lunsford, who were editors of the official report) was not even chosen till the last day. You might say that we all disqualified ourselves as bona fide academics by passing up so many opportunities to quibble over wording. We ended up on the last day with documents that I admired for their roughness—that did indeed express the spirit of what people were figuring out and agreeing on among themselves. ("Admirably rough" isn't fair to those groups that wrote skilled and even elegant pieces—most of them from the elementary group.)

The original plan was that these drafts would be ratified only by the strands that had produced them, but in the final two days, we found we wanted to get all documents ratified by the whole conference of sixty.

Thus my sense of the spirit of the conference as a whole was this: lively, perky, a bit fractious at times, but also with an instinct for play; an intense commitment to teaching, students, and the health of the institutions that educate our children and older students; a deep underlying hunger to "get somewhere" or get something done or make progress.

About me and my point of view: I was very much a participant and member of the conference, not just an observer (and also, not at all a planner). I toyed with the idea of sitting back and mostly observing and trying not to affect the conversation, but after the first half hour I realized I couldn't play that role. Participants knew from the beginning that I'd been invited to write my observations and reflections about the conference, but I didn't sense that this much influenced how I was treated. Thus, I write as a member of the Coalition Conference but also partly as an observer—referring to participants sometimes as "we" and sometimes as "they." I've become more of an observer in retrospect as I spend so many months going over my notes and reflecting on what I see.

My decision to be a participant led me to stay in the college section and for the most part not to observe elementary or high school section meetings. In short, my view of the conference is that of someone most concerned with university issues in English—and someone who has never taught in elementary or high school. My assumptions and biases will show through clearly enough in the chapters that follow (and people came to make fun of *situate* as a jargon term from the theory game), but it also feels important for me, as reporter and reflector on this conference, to describe more explicitly the particular life situation from which I participated in and observed the conference and from which I write these reflections. I do so in appendix D.

NOTES

[1] Paul Armstrong, in a response to a draft, makes an interesting observation about the position of many participants vis-à-vis the profession and our institutions. He says that in my writing I "betray a sense of being an outsider," and he goes on to say he shares that sense too:

> Isn't this a paradox that characterized many of us at Wye? We were there because we were marked as "authorities" in various ways, but most of us also feel we're antiestablishment, or at least reformers—"outsiders" in some ways to the institutions we're "inside."

[2] Shirley Brice Heath remarks (in a response to draft, 24 Jan. 1989) on

> the dominant conversational nature of the group; even in many of the large sessions, people grouped their chairs as though primed for conversation. The setting certainly supported that mode, but I sense something deeper going on in a group whose members knew they were there to converse and learn and not to reach consensus and write administrative reports.

Our Challenges: The Academic Problems Students Face

Jane Peterson
(college section)

*F*OR FIFTEEN YEARS, I have taught at Richland College, an open-door community college that draws primarily middle- and upper middle-class students. Most of our thirteen thousand students work, take fewer than twelve hours a semester, and are white. We have a few blacks and Hispanics, some refugees from Southeast Asia, and a small but growing number of international students. Although the average student age is 27.5, most day students are 18–24 years old and most night students 25–40 years old. Within the seven-campus Dallas County Community College District, Richland is seen as the "academic campus," with a high percentage of students enrolled in transfer courses or two-year technical programs with strong ties to traditional disciplines (e.g., management, educational paraprofessional, robotics). In short, the students whose problems I describe are more advantaged than many community college students, yet they face a range of academic problems.

These middle-class students exhibit most of the problems receiving public attention. Their papers contain misspellings, incorrect word forms, comma splices—all the usual surface errors. Their comments and questions reveal limited vocabularies, a lack of much of the shared background information E. D. Hirsch considers part of cultural literacy, and ignorance of current local, national, and international events and issues. This litany of what students do not know could go on and on, for these problems are increasing not only in number but in intensity (e.g., individual students make more surface errors on papers) and scope (e.g., native speakers as well as ESL students have difficulties with prepositions).

Though the litany grows longer, its essence remains unchanged. For students, it represents difficulties, the level of information and skills that they lack but expect to acquire in college. For teachers, it represents symptoms of another more serious level of academic problems. Let me use a new and rather trivial comma error to illustrate.

Ten years ago, students had problems with commas, but they were familiar enough with basic print conventions to know that "it looked funny" for a line to begin with a comma. Now I see lines that begin with commas—and not just from basic writers and ESL students. When I ask about those commas, I am sometimes told that they have to be there because "the comma goes before the conjunction" and sometimes that they have to be there "for the space on the other side to be right." What bothers me is not the error, which is a variation of a familiar difficulty and easy to remedy, but the explanations of it that suggest a second level of problems—tremendous literalism, a love of rigid rules, and a focus on physical attributes.

Difficulties in reading reflect similar problems. If asked to read pages 63–78, many developmental students will begin reading at the top of page 63, not at the heading. Freshman composition students will read the text pages assigned but won't look at examples that appear within those pages. Both groups of incoming students resist making notes in their textbooks or highlighting, not because (as I first thought) they have extended high school prohibitions into an "it is wrong to write in books" rule, but because (they say) they will lose money when they sell their books. Literalism and pragmatism (today's brand of relevance) abound, and few students see textbooks as tools for learning or reading as an active process of making meaning.

This suggests another set of serious problems: the limited concepts students have of what an education is and what writing, reading, and learning involve. Our students approach college more as consumers than as learners. They enroll in courses to get an education. For most, getting an education means receiving credits or a degree that will increase earning power; learning means attending classes, doing assignments, and going through other motions that lead to credits. Along the way, students expect to pick up discrete pieces of information and develop isolated skills, but they do not expect to engage in the exciting but often risky and frustrating process of learning. They seldom seek connections between example and text, exercise and assignment, the current assignment and the previous one, skills developed in one course and their uses in another, ideas discussed in one course and their implications for another, or the analytical and evaluative skills they use at home and work and those they need in college. Most define learning in concrete, additive terms, as a series of isolated activities, not as an interactive process of questioning, generating possibilities, and seeking connections to make meaning.

Because writing and reading are integrally related to one another and to learning, this limited concept of learning also means limited concepts of what writing and reading involve. Most students conceive of writing primarily as a series of physical activities—putting words on paper, correcting errors, recopying—not a complex process of making and communicating meaning. They cast thinking in a subordinate role, limited to "getting an idea" (i.e., finding one, not generating and playing with possibilities) and remembering and applying rules. Their concepts of reading are similarly limited. Instead of seeing reading as a dynamic, interactive process of questioning, predicting, and seeking connections, they view it as a matter of recognizing and decoding words.

Evidence of their concrete, limited concepts of both writing and reading abounds in our classrooms, but I can only offer a few examples here. For writing, consider their first questions about assignments. Basic writers ask if they can use pencil or write on the backs of pages. Freshmen and sophomores ask, "Does it have to be typed, or can I use a dot matrix printer?" Students in every class ask, "How long does it have to be?" When I respond to questions about length with "it depends" or "long enough to communicate your point clearly to your readers," students listen politely and say, "yes, but how long does it *have* to be?'" They are far more concerned about the physical attributes of final products than the content, and the idea of subordinating physical concerns to making and communicating meaning is foreign.

Their concepts of reading vary from the almost purely physical view of developmental students (who often see reading as a matter of moving their eyes over every word on the assigned pages) to the functional view of second-semester freshmen and sophomores (who see it as a matter of literal comprehension, of being able to summarize). Tom Dodge, a colleague from a sister campus, described a typical result: students who dismiss "The Lottery" as "a stupid story about a stupid town that selects someone every year to be stoned to death so the corn will grow." When given models for critical reading and pressed, most students can and will go through the motions that take them a bit beyond the literal, but they do so grudgingly, seeing neither value in the process nor use for the ideas discovered, and making it plain that in their eyes this interpreting, reaching for meaning is not a legitimate part of reading and not a legitimate demand.

Given their limited concepts of writing, reading, and learning, their resistance is understandable. They have enrolled in our courses with their own expectations and concepts, and they do not expect or wish them to change. They expect only to acquire the information and skills that will make them "better writers" (i.e., more proficient with surface features) and "better readers" (i.e., able to read more quickly and summarize the literal meaning accurately). They do *not* expect to become fully involved in the demanding, uncertain, and complex processes of learning and making meaning. In effect, most want to acquire an education that will increase their earning power, not engage in learning that might transform their beings.

The problems I have sketched that concern us most as English teachers are so closely connected they reverberate. The limited concepts students have of reading and writing reflect values and foster characteristics antithetical to real learning—the literalism, love of certainty and rigid rules, focus on physical activities and attributes, and pragmatism that we find when we scratch the surface of problems receiving public attention. What seems new is not the fact that students have limited expectations and concepts (when has it been otherwise?), but the effect of problems that are both widespread and closely connected. That effect is a critical gap between the liberal arts view of education held by most English teachers and the training view now held by most students.

Recognizing the gap is easy; interpreting it is not. And though I have taken a traditional approach here, assuming that the limited views of students are the problems to be solved, I want to conclude by questioning that assumption. For community college teachers whose institutions "market" programs and "sell" courses—not only exploiting the training view of education to recruit students but, in an important sense, validating it—it becomes increasingly possible that it is we, and not our students, who have serious problems. Our challenges may be greater than we have imagined.

Pat

Nancy McHugh
(secondary school section)

*P*AT WAS A gang leader. He said nothing, but others smiled or trembled as he walked past. The teacher was notified only much later in the semester about Pat's past and current status with the probation department and a string of other schools where he had either failed or been kicked out. He would have been a prime candidate for the lowest-level class in a tracked system because his skills were very poor, even though his ideas were good. He was a first-rate thinker and strategist.

In our nontracked school, he was placed in a senior writing class with all levels of students. At first he appeared to sneer at group work and assignments of any kind. Gradually, in spite of himself, he became interested in discussion groups preparatory to writing and in read-around groups between writing stages. He began to argue issues and logic with other students who were writing on argumentative topics. He helped one girl organize arguments in a very weak paper that had no real focus and thrust. In return she offered to proofread his paper. He had none, but he told her that he would "bring it tomorrow." They formed a team during most of the rest of the semester. She learned to organize better and to think and to value her ideas. He learned to teach, to revise and proofread, and to share. He was transferred again from our school before the end of the year, but he left with a B and with some extra facets to his education, none of which he would probably have had in a tracked class.

2 | A Remarkable Consensus about a Main Theme

A small group is talking after Shirley Brice Heath's presentation. People reflect on an interesting fact: no matter how much research seems to demonstrate that teaching grammar doesn't help speaking or writing (for a summary, see Hartwell), nothing seems to allay the deep impulse to teach grammar. Greg Ulmer makes an interesting suggestion: grammar shouldn't be taught till college; finally, he argues, students will be ready to appreciate its cognitive power and deep implication. People are intrigued but are scratching their heads. (More intriguing still, I recently noticed that this same proposal was put forward 150 years ago in an essay in the North American Review *[See "Popular Education"].)*

Heath cuts through the issue in an interesting way: "It's not a question of whether or when to teach grammar but how." *Teaching grammar makes sense even in kindergarten (she goes on to say), but it needs to be taught through an active, empirical, inductive process. Students from the youngest level can be asked to collect language usages (e.g., instances of asking, suggesting, inviting, and ordering), to work together to examine them up on the board, and to suggest hypotheses about forms and how they relate to different speakers or situations. "Language is a puzzle that kids of all ages can enjoy exploring. They can enjoy trying to state some of its more obvious rules—yet also gradually realize that we can never capture its full complexity." Heath is suggesting (and she acknowledges this and has tried it out extensively) that we can show even small children how to work like little participant-observer linguists or anthropologists—little linguistic hypothesis makers.*

IT WASN'T the mission of the conference to reach consensus—not even to produce an official report. Thus it was an event of note for sixty educators from kindergarten through college to reach consensus. I can't resist the narrative or mythic mode to set the context for how it happened. (One of the important texts for me and many others at the conference was Bruner's *Actual Minds, Possible Worlds.* I love to see how someone who gave us the classic research on thinking as categorizing or generalizing—looking for superordinate principles [*A Study of Thinking*]—now emphasizes narrative or storytelling as a central form of thinking.)

We were sixty of us holed up in a fortified castle or an enchanted garden. It was a lovely castle or garden in eastern Maryland, but we were stuck nevertheless for three weeks. A succession of knights came by to visit. The little drama I want to focus on here was that of Chester Finn and E. D. Hirsch laying siege to us and Shirley Brice Heath riding in on a white horse to the rescue. (Finn was assistant secretary for research and improvement, US Department of Education. Hirsch, professor of English at the University of Virginia, wrote *Cultural Literacy: What Every American Needs to Know*. Heath, professor of anthropology and linguistics at Stanford University, was awarded a MacArthur Fellowship for her ethnographic studies of literacy, such as those described in her *Ways with Words: Language, Life and Work in Communities and Classrooms*.)

Finn came on the first official day and gave a talk summarizing the history of recent educational reform movements. (He didn't say this, but most of them were movements or approaches that various government agencies had invested in heavily.) He implied that all the movements but one were spent, problematic, indeed discredited. But he argued that the last one—the reform movement centering on Hirsch's work on "cultural literacy"—finally represents a reform movement we can trust.

He ended his talk with some strong jabs at us. He fell into recounting examples of things that "kids don't know," talking, for instance, about the proportion of students who checked the box saying that Toronto is in Italy. (When people recount student blunders like this, I often get a whiff of tacit outrage and luscious prurience—like the flavor with which the puritan describes sexual sin. Perhaps I react this way because I teach writing.) People always come up to writing teachers to vent their sense of scandal at the latest grammatical mistake they've just seen a student commit—as though mistakes in grammar come from teachers and workbooks *not teaching grammar*. Finn said he wasn't blaming students—maintaining that this ignorance was the fault of schools and teachers. He ended by saying, "I implore you to catch up with the general public!" (He also "implored" us to make a list of the fifty to one hundred core works of literature for schools to teach and to figure out better ways to assess knowledge of literature. See appendix B.)

There are lots of arguments in the sessions that follow. Should we try to get Hirsch to come? Many people bash Hirsch; not a few stick up for him. Wayne Booth in particular maintained (what seemed right to me too), "Of course he's right underneath all this silliness about lists; you can't have reading without knowledge; 'schema theory' is obviously right; we all agree it's no good teaching empty skills without content." And even after the invitation to Hirsch was worked out, the bickering went on: "Let's not just fight him and make it nothing but adversarial." "Well why not? Are you trying to tell us we have to be on our best behavior for the famous visitor?" And, "Why should we waste all this time talking about Hirsch instead of about our real business?" At the session before he was to address us, we were supposed to be talking about a different topic; but as Chaucer says, the tongue returns to the aching tooth: "We're getting Hirsch at 10:30. Do we have to have him at 9?" (Betsy Hilbert).

By 10:30 he had indeed flown to our castle in a private chartered plane. The form of his argument troubled even those of us who had been sticking up for the basic cognitive case he was making. He put his emphasis squarely on what seemed most wrong-headed and peripheral to his case. He asked for a *narrowing* of national culture just at a time when most of us feel the need to affirm a multiplicity and plurality of cultures. He asked for a more restricted catalog of information and books to be taught just at a time when most participants feel that the list of what we should teach as literature must be wider. He emphasized one mode of reading (for information) just at a time when we all sense agreement in the profession that narrowly "right" and "proper" modes of reading are most problematic. He emphasized teaching small bits of information (putting the student into the position of passive recipient, and this is teaching *literature*, mind you) just at a time when participants feel the importance of opposite processes: reflecting and chewing on information, connecting larger units of study, and in general being cognitively active rather than passive. He stressed the teaching of a list—which invites teaching to be driven by objectively scored exams on small bits of information—just at a time when teachers feel enormous danger from school curricula that are being driven by testing. A telling moment came when he said it wasn't so important to read Shakespeare or see performances of the plays themselves—plot summaries or "Lamb's Tales" would do fine.

He acknowledged, of course, that his goal of teaching cultural literacy by teaching a list of terms and facts does not constitute all of teaching. "This is only extensive learning. Of course I'm for intensive learning too. But for cultural literacy we need this more surface-oriented extensive learning." However, he kept refusing to talk about intensive learning or learning for understanding. He kept stressing nothing but terms and information. And then his plane lifted him away.[1]

It was in this context that Shirley Brice Heath arrived a couple of days later to give a talk and meet with the smaller groups. She provided a conception of literacy and learning and teaching that was seminal for the conference. In effect she said that the central business of English studies has three main parts:

Using language actively in a diversity of ways and settings—that is, not only in the classroom as exercises for teachers but in a range of social settings with various audiences, where the language makes a difference.

Reflecting on language use. Turning back and self-consciously reflecting on how one has been using language—examining these processes of talking, listening, writing, and reading.

Trying to ensure that this using and reflecting go on in *conditions of both nourishment and challenge*, that is, conditions where teachers care about students themselves and what they actively learn—not just about skills or scores or grades.

What was important here was that Heath provided not only a train of thought but, above all, a set of terms that united people from elementary school through college. For until this point the different sections were talking different languages. The college section participants tended to use language that reflected a somewhat theoretical perspective: that we can't see things directly or know things in themselves; that we can never see stories or poems unmediated; that there are different kinds of reading, knowing, and interpreting that depend on our position or point of view; that knowing is mediated by language and by the other people around us; that therefore the business of college English studies is not just writing and reading but reflecting on the cultural scene of writing and reading and questioning what's really happening—"problematizing" these activities by seeing how they are always ideologically situated.

The elementary-strand participants, however, tended to use language that reflected a more practical pedagogic perspective: that the teacher's job is not just to get children to write and read but to write and read in such a way as to highlight the child as world builder or hypothesis maker.

The way of talking that probably best sums up this idea for all participants is this: learning involves the *making of meaning* and the *reflecting back on this process of making meaning*—not the ingestion of a list or a body of information. At all levels we stressed how this central activity is deeply social.[2] (It is worth noting that Heath and the conference participants were reinforcing a theme that has been emphasized for quite a while by Ann Berthoff. See her *Making of Meaning* and *Forming/Thinking/Writing*.)

In short, the main conclusion of the conference may be that we see the same constructive and social activity as the central process at all levels of the profession of English. Inherent in this overarching emphasis on making meaning is the principle of getting the learner to be active, not passive: learning as hypothesis making, world building, experiential—and active, especially in the process of questioning and reflecting back on what one has been doing.

Hirsch and Finn tended to frame the conversation in terms of a debate or a dichotomy between "solid content" and "empty skills." Participants kept trying to dismantle this dichotomy, stressing that you can't make meaning unless you are writing or reading about *something*; that practices are always practices *of* a content. (As Michael Halloran put it later, "It does seem to me we've been snookered a bit, conned into opposing general ideas that are sound, simply because the specific form in which they're presented is unsound. William Bennett has been particularly clever . . . about defining a battlefield where there ought to be something more like a seminar table" [personal communication, 9 Jan. 1989].)

On the last day of the conference I read a protodraft of my sense of this consensus to the participants themselves. Gary Waller and a few others had serious reservations that all my emphasis on "making meaning" and "active learning" implied too much that we are "free autonomous subjects"; that I wasn't doing enough justice to the constraints and limits on human beings—the forces that circumscribe us; that I imply too naively that we write and not enough that we are written. There was very little discussion on this point, and we had to move on, so it's not quite clear to me how most participants felt about it. Certainly Waller's misgivings point up what could be called my bias. But I sensed that there was more emphasis at the conference on the student as an active learner who constructs knowledge. I resist calling this emphasis politically or philosophically naive. I can't help seeing it as characteristic of good teachers to emphasize the student as more subject than object—to stress the real possibility for change in individuals and society as a way to fight the passivity and helplessness that students fall prey to. This question of freedom and agency versus constraint is a bit of a crux, and I will explore it more in chapter 5, "What Follows from Taking a Theoretical Stance?"

Another observation about my summary of the consensus: I give equal emphasis to using language and to self-conscious reflecting on the process of using it. I actually didn't hear as much explicit emphasis during the conference on that first element—using language—but I sensed just as much implicit focus on it. To support my contention, I point to the following things from our three weeks together:

> There was a constant refrain from elementary and secondary teachers on the need to get students to be habitual writers and readers; only then can we be effective at getting them to be reflectors and examiners of language.

Virtually everyone acknowledged repeatedly that the main practical finding of the last ten or fifteen years' renaissance in composition has been that students (and teachers!) should engage in more writing—even in class. This movement has taught us that we can't teach writing by just looking at models of others' writing or even by just talking about our own writing process: we have to emphasize production—the practice of writing—and devote plenty of time to this oddly neglected activity.

Similarly, college people stressed repeatedly that we should focus not on asking students to study theory as a content but on using theory as a lens through which to look at our actual reading and writing. Implicit here is the need to get people to *engage* a text. We can't effectively examine ways of reading until someone *has* a reading that carries some investment or moment. Otherwise there's no purchase for the act of reflecting or calling into question. (Robert Scholes in *Textual Power* shows us beautifully how to help students get out from under the power of a literary text, but he presupposes what is not so easy: that students should allow such texts to *have* some power over them.)

What then does this consensus look like in practice? I provide stories or snapshots in many of the interludes between my chapters. But for another example, Susan Stires told of her first- or second-grade student reading *Mop Top* in the original book—but then also seeing it in a textbook reader and being intrigued. The child noticed how at one point the word *soared* had been removed and replaced with the phrase *high flying* instead. "Maybe some kids need help with *soared*," she said, "but I can read *soared* just fine." That's a lovely example of a teaching-learning moment of the sort that Heath was trying to call to our attention. A tiny child reads for pleasure but, with encouragement from the teacher, she is also curious to see how the story might be in a different published version: a story of how first or second graders can do textual scholarship out of natural curiosity.

For an extended picture, here is Carol Avery describing her first-grade classroom in her position paper:

> Several years ago, with my school district's support, I stopped using the designated reading program. Instead I implemented a process approach to teaching through daily workshops in writing and reading and a daily literature period. Today, children in my classroom know that each day they will write on self-selected topics, they will read books of their own choosing, and they will hear me read to them. They know they will explore topics and share questions and ideas with class members. They use language throughout the day in

purposeful ways as they read, write, and talk together in a continual search for meaning.

My classroom has changed. Children are readers and writers and thinkers who use language to question and to understand. They become members of literate communities using language in real ways for real purposes. Classroom shelves are no longer piled with workbooks and stacks of seatwork papers; rather, they are filled with books authored by children and professional writers, as well as projects and interests initiated by the children.

I have changed; I learn in this environment too. Through my own classroom research, I have learned to listen to children, to observe the multitude of ways in which they learn, and to examine the elements that encourage their growth.

What are the elements of this literate environment and how is a literate community established? A predictable structure is carefully, slowly built beginning with the first day of school. On that day children write using invented spelling; they read by browsing in books and reading pictures; they listen over and over again to familiar and new stories that I read to them. As we talk together during these activities, the focus is on forming meaning, on making sense of the written word. As the days and weeks unfold, we share and respond to each other, always moving toward understanding. . . .

To maintain this environment, chunks of time each day are devoted to writing, reading, and interacting with literature. Children learn to write by writing. They learn to read by reading. Listening to and talking about literature enhances both processes. Children learn to think, to question, to reflect on what they write and read and listen to, in a classroom that allots a significant amount of time each day to these activities.

The children are exposed to a variety of styles and genres of literature and a range of strategies for writing and reading processes. Children make choices as to what to read, what to write, how to accomplish a task. . . . Children who make their own decisions take ownership of their learning and are better able to make meaning within their worlds.

Teacher responses are a critical aspect of this environment. Theodore Sizer speaks of *coaching*; Donald Graves and Mary Ellen Giacobbe refer to *nudging*. Effective responses enable learners to explore options, make choices, and participate in meaning-making experiences. Teachers ask questions to stimulate thinking, and children become adept at generating their own questions and seeking answers. Peers also learn to make enabling responses in a literate community. Children need and deserve these responses and to hear the ideas of others in order to expand their own.

At the other end of the spectrum, Janet Emig described an activity she uses in college and graduate seminars: she has everyone read some critics or theorists and then look at a poem. Students draw names of critics or critical concepts from a hat and then are asked to talk about what that critic might be most likely to notice in interpreting the poem; or how a concept bears on the poem; or how someone from a particular race, class, gender, or historical period might be likely to see it. This is an exercise in helping people see multiplicities of readings—heightening their sense that there are choices to be made.

See the official record of the conference (Lloyd-Jones and Lunsford) for other agreements about what this consensus looks like in practice. The college report, for example, gives accounts of the English major, a freshman reading and writing course, and general education courses. The primary and secondary reports give accounts of what follows in the classroom from this consensus. The conference record has a section of "Illustrations" devoted to short concrete accounts. The primary teachers, in particular, have gone on to publish a book that consists mainly of accounts of classroom practices that follow from the consensus of the conference (ed. Julie Jensen).

It's important to realize, thus, that this consensus represents a kind of teaching that is already going on. The conference participants did not spend three weeks dreaming up some new and splendid vision: "Hey, wouldn't it be neat if. . . ." The consensus was around principles and practices that have been used in more than a few classrooms for more than a few years (indeed, principles and practices not so different from what good teachers have traditionally used). Our discussions were grounded in the initial position papers in which most participants wrote of their actual teaching practices. In short, these are not "new," untested ideas. I'd call the participants second-generation idealists or tempered visionaries. Participants sometimes worried (correctly enough, no doubt) that some elements in this consensus might strike some people as too reminiscent of the 1960s or of Dewey (e.g., "active learning" or "learner-centered"). I can't help stressing, however, that these elements are part of a broad conception of literacy and English teaching that have been worked out and tested by people in the 1980s in a spirit of sophisticated pragmatism. (For more on the problem of things sounding like "the 1960s or Dewey," see chapter 11, "The Danger of Softness.")

NOTES

[1]It strikes me that Hirsch's agenda is perfect for television, a medium that is ideal for the transmission of small segments to passive receivers. If Hirsch would take his sophistication and energy (and financial and governmental backing) and put pressure on television, he could go a long way toward getting every item on his list into cartoons, game

shows, adventure shows, and sitcoms. He's the one who stresses that the medium needn't be high-toned; he's the one who doesn't care whether they read *Hamlet*, only that they know who Hamlet was. With TV, he could make us all "culturally literate" (in his sense of the term) and avoid pushing schools to be arenas for list learning.

[2]From the report of the college section, 15 July 1987:

> What we did discover as a point of assent was considerable unity of aims at every level, whether expressed in the common language of practice or the more specialized language of theory. Our aims are to inquire into the questions of what is a reader, what is a writer, what is a text, and how do we make meaning. On the theoretical side, some of us are willing to say that we problematize these questions in our courses; others prefer to say that, because we live in a world in which there are multiple modes of reading, writing, interpreting, and thinking open to students, we want them to know these modes in order to make informed choices among them; and that, in a world of multiplicity, we want to extend their knowledge beyond the canonical, that is, beyond the elitist and school-hallowed list of "masterpieces."

Are Teenagers Different?

Candy Carter
(secondary school section)

O NE OF MY best students came in to ask for an extension on a paper. She said, "My dad was with us this weekend while my mom left. I guess we're 'time-share kids.' " The proportions of students from nonnuclear families are overwhelming to those who haven't been in a high school classroom lately: In my friend's class of twenty-three eighth graders, only four students live with both of their biological parents. In another friend's sophomore English class totaling eighty students, fifteen students did not even know who their fathers were. (Our community is considered middle class; we have only a handful of minority students.) In our senior class, about ten percent of the students were "emancipated minors," that is, students who lived alone or with other students or with other students' parents.

It is foolish, presumptuous, and unrealistic of educators, particularly university professors, to assume that we can reform American public schooling by simply returning to universal truth and the classics. In fact, the truth that lies in great literature has the potential to bring solace and direction to students whose emotional base, the family, is disintegrating. However, the approach to literature must change radically if we are going to expect students to make the connection between the classics and their own lives. Most important of all, teachers must be listeners. The journals of my students make me weep with my own powerlessness.

From a student journal:

> I wonder if my parents realize how much pain and grief their divorce has caused. I know that they are individual people with feelings and concerns of their own, but they don't seem to realize that it's not a matter of being away from their kids, it's a matter of us having to choose between our parents. . . . I feel like there is a huge volcano, close to eruption, and the molten flowing from within is the blood in my heart. . . . If I get married, I will never have

kids. . . . I will never put them through the heartbreak of divorce. Marriage is not guaranteed, so I will never have kids.

When your parents get divorced, it is really hard to have something to grasp or count on to be there for you. You can't go to one parent or the other because they just play immature games. They tell you that you shouldn't feel the way you do, but it's hard. Then you find yourself trying to justify these feelings . . . and you feel everything is your fault. As far as I'm concerned, *divorce* is a four-letter word.

. . . I want to have a complete normal family now more than ever. It's so hard talking to your dad on the phone, and even though I never really got along with him, knowing that he's not coming home again, ever. I feel so frayed, like I can't grasp anything. I look at families that are together and I got so . . . maybe jealous . . . that I can't even function. Today I wanted to yell at Mrs. P_____ and ask her if she could function in a normal way if she was watching her family break up right before her, knowing that nothing would ever be the same, ever, and there is nothing anyone can do except watch. I feel so damn useless. It's hard to get up in the morning. Just at that first instant that I reach consciousness, it hits me.

But testimonies at the end of the year say it all: "You were there when I needed you." "Thank you for 'listening' in this journal." "Thank you for caring." "I never had anyone I could count on before." Any compassionate teacher hears the same words.

There are some interesting manifestations in the disintegration of the family. These outward "signals" of the change in the family are what cause high schools the most grief.

The media: It is not necessary to rehash the well-publicized impact of visual and musical media on the reading habits in the country, but the long-term effect also is that students get very mixed messages indeed about everything from sex to family life from television, music, and films. In one day, students can see several episodes of casual sex, see people "blown away" in several different ways, and yet be confronted with ideal 1980s families in "Cosby" and "Family Ties." One of my students reflects on the impact of media:

I thought about why I am a geek after seeing some lame sitcom on the tube. It was about this guy who was the complete stereotyped geek. The look, the hair, the glasses, all the way down to the voice and manner of speaking. It was funny because people were giving this geek the same advice and encouragement they give me. Interesting. Only at the end of the show it turns out that this geek was a marvelous dancer, so everybody liked him, including a really cute girl. Wouldn't it be nice if real life was like TV? . . . While I'm on the subject and before I put down my lapiz there is one more important factor of geekhood I left out. A geek has to rationalize things to keep them bearable. A geek has to keep his guard up. If he lets himself start liking a girl, it could be dangerous. I guess that is one of the two big factors of geekhood—girls and the future. A geek's standards are always much higher than realistically attainable. If I let my guard down, I could really fall for _____. But I won't, because I am an experienced geek and I know what to do to make my life bearable. Yeah, I guess that's it—disappointment. That's the main word one would use to describe the life of a geek.

A student coming from a family that monitors viewing and discusses issues with the children in the home will probably come away from the diet of television shows relatively unscathed, but such families are not necessarily typical.

Part-time jobs: The media, among other things, make us want and expect more. Now no longer able to provide all the "must haves" for their children, parents are allowing, and in many cases encouraging, part-time jobs during school. Even in my honors classes, the vast majority of students work ten or more hours per week. If a student has nothing else going on, this is not too much, but picture the life of a high school athlete-scholar: he plays football (or basketball or baseball) in the afternoon, comes home at 6:00 (exhausted), studies three hours (probably not doing a very good job at it, either), and works on weekends (except for game days). He might even work a few nights, too, during the week, studying between turns at pumping gas or working the cash register. The same schedule applies to girls; just substitute volleyball or soccer for football and waitressing or store clerking for pumping gas. (Sexism still applies in the teenaged workplace.) . . .

One of my favorite students is oddly inspiring and frighteningly typical. During his senior year, Lewis worked 25–30 hours per week as a graveyard cashier at a gas station mini-mart. He paid $80 a month to his father for "rent." (It is also not unusual for my students to pay their parents for a portion of their "upkeep.") He bought all his own clothes and paid for all his own entertainment. His mother had deserted the family several years earlier, so his diet consisted of fast food (which he paid for) and menus he put together himself. Lewis was vice-president of the student body, which involved running the representative council. He was active in three school clubs. In his first semester of his senior year, he got a 3.8; in his second semester he got a 4.0. He was salutatorian and is now a sophomore at Stanford on a full-ride scholarship. After high school, his college program is a relief.

Drugs: . . . The teenager who hasn't been confronted with opportunities to use drugs or drink to excess is rare. The pressure to experiment is intense. At a neighboring high school, tickets are sold at the door to be used for lines of coke; parents often serve liquor in their home to their children's friends on the pretext that "they're not using drugs." It takes a very strong adolescent to go against the crowd and say "no." . . . I applaud the efforts of the media and organizations to educate children about the effects of drugs, but the programs are meaningless unless kids have the "inner core" of self-belief to go their own way.

This inner core comes ideally from a good base, which leads us back to the subject of the family. When you consider the lives of many of our teenagers today, you marvel at their resilience. Rather than resenting them, you admire them for the guts they must have. Students such as the ones I teach continue to put one foot in front of the other, marching through classes, learning French, memorizing the first ten amendments, understanding logarithms, reading *Antigone*, contemplating $E = mc^2$, proceeding on to tedious jobs to put gas in their cars and in some cases food in their mouths. In their spare time, they might play a sport, participate in student-body activities, star in the school play, or be part of the school orchestra. The pressures are there, but often the foundations are not.

The implications for the teacher of English can be overwhelming. On the one hand, literature, writing, self-expression can provide the necessary "great truths" to help these courageous but confused adolescents make sense out of their world. On the other hand, students often come to school with so much unfinished business from home that it takes a real master to bring art and life together. Most teachers try, some more than others. Others live in the time capsule dated 1965, in which Mom made lunch, took the kids to the library for research papers, and set a curfew at 10:00. Yes, kids are different but oddly and sadly the same too. It is the world around them that has changed rather than the students themselves.

An Interactive Literature-Writing Class

Larry R. Johannessen
(secondary school section)

*T*HAT'S NOT what the author is saying at all," Mary said, interrupting Dan's rather long explanation of what he believed the author was trying to tell readers about love. Mary and Dan are two of the twenty-seven students in my American literature course. The class is involved in a discussion of John Collier's short story "The Chaser." They are attempting to determine what the author's message is about romantic love relationships.

"Okay," Dan said, "What do you think he means?"

"Our group decided that the author would agree with statement 13, 'Love never changes,' because Alan [the main character in the story] wants to buy the love potion and give it to Diane to make her love and sort of like worship him. He wants a love that never changes."

"Yes, Charles, you had your hand up," I said.

"Our group saw this differently. Alan would agree that 'love never changes' but not the author. That's the point of the story. That's why the old man who sells the potion to Alan says, at the end of the story, 'Au revoir.' Jenny, the French student in our group, told us that it means 'till we see each other again.' The old man knows that Alan will be back to buy the 'life-cleaner' or poison to kill Diane—"

"What? Come on!" a number of student voices chimed in.

"Let me finish!" Charles said. "See, the old man knows that after a while Alan will get sick of Diane adoring him—like the old man tells Alan, she will be 'jealous' and 'want to be everything to you.' See, the author wants us to realize that this isn't true love at all. Love does change."

"Oh, I get it!" Martha said. "That's why he sells the love potion so cheap and the poison is so expensive. He knows Alan will get sick of this love and be back to buy the poison to get rid of Diane."

"Yeah, and now I get the title," Bill said. "The word *chaser* has two meanings here. It means someone who chases after someone or something, like Alan chases after Diane and what he thinks will be perfect love. But it also means a drink taken to wash down another drink, such as a drink of beer to wash down a shot of whiskey. So, like the poison is the beer or chaser to wash down the love potion whiskey."

"He wants us to see that you can't force anyone to love you," Sharon added. "It doesn't work. The author wouldn't agree with statement 13."

How did this group of eleventh-grade high school students get to this rather sophisticated textual analysis of this short story? And why were they so involved in the discussion? And how could they have possibly understood the irony or ironies in the story without my lecturing to them or telling them what irony is or at least what theme is?

The answer is at once simple and not so simple. First, I long ago gave up the notion that lecturing to students about irony and/or having them read *the* definition of irony in their literature anthologies and then having them try to apply it to works of literature would produce much real learning. Oh, sure, one or two students would "get it," but then they usually "got it" anyway. Real learning happens only when students become actively involved and can internalize knowledge or understanding by arriving at the realization themselves.

It is important to understand that the excerpt from the class discussion did not happen by accident. I began this bit of instruction by first giving students fifteen generalizations about love, everything from "Love is blind" to "If you are really in love, physical appearance doesn't matter." I had students decide individually which generalizations they agreed with and which they didn't. Then, I compiled the results on the board and we discussed the generalizations.

This discussion was heated and generated considerable disagreement. Of course, every teenager is interested in the subject of love, but they were surprised to discover that their classmates held some very different views about love. With their enthusiasm ignited, I introduced the story. I suggested to them that authors who write love stories also have particular views about love and they sometimes want to convince us that their views are right. "Let's read this story," I said, "and see if we can figure out what statements this author would agree and disagree with from our list of fifteen."

We read the story. Then, the students got into small groups I had assigned them to and listed on the board. Their assignment was to answer the question I had posed before we read the story. My students did not disappoint me. They enthusiastically debated various viewpoints. When they had arrived at agreement or could not agree in their small groups, we reconvened as a class.

The excerpt illustrates the nature of the debate or class discussion: healthy, vigorous disagreement that took students, time and time again, back to the text for evidence to support their interpretations. In addition, a questioning audience encouraged students to carefully explain how their evidence supported their interpretations.

I merely guided, directed, and made sure we moved forward toward a more complete understanding and comprehension of the text. I encouraged them to inquire, solve the problem, and synthesize.

The excerpt is only part of the story. After we discussed their understanding of the story, we then examined each of the fifteen generalizations about love and discovered that there was still disagreement about exactly which ones Collier would agree or disagree with and why. "Tomorrow," I said to them, "I am going to ask you to write an essay explaining why you think Collier would agree or disagree with the statements we are having a problem with here. Write it as a letter to one of the people in the class who disagrees with you. Try to convince this person that he or she is wrong. Yes, Steve, do you have a question?"

"Can we use things from the story to prove our point? You know, like Charles did when we discussed?"

"Can you? That's exactly what I want you to do."

The bell rang and I knew that some of the enthusiasm would be gone when they came to class the next day. One or two will have forgotten their stories, and another one or two will have forgotten their list of generalizations about love. I will also need to review the end of our discussion and the assignment. I'll have to cajole one or two to get busy and stop talking, but I know that the momentum will still be there.

Even though the new problem of writing their interpretations will present new anxieties and struggle for them and me, I know this is real learning. I know, too, that we have what they learned *today* to fall back on and remind them that they can do it. And I know there will be additional anxieties and struggle when we begin working on Max Shulman's story "Love Is a Fallacy" two days from now, but I also know that they are already halfway there.

3 | Democracy through Language

*I*n *his talk to the assembled coalition, E. D. Hirsch, Jr., argued that for the sake of literacy, we need to push harder for a single common culture, not multiple cultures. In the question and answer session afterward, Marie Buncombe, a black faculty member, asked, "But can't I be literate and different from you?" I expected to hear Hirsch argue that a common core of shared information and shared culture would of course permit enormous cultural diversity. But in fact he replied by talking about the loss of cultural diversity as a "downside" (his word) of cultural literacy. Echoing Richard Rodriguez in* Hunger of Memory, *he argued that we must choose between cultural pluralism and cultural literacy.*

THE CONSENSUS I described in the last chapter was not formally ratified. In a sense it is a product of my perception, one that was informally ratified by participants on the last day. But the coalition members formally ratified a different consensus around a phrase voted as the theme of the conference: democracy through language. This was chosen to sum up the three weeks and was chosen for the title of the official published report of the conference (Lloyd-Jones and Lunsford).

Of course, the phrase is hopelessly general and has a patriotic if not sloganeering ring to it. Voting on it was one of the more overtly political moments of the conference: people were consciously looking for language to reach the general public. With this patriotic phrase, we were trying to fight against the way Hirsch and many educational conservatives claim a monopoly on patriotism—that anyone not interested in teaching lists and a single culture (and "English only") is anti-American. Despite the apple-pie ring, however, "democracy through language" had some very substantive meanings for the conferees. These meanings need spelling out. That is, we weren't so naive as to pretend that we can make society wholly democratic by how we deal with language in our research and in our classrooms; rather, we were insisting that there are specific places in our research and teaching where concrete choices can be made.

Participants returned repeatedly to their concern about how our culture nudges citizens into passivity and helplessness: how insidiously the media mold values and attitudes; how often schooling makes students feel that being a good student means passively accepting what's in the book or what's said in an authoritative tone—following orders and feeding back material on tests in the form it was given. In short, the consensus was around a vision of what education must be if we are to make thoughtful citizens who are not prey to propaganda by what is authoritative or seduction by what is sincere or glossy.

Thus participants came to a more frankly activist, political, Jeffersonian view of education than I expected: that one of the main goals of the kind of language-oriented teaching and learning I described in the consensus chapter is to help make better citizens. What children need to become good citizens is the ability to interpret, question, and evaluate information rather than just passively receive a list of terms or concepts—to be producers of knowledge rather than just consumers.

It is important to note here a third consensus at the conference, one that participants *shared* with Hirsch and that is argued most powerfully by Theodore Sizer in *Horace's Compromise*: that "less is more." Schools must stop taking on all the jobs neglected by the rest of society (family, culture, politics) and instead concentrate on a smaller, more manageable core of important learning. Yet despite this belief that schools should not dissipate their energies trying to do too many things, participants consciously affirmed the Jeffersonian assumption that good work in English needs democracy and democracy needs good work in English.

That is, on the one side, for the sake of good scholarship and learning we need an atmosphere of free thought where all ideas are invited to compete; we need talk-rich, interactive classrooms where students are invited actively to make their own meanings, form their own hypotheses, and test them autonomously and in open discussion (all this in contrast to just getting right answers from lectures, textbooks, and workbooks). On the other side, for the sake of our democracy, we need students who can fight for their own point of view yet still understand and appreciate the points of view of others, students who understand how different ways of reading the same text or looking at the same data can yield completely different meanings.

Important in this regard was the time we spent talking about television (a number of the position papers were devoted to people's thinking about it) and the visit by Jerome Singer, who spoke about his research. (Singer is professor of psychology and director of the Clinical Psychology Program at Yale.) There was some interesting and unresolved debate about the effects of TV ("it scrambles their brains"; "it opens up new and neglected forms of literacy"). But I think Singer's presentation of his (and other) research was powerful to many participants: that heavy TV watching seems to decrease children's tendency (if not ability) to make up their own images and to tell their own stories—and even to play with other children. Most telling to me was his finding that heavy watchers don't even understand the TV stories themselves as well as children who watch less TV. These effects appear to be somewhat mitigated if children watch with adults and discuss what they see (reinforcing Heath's emphasis on the need for conversation). I read all this as a story about activity and passivity: that making meaning is an active process, and if conditions encourage children to be passive and try to just "take things in," they don't figure out even simple meanings so well. Thus I think participants felt that the kind of teaching that asks students to be active and analytic and to question (as opposed to trying to take in right answers) is particularly important for students so heavily influenced by television watching.

Tracking

One of the strongest reports is the one that speaks out against tracking. For the phrase "democracy through language" also grew out of a recurring sense that a country, like a school, is only as strong as its weakest link. One of the clearest themes in position papers and discussions during the conference was that we can't just give up on certain students in our classrooms or schools—or classes of people in our society. I saw in this attitude at the conference an insistence on the nation's traditional ideals, an insistence that unless everyone learns, we all suffer.

I wouldn't have been surprised if the college faculty members had made this stand, because we in college are more susceptible to easy nobility about tracking—forgetting that we already have tracked classrooms. (De facto tracking results from test scores and financial ability. Even community college faculty members don't have to deal with the many students who don't go to college at all). But college faculty members rightly held back on this issue, and it was the primary and secondary teachers who came out against tracking. Here then is the coalition report on tracking. It was written by a subcommittee with more members from the schools than from the colleges and approved unanimously in a final plenary session:

> The teachers at this conference cannot endorse tracking in any of its forms or disguises as a viable educational practice in English language classes.

As John Goodlad has pointed out, "the circumstances which tracking in secondary schools is intended to address have their beginnings in the primary grades" (295). Tracking by reading level in the elementary school begins a path toward failure for slower learners that is very difficult to reverse and usually leads to increased failure and frustration for those learners in the upper grades.

Tracking and ability grouping are perpetuated by the assumption that the teacher can better meet individual needs of a more homogeneous component of students. Goodlad calls this "a retreat rather than a strategy" (297)—noting the differences in teaching modes that emphasize rote learning and skill practice in low tracks and that result in the denial to low-track students of "types of instruction most highly associated with achievement" (155).

Tracking systems in many schools have the effect of segregating learners along lines that are primarily racial or ethnic. In this way, and because such segregation prevents a richness of experience for high- and low-track students that mixed classes provide, the hidden curriculum demonstrated by tracking promotes elitism of certain learning styles, modes of expression, and cultural or ethnic views.

When learners are separated by ability or skill level into reading groups or ability-grouped classes, they suffer from the lack of interaction with learners of different abilities. All learners need the interplay of thought, the motivation, and the sharing of diverse experiences.

We recommend, therefore, that students studying the same subject not be assigned to classes on the basis of past performance or testing and that teachers be trained to modify classroom practices to offer equitable educational opportunities within heterogeneous groupings both at the classroom level and within classrooms.

I need to stress again the element of 1980s pragmatism and worldliness at the conference. That is, when these public school teachers argued against tracking, they weren't just sticking up for underdogs (though of course they were doing that too). They argued just as strongly for how much the *better* students suffer for being in homogenized classrooms and schools; how tracking tends to make classrooms and schools not only more culturally narrow but also intellectually narrow; how students in the top tracks often show not only a kind of smugness but even a downright denseness. Isolated top-track students often fall into thinking that all learning is a matter of right "school answers" on tests rather than a matter of integrating academic or book learning with their wider life experience.[1] Isolated top-track students often remain blind to many of the realities of society and class that low-track students see very clearly. Sometimes high-track students pay a psychological and moral price: teachers spoke of high-track students often being more driven to cheat, more anxious and depressed, and more likely to commit suicide.

Tracking tends to deprive weaker students of the very things they need to become stronger. For example, it's almost inevitable that higher tracks are used as rewards or incentives for the most skilled or senior teachers, and so the best teachers go to the best students and the worst go to those who need most help. Tracking also robs the lower tracks of students who have more hope and expectation of learning—making failure and dropping out more likely in the lower tracks. Teachers spoke of the burden of trying to teach a class from which the system has removed any students who experience themselves as bright or successful or who get any satisfaction from school. Perhaps worst of all, tracking is self-fulfilling, making low-track teachers see their students as stupid and making the students have the same view of themselves (see Rosenthal and Jacobson).

What's ironic, in addition, is when tracking robs the weaker students —in the name of trying to treat their "deficiency"—of the very teaching activities and approaches they need for learning. There's a long history of this in the field of writing: teachers have traditionally asked higher-track students to write whole pieces of discourse of diverse genres to diverse audiences and asked low-track students to write only exercises and disembodied sentences and paragraphs. It seems clear, however, that what students need most for learning to write is to write whole pieces of discourse to varied audiences (not just writing "dummy runs" to the audience of teacher-as-examiner)—and that, of course, weak students are just as capable of writing whole discourses as strong students, despite the mistakes they may make (see, for example, Farr and Daniel).

Tracking is also unfortunate in the way it tends to reinforce a problematic "banking" model of education. Because the students sitting in the room are allegedly "at the same level," it invites teachers (and parents and school boards) to think of education as a matter of pouring the same ingredients into similar heads. Heterogeneous or mixed classes are more likely to encourage teachers to a more fruitful model of education: diverse students practicing complex activities together so that they learn to some degree from their own efforts and from each other (not just from the teacher), and all with different paths of learning. As experienced teachers in tracked and nontracked situations, conference participants asserted that the same educational approach is right for both the best and the worst students: a learner-focused, interactive approach.

But participants also recognized that tracking cannot easily be removed: it makes life easier for schools and for teachers—especially in chronically overburdened institutions of low prestige and poor resources. If a classroom contains children of widely different abilities, the teacher may have a harder time building a learning culture, a culture where students listen to each other with respect and learn from each other. Thus it's important to note that the report ends not with one recommendation but with two: to end tracking and to give teachers the training they need to deal with classes of mixed ability.

Though I have taught a wide range of students at a range of institutions of widely different prestige, I don't feel I can speak about tracking with the authority of many of these public school teachers, for example, Nancy McHugh, a long-time high school teacher (president of the National Council of Teachers of English at the time of the conference and formerly president of the California Association of Teachers of English):

> I have taught in three different schools (all highly academic); two had tracking and one did not.
>
> Tracking is easier in some ways. It allows the teacher to select materials and strategies specific to a particular ability group and to be able to teach "whole class" lessons fairly effectively. I believe that there is often more synchronicity in such a class. Often the students have been together for several years and know and accept each other fairly well (at least I enjoy my Advanced Placement English class for those reasons). But, if I am truly honest, I have to admit that tracking limits teacher perspective (the teacher sees students in certain categories with certain expectations), and the children may suffer. Also, there is a great variety even within a tracked class. Meanwhile no one even mentions the many, many students who have been misplaced (underestimated or overestimated) and who accept these labels. Those who are "underestimated" fall far short of their potential and may end up with a false concept about themselves, may even be convinced that they should not aspire. Tracking also allows the lazy or noninteractive teacher to use the same old method (lecture, total class assignments, etc.) without any attempt to meet individual needs.
>
> When I went from a highly tracked school (honors, academically enriched, regular, remedial, basic) to a nontracked school, I was forced to do a number of things that I feel were very good for me. I was forced to see each student as an individual and to expect the best of every student. I was forced to use groups (because of the tremendous diversity of learning styles and behavior patterns in these nonhomogeneous groups and rather large classes of thirty-eight), and I discovered by trial and error how much more involved students could be, how much some students could "grow" or "bloom." I also discovered things that I should have recognized previously: the verbal strengths of many "lower-ability" students, the leadership qualities of both those and otherwise shy students who in a heterogeneous setting felt more free to express themselves, the shock of recognition that came to many "gifted" students when they discovered that "lower-ability" students had smarts, good ideas, clever reasoning, even if sometimes they were less able to express those ideas in writing.
>
> I believe in nontracked classes (even though I am now in a high school that has tracking) because I feel that every student should be

looked at as a person of great insight and potential. Tracking skews teacher perspective about students in very subtle ways. "Lower-ability" students can learn a great deal from interacting with "higher-ability" students: they are to be more challenged, and they may also see themselves as being more capable than they had thought. "Higher-ability" students need to appreciate and interact with "lower-ability" students to be reminded that their differences are relatively little and to be better conditioned to live in a democratic society. The mix keeps everyone more real and more open and leaves open options for all parties concerned.

Business interests tell us that they want two things from our graduates: that they be able to think both logically and creatively and that they be able to work cooperatively in groups. These are highly valued in business and industry at the present time. Heterogeneous classes provide these opportunities in a real world setting. Sometimes otherwise selfish and elitist students learn how to share and help. The labels that we put on students are at best inaccurate and at worst damaging—and totally unnecessary. (response to draft)

(I have put some of the stories that bear on tracking in the interludes that precede and follow this chapter.)

Perhaps we wouldn't have come out so clearly against tracking if we were teachers of a more precise and quantitative discipline like physics or math: in such disciplines teachers seem much more confident than we are in English that they can diagnose the exact level of students' knowledge and skill and more confident that there is a single necessary sequence in which the elements of a discipline should be learned. Therefore many teachers in those disciplines don't question the assumption that students in any given classroom should all be at the same level. Is there something special about English? Despite some exceptions, most of the texts we teach are appropriate for both strong and weak students (Shakespeare and Emily Dickinson are both "advanced" and "remedial"), and most of the writing assignments we give are also appropriate for strong and weak students (e.g., "persuade someone of your view" or "compare how you read this work with how someone else in the class reads it"). Perhaps it's simply not feasible to aim strong and weak students together at quadratic equations. Nevertheless, perhaps people in other disciplines could learn from us to be less preoccupied with having all students in the classroom at the same level of knowledge and skill and to be less likely to assume that everyone learns things in the same order. (Interestingly enough, mathematics seems to have a double tradition here: on the one hand, a tradition of using more tracking in earlier grades than other disciplines; yet on the other hand, a tradition of pioneering in nontracked classrooms in those early grades where students do individualized work and study at their own level and their own speed in the same classroom. But this latter individualized practice seems to be built on an assumption of one right route—following a textbook/ workbook step by step—and is therefore highly individualized and often involves no interaction among students.)[2]

As for me, I like heterogeneity for exactly those English classes where most people assume the need for tracking: freshman writing. It strikes me that we waste lots of time and money giving placement or diagnostic tests to entering freshmen in order to separate remedial and advanced sections, when it might be just as good if not better to mix them all together. Putting extremely weak and strong students together tends to make everyone nervous, teachers and students alike—sometimes making weak students ashamed and strong ones snotty. It is a struggle to fight those attitudes. But once you segregate remedial students into separate courses by themselves, there is an insidious temptation to teach forms (small grammatical forms and larger predefined genres or structures for essays) instead of giving the weak writers what we give to stronger writers: lots of practice in writing out their thoughts into exploratory and revised pieces of whole discourse for a variety of readers. The large sums that most colleges and universities spend on placement testing might be better spent on helping bring about the kind of teaching—usually a better kind—that is needed in mixed classes; that is, we should spend the money on workshops to help teachers deal with mixed classes and on reducing class size.[3]

Difference

The consensus on the idea of democracy through language was bound up with what might be called the major unifying theme of the conference: difference. Conference participants simply resisted Hirsch's view that we must choose between cultural literacy and cultural pluralism and insisted rather that we can work for *both*—insisted that a society that teaches only one culture is culturally illiterate: cultural literacy means the teaching of difference among cultures.

Hirsch and the members of the coalition start from the same base: that our society has enormous cultural diversity. (Although Heath at one point questioned this, suggesting that perhaps, with TV and other national forces of homogenization, we have *more* common knowledge now than twenty or fifty years ago—even if it's not about Hamlet, Keats, and Wordsworth.) But Hirsch's premise is that no society can survive if it has too much cultural diversity, and therefore he argues that we must enforce cultural commonality through our curriculum. The premise of the members of the coalition is that enormous cultural diversity is not a problem but a good thing, but it forces on us the obligation to teach students how to deal with diversity—how to understand diverse points of view and how to communicate across cultural boundaries.

"Difference" can be a jargon cliché in poststructuralist or cultural criticism, but in the context of this conference of teachers, the term was grounded in the concrete realities of our lives and those of our students. Of course, there was some sentimental desire for diversity as "a good thing" (why must *sentimental* be a term of disparagement?). But mostly the commitment to difference was a commitment to the specifics of classrooms.

For example, I think that the most important, concrete outcome of the conference was an agreement about a model for the typical English classroom: not a class that pushes for a single or best reading of a text but rather a class that pushes for multiple and various readings of the text and then devotes some time to reflecting on how one got to these readings. This is a call for teaching with less closure and less criticizing of bad or wrong readings and more affirmation of differences among readings.

Although this emphasis on difference in the classroom asks us to hear and respect rather than merely criticize student views that strike us as marginal or deviant, it doesn't mean merely inviting students to stay complacently stuck in careless readings or idiosyncratic views. The approach may be "soft" in saying yes to marginal views and ways of reading, but it's "hard" and analytic in pushing students to interrogate each reading and uncover its premises, implications, and interests—and in pushing students to practice and learn to use a variety of kinds of reading and writing and knowing. (See chapter 11, "The Danger of Softness," for reflections on "hard" and "soft.") Implicit here is a kind of intellectual bargain that says, in effect, "We'll try to enter into the kinds of understanding and reading that you do; but in return you must try to enter into the kinds of understanding and reading that we do" (Elbow, "Methodological Doubting"). If this picture of teaching doesn't sound so different from the way some teachers already teach (and it is not), reflect for a moment on how deeply we as academics have ingrained in ourselves the impulse toward closure and right answers—the impulse to criticize our colleagues and correct our students, an impulse not absent even in those of us most devoted to difference.

Thus Hirsch is sincere in his commitment to democracy, but for him that means helping everyone to the "right" information and language and thereby to the right culture. The coalition members' idea of democracy is to insist (as scholars) that there is no right information or right language or culture; that we have to learn to see the limits or parochialness or "interested" quality of any view or language or dialect;

and that the ones that seem "normal" or "sensible" or "default" are just as limited or interested. But of course the conferees also recognized that society, as it exists, does indeed sanction a language or dialect (and culture) that is most "correct" or privileged (standard written English) and therefore most useful for people to know how to use. How can we have "democracy through language" if there is nothing but "difference"? Don't we have to get our children and citizens to speak and read and write the same language—and, in particular, to write the common code (what Hirsch calls the grapholect or standard written English)? Most participants were in fact happy to stick up for some sameness in addition to difference: to affirm that all citizens need command of standard written English.

But while thus agreeing to some extent with Hirsch's goal of teaching a common literacy, most coalition members flatly refused to say we have to choose between it and celebrating or nurturing difference. These veteran teachers pointed to their own experience and to evidence around them that both goals are important and need not be at odds—and in fact the two goals can reinforce each other. What children from non-mainstream cultures need to acquire in order to master standard written English are those crucial linguistic skills and motivations that are difficult to acquire unless students feel supported in their own culture. This means spending some school time *not* trying to hammer home standard English; taking competence in standard English as a final goal, not the goal of every class or every written assignment; having the patience to see that students need to learn to trust and build on the language skills they already have before they can master dialects that are foreign to them. In short, these teachers were recognizing the crucial fact (from their own classrooms and from their positions of leadership with other teachers) that we have little hope of getting students invested in the effort to learn a common language or common written dialect if it means "trading off" their own language, dialect, and culture.[4]

Thus participants were frankly arguing that even though we can teach certain common literate practices, we no longer have the option to live in a nation with a single common culture. They established this theme even before they met, noting often in their position papers that our classes are already full of different cultures and languages. To walk down the streets of our cities and towns and down the halls of our schools is to see that difference and heterogeneity are givens. "ESL/EFL students will constitute approximately forty percent of the student population by 2000. . . ." (coalition report on English as a foreign language, in Lloyd-Jones and Lunsford 39). In higher education, enrollment figures changed as follows from 1976 to 1986:

American Indian enrollment increased about 20%, foreign enrollment increased about 55%, Hispanic enrollment increased about 60%, Asian enrollment increased about 125%—while black and white enrollments stayed about the same (white increasing a bit; "National Snapshot").

It's my sense, then, that when the conference participants adopted "democracy through language" as their official theme, they were not just sloganeering. They were using a phrase that summed up a number of important, concrete principles. First, our goal must be to produce active and questioning students who inquire and make meaning rather than just receive meaning. Second, difference is to be welcomed even if it is something we need practice in learning to live with: difference of language and culture in a nation, difference of opinion and view in scholarship and in a classroom, difference of skill and experience in an untracked classroom.

Of course, people did not fail to acknowledge that democracy is an ideology—not built into the universe or natural or neutral. Indeed, I heard some recognition of the vexing tension between the ideology of democracy and the almost inevitable authority imbalance in most classrooms or institutions of learning. Trying to do away with "right-answer teaching" is not the same as doing away with authority in classrooms. (These seasoned teachers from different districts were not advocating that parody of Dewey's idea—"do whatever you want, kiddies"—nor was Dewey.) Teachers emphasized carefully worked out classes and assignments—often experiential or workshoplike activities, often individualized for different students—and emphasized how this kind of teaching takes an enormous amount of authority and control. Indeed, I sometimes think there is a paradoxical cross-relationship here. Insofar as I run a class where I mostly lecture and the main thing is right answers that I possess and am judge of, I don't have to wield much authority and control: the authority is in the material and the right answers; I can just ride with it, things run themselves. But insofar as I try to set up a workshop class or discussion where there isn't a single right or best way and where I want to produce an interplay of different readings, different ways of writing, then I really need more authority and control in managing the class and the learning.

Putting the burden of this chapter in yet another way: the main theme of the conference was not "save our subject matter from the ravages of vulgarity" or "save Western values" or "save culture." It was "save our society and our children." This doesn't mean giving up on subject matter or even high culture. But what most distinguished the participants, in my view, was a deep caring for students.

NOTES

[1]From Carol Avery (response to draft):

> My most recent student teacher is a perfect example. She graduated [from college] summa cum laude in December, was a top student at one of the best local high schools, yet she came to me not knowing how to learn. She did not know how to use writing as a tool for reflection and learning. She lacked creativity and innovative thinking skills. She relied on me to suggest virtually all her lesson plans—a role I resisted. Because she had no awareness of how she herself learns, she was unable to address ways of teaching and learning with six-year-olds. She was so used to working for evaluation—one awareness she openly admitted—that she could not make a decision on which of two different colors of paper to use for a project. We struggled together and she did grow and begin to trust herself and take some risks. But I still have concerns about young people like her who are coming out of our schools today. And one of the sad things is that many administrators and teachers want people like this who will not question.

[2]From a recent *New York Times* column about tracking:

> [Tracking] is a practice notable for its pervasiveness and for the absence of scholarly evidence that it works.
> Last June [1989] the Carnegie Council on Adolescent Development called for an end to tracking in middle schools, characterizing it as "one of the most divisive and damaging school practices in existence. . . ."
> Robert Slavin of Johns Hopkins University recently surveyed research in which students were randomly assigned to heterogeneous and tracked classes and concluded that "as far as achievement is concerned, the effects for both high- and low-achieving students is neutral."
> Adam Gamoran, a sociologist at the University of Wisconsin in Madison, questions Mr. Slavin's reading of the evidence, arguing that high-achievers gain by tracking and low-achievers lose. "The overall result is no change, but the resulting inequalities are considerable," he said.
> In a 1986 article in the education journal *Phi Delta Kappan*, Jeannie Oakes, a Rand Corporation social scientist, argued that the students in the lower tracks—that is to say, most students—"suffer clear and consistent disadvantages" from the practice, including low self-esteem and low expectations that become self-fulfilling prophecies.
> A major reason, she said, is that the top tracks get the best teaching. . . .
> Albert Shanker, president of the American Federation of Teachers, argues that, given its deep roots, tracking will never be eliminated from "didactic" classrooms where teachers do most of the talking. But why not reframe the issue by getting away from "didactic" classrooms?
> A number of solutions have been proposed. Mr. Slavin's research has produced abundant evidence that cooperative learning—in which small groups of students work together on problems—is highly effective. "Say you're working on solving simultaneous equations," he said. "The slow students do well, so that the high achievers, who probably do a lot of the explaining, get a deeper grasp of the material."
> Schedules can be changed. In Bolton Landing, N.Y., on Lake George, all high school students take the same high-level Regents courses in English and

social studies for five periods a week. Then a sixth period is devoted to individualized instruction—enrichment for the top students and remedial work for those having trouble. "Getting rid of tracking has made for a much more harmonious social climate in the school," the Superintendent, Dalton F. Marks, said.

Computer-assisted instruction offers another alternative by allowing students in the same classroom to work at different paces. Steve Anderson, principal of the Cougar Valley Elementary School in Silverdale, Wash., said this could solve the problem of what to do with bright but socially immature students who typically skip a grade or two. "Now you can meet their intellectual needs without sacrificing social ones," he said. (Fiske)

³There is an interesting final paragraph in the coalition report on tracking that didn't make it to the published report of the whole conference (where there was a need for editing and cutting). The paragraph seems to exempt college teachers from having to teach heterogeneous classes: "Developmental placement at the college level is viewed as one possible route by which a student may attain a level of language, reading, and writing proficiency defined as acceptable by the institution. Each student begins in a course or program that meets his or her entry-level language needs and moves beyond that level to the defined level, which must be met by all students in the institution." I wasn't at any of the meetings of the committee that wrote the report and don't remember this point coming up in the discussion of the report by the whole conference. I'm not sure what assumptions lie behind this paragraph. Is it an attempt to distinguish between differences in knowledge and differences in ability? Or just a cop-out by college teachers? Or a tacit admission that college teachers can't learn the kind of flexible teaching required for heterogeneity and will always fall back on, say, lecturing?

⁴For the sake of the discussion, I've been granting Hirsch's premise that there is a single "grapholect" and that we can thus talk of standard written English as an unchanging or monolithic entity. But in fact this premise is debatable. What we see as standard written English contains more variation and flexibility than it did even a decade ago—more options. Look at the range of discourse that turns up in newspapers, magazines, and books compared with that of a decade or two ago. Notice too—perhaps even more surprising—how there are many more options even within "scholarly English" than a decade ago. A look at the journals shows us a striking range of published "dialects": for example, the old-fashioned heavy "Germanic" scholarly discourse; the somewhat lighter, more conversational and allusive British/rhetorical scholarly discourse; some kinds of feminist scholarly discourse that insist on a personal grounding; and a deconstructive or poststructural playful/difficult scholarly discourse. Note, in this connection, Wittgenstein's metaphor of language as a diverse, expanding city.

The Story of David and His Experiences with Tracking

Carol Avery
(elementary school section)

*I*MET DAVID when he was a first grader in my classroom. He is one of the most intellectually gifted children I have encountered in my years of teaching.

Now, ten years later, David regularly sends me packets of his writing to read and respond to—a whole year's worth at a time! He's bored, turned off, and radical. Right now his hair is punk—half purple and half black—and the first part of this year he failed most of his subjects in school. He told me the other night that he's brought those grades up this last marking period to B's and C's. I asked how he did that and he said, "Oh, I just decided to do it. That's all." But I didn't sense much commitment in his voice.

In first grade he was a student who remembered everything precisely as it was stated or read or discussed and who synthesized, analyzed, and produced fresh insights and conclusions to concepts we addressed in the classroom. He was also sloppy, lazy, and challenging of the expertise of those in authority and of the system. His desk was continually overflowing with papers, pencils, drawings, and late assignments. When he saw no value, or was uninterested, in assigned work, he dashed it off with little regard for precision or possible error.

David did not make teaching easy. He seemed to enjoy an intellectual game with me that said, "Can you find what I don't know and you do? Can you discover something you understand and I don't?" I chanced upon my best move in this game with David when I asked him to write. Writing provided the challenge to David. Writing was solving a mental puzzle: integrating all the polished knowledge, immature emotions, and emerging concepts that teemed in his mind and putting them down on paper in concise form. When I asked David to write (an activity he had not really engaged in before this time), I won his respect—and began a relationship with him that continues as a friendship to this day.

David, even at age six, was quite aware of his abilities and the value society placed on them. David was an elitist. But David was not a snob. He enjoyed and appreciated other children. He liked working with them. Compassion for others was a definite strength for him. And the other children liked David. He could answer their questions when they were stumped. He liked to play, and he was a creative leader and good competitor. Although they did not entirely understand him, this did not matter. David possessed qualities they admired, and he did not flaunt these talents. He was a resource for them, a strong peer model, and they all learned from him. I think David learned too. He learned something about relating with others, about valuing all people, not just those with the talents society values.

Throughout his schooling David has qualified for gifted and talented programs. (Even in my first-grade classroom he and four other children were assigned as a group because they were all fluent, self-taught readers.) Today, David's mother, Nancy, does not see the value of these programs for her son. "His elitist attitude is still alive and well," she reported to me in our phone conversation.

The programs for gifted and talented youngsters are supposedly designed to meet the special needs of these children. Nancy finds that, despite the best of intentions, oftentimes this means "more is better." "What is expected in the educational system is *more*, not *quality*. There is a lack of tapping creative abilities. Because there is no academic challenge, complacency sets in, and with it arrogance." David's attitude of "I really don't have to do this because I know this stuff, and I know I can test well" is one the family lives with on a daily basis and one they have struggled with for years.

I asked Nancy what differences she might envision if her son had not been in tracking situations. "The lack of motivation may not have changed," she replied. "But maybe he would have maintained some humility and learned those things that we, who are not as capable, rely on: hard work, responsibility."

The special programs promote David's self-esteem. "But that self-esteem works against him," says Nancy. "Enhanced self-concept either dampens his spirit further or builds arrogance." David enters these programs anticipating a challenge that never materializes. Often, the activities are more of what he has already done in the classroom. His creative energies—his spirit—are thwarted and his attitude of "I don't have to prove this" (and do this work) results.

David's mother does not feel that programs that remove David from the mainstream have made him unaware of others and their needs. "He's sensitive. He accepts others more than they accept him," she comments. "Tolerance is a strength for him." However, tracking programs prevent David from acting on this keen sensitivity to others and from developing skills in communicating with less able individuals. Peers are also denied the opportunity to learn from this talented child.

David has a brother three years younger than he. Carl is also in special programs. He is another exception to the norm in American schools—he is "learning-disabled" and has spent most of his school career in the "low group" even though his intelligence tests above average. "Once you are in the low group," says Nancy, "you are pigeonholed because that's what the system says you are."

"We've had both ends here," she continues. "What we've seen is that if you tell a kid he's good, he's good. If you tell him he's rotten, he's rotten. Each boy works best when the teaching presents a level of challenge. Special programs or tracking don't make that happen. In our experience it's been a few specific teachers along the way who treated each child as an individual."

I think of other special-needs children I've worked with. No two have been alike. Jenny, the learning-disabled child who spent two years in my classroom, was later put in a private school by her parents when they felt that the tracking program did not adequately meet her needs. Megan, the brilliant but isolated loner, became even more isolated in a gifted program that denied her ready access to her peers and the opportunity to develop everyday social skills. Joshua, whose strong artistic and story-telling abilities delighted his classmates, was shuttled into a tracking system that did not value his original ideas and that subsequently left him frustrated and discouraged with school.

Tracking seems to promote a narrowly defined norm of excellence in American culture. What are the costs? What talents remain undeveloped? What do we neglect to nurture in young children when we set them on specific courses so early in their educational careers? What opportunities are we denying our children? The answers are probably as unique as the children themselves.

At the end of our phone conversation, I told my friend Nancy about the English Coalition; our theme, "Democracy through Language"; and our statement against tracking. She reflected on all I had just said and responded, "Yes! It seems to me that in a democracy the educational system ought not to limit kids by defining who they are but rather present the challenge of learning to *all* kids and encourage them to learn *from* each other and *with* each other."

Sydney

Brooke Workman
(secondary school section)

*H*ER NAME WAS Sydney. She taught me about ad-
justing to individual differences. It was 1956, the second year of my teaching. And I was teaching eighth-grade civics to five
sections. On that first day, I reviewed the nature of the course and the
textbook. Near the end of the period, I asked students to suggest their
future occupation.

"Race car driver," "baseball pitcher," "nurse," "housewife" (remember, it was 1956), "engineer," and "psychoanalyst."

Psychoanalyst? I looked at my seating chart. Sydney Diamond.

The bell rang. All but Sydney left the room. A very physically mature
eighth grader, Sydney marched to my desk and asserted, "This civics
book is too immature."

I was twenty-three years old, had just finished a thesis on the com-
plexities of the Interstate Commerce Act, and was confronting my first
experience with eighth-grade genius. My first reaction was to engage in
postgrad sarcasm. "I'm sorry to hear that." But here was a kid that looked
"mature."

So I mumbled something about thinking about her concern as she
rushed off to second period. Then I rushed to the office files and her
folder. Results: plays in civic orchestra, teaches Hebrew, and has an IQ
(remember, it was 1956) that hit the top of the chart.

A Jeffersonian, I did not want to lose Sydney. And so I put her to work
on "political science" research, a synthesis of famous utopias and personal choice and creation of a new utopia. She was also a classroom
defense attorney in our mock trial and started a school creative writing
magazine called "It."

Thirty years later I heard that she is a psychoanalyst in California.

Mario

Nancy McHugh
(secondary school section)

MARIO WAS SMALL for his age and very insecure. He had been in special reading and remedial classes until the eleventh grade when he transferred to our school, which did not use tracking. At first he was unwilling to try any kind of writing. He said that he was "dumb," and he didn't think that he had anything to say. He was dyslexic, but he was far from dumb.

Under the group and partner work of an eleventh-grade contemporary composition class, he was gradually emboldened to try to imitate poems and prose passages. He read with interest the work of other students. Next he began bringing snippets of poems to class to show the teacher, poems he had written at home, outside of school work. As the teacher welcomed and praised his work, he began to enter more fully into the work of the class.

He ended up going first to a community college to make up credits and then to a university. He was the first in his family to do so. He might never have had a chance to catch fire or see the possibilities in himself and in the subject in a tracked class.

4 | Taking a Theoretical Stance

*A*n afternoon in the second week: Janet Emig conducts a workshop for everyone in the large meeting room. She gets us into groups of five and provides large sheets of paper and an assortment of markers and crayons.

First activity. Draw your theory of learning—a picture that illustrates your notion of how people learn. Some of my process notes about my efforts: "Feeling inept. How to do this? But a feeling of liberation too. I'm so out of my element I can't be judged. I'm frustrated that my picture needs explaining. We can think nonverbally, even if it's not communicable, but I'm sad that I drew 'from' a 'meaning'—clearly translating something already verbalized in my mind. Why should I mind this? Mine is not social, more internal and private. Old-fashioned."

She asks us to talk in our small groups: look at each others' drawings and discuss what we notice, both in the drawings and in the process of making them. Some interesting things emerge: there were no teachers in anyone's image of the learning process in our group. (No teachers, in fact, in almost any drawings of learning.) Also, when we discussed one anothers' pictures, we all took the maker's intention as the governing criterion for deciding how to "read" it.

Bob Scholes declares his crude drawing to have won. What cracks everyone up is how his quip tacitly articulates something in the air: so many of us feel inept at this classroom activity that "of course" is not competitive—just a "learning experience"—yet so many of us habitually try to get an A or prove we are good.

Second activity. Write your theory of learning—but in a metaphor of any length. I play with various metaphors in my exploratory jottings. Corny, purple. Eventually I write, "Learning is the gathering cyclone fragmenting and going through struggles—and waiting; self-agency; something emerges." My process: "Yuck! I can never think of metaphors that work when I try."

Again, useful discussion in small groups of the process and product.

Third, write your theory of learning in literal language. I write, "Learning is what people naturally do when supported and cherished: it involves following perplexity and letting it heighten—inviting maximum chaos and dissolution and allowing the process to

49

*go—percolate—riding the horse without fear—and trusting that new gestalts and mean-
ings will emerge. It is heightened if there's a dialectic between private and social dimensions." My process: "I can't find an alive metaphor till I try to write literally. Metaphor
came entirely unbidden."*

*Interesting discussion in small group and then in large group about modes of repre-
sentation. She asks us to think about how changes in medium or symbol system affected
our thinking. She spells out her own constructivist assumption: that using different symbol
systems seems to change what we see or say and thus suggests that we don't have direct
access to some fixed reality. But she manages to say it in an inviting way, making it an
invitation for us to articulate our own assumptions and theory rather than feel we are
supposed to agree with hers. She doesn't push for closure or right answers.*

IN MY SECOND chapter I described what I saw as a consensus about the
central practices of English: using language and looking back reflectively
at how one uses it. In my third chapter I described another agreement: a
potential connection between democracy and English studies. This second
agreement is related to the first one by a number of links. The centrality
of making meaning connects with the centrality of students making up
their own minds in both writing and reading—not copying down or rep-
licating the meanings in authoritative books or in teachers' minds. Students
should question not only their own writing and reading processes but also
those of others, even those in authority, to see what assumptions they rest
on and what consequences follow from them. This approach leads to an
affirmation of differences among interpretations and diversity among
points of view as inevitable and positive facts of classroom and society—
not features to be reduced or gotten rid of.

But I felt a third large area of agreement at the conference—fuzzy
yet important: an agreement that theory is a central and unifying focus
for English studies. Indeed, I wouldn't be surprised if the word *theory*
popped into many participants' minds first when someone asked them,
"What was important at the Coalition Conference?" It will become clear
how this agreement is related to the previous two.

Theory is a slippery and loaded term in the profession and has become
a point of contention in some departments. So what did theory mean at
the conference? Participants who hadn't studied literary theory carefully
(most of us) learned most about it from a few position papers devoted
explicitly to theory.[1] The closest thing to an official statement about
theory is the "Rationale" section of the final report of the college section
on the English major:

> Over ten years ago, Jonathan Culler ["Beyond Interpretation"]
> called for teachers of English to mitigate their near obsession with
> interpretation, a concern that, he argued, is "only tangentially related
> to the understanding of literature," and to focus on the "conventions

and operations of an institution, a mode of discourse." Other such proposals have been heard over the past few years, as the issues that have altered the thinking of the profession have begun to be translated into curricular and pedagogical practice. Robert Scholes wants the object of our study to be textuality. Arac, Messenger, and Sorensen argue for hermeneutics, poetics, and criticism. McCormick, Waller, and Flower suggest language, history, culture, and a focus on the cognitive and cultural aspects of reading and writing. Nelson emphasizes textuality and culture.

While there are differences among these positions, what each has in common is the recognition that as students learn to reflect on their own practices in reading and writing, they will become more self-aware, more independent and strong as readers and writers. It is significant that a number of these positions have already been translated into curricula: In *Professing Literature*, Gerald Graff lists more than a dozen departments that have moved in the directions we propose, specifically from programs in literary studies to programs in literary and cultural studies.

The issue of history (or more accurately, histories) is especially important. In the past, while literary history has often driven the curriculum of English studies, the idea of history—and how we make sense of the past—has been missing; rather, it has been assumed that coverage of a chronological span will add up to a sense of history. Coverage alone is an undesirable goal if it takes the place of serious inquiry into the problem of history. Coverage is also an increasingly unrealistic expectation: While complete coverage of a period in a course has never been fully possible, the recent expansion of the canon makes the notion of coverage even more problematic.

What students have to infer from period courses should become part of the curriculum. The alternative proposed here is to make literary history itself an object of study by investigating the nature of historical inquiries, historical transitions, and periodization, so that students can begin to recognize how they themselves are involved in them. For example, a course might begin by looking at some competing or overlapping descriptions of the shift from Renaissance to Classical ways of thinking and writing. T. S. Eliot's term for this shift—"dissociation of sensibility"—could provide a point of departure. The first hundred pages of Michel Foucault's *Order of Things* could be used to challenge and complicate Eliot's scheme by introducing a description of the Renaissance and Classical "epistemes" or ways of making sense of the world. These could be tested by contrasting texts of such Renaissance writers as Hooker, Donne, and Sidney with those of such neoclassical writers as Pope, Hume, and Fielding. Depending on circumstances, texts in the other media such as architecture, painting, sculpture, and music might also be included, along with the periodizing terminology of art historians, music historians, and social, political, and economic historians. The point of such a course would not be to apply Eliot or Foucault, but rather to test their theories and refine or even refute them. (Lloyd-Jones and Lunsford 33–34)

I'm struck that although this was written by the people at the conference who were most interested and knowledgeable about theory, they hardly use the word—making for an admirable concreteness and directness. In contrast, the word was commonly spoken by people not so knowledgeable. The professionals used it too, of course—and, interestingly, didn't go around saying, "Stop using the word *theory* unless you know how to use it professionally" (something that has been said to me a number of times by readers of my drafts). In short, people sometimes talked about theory in general as opposed any particular theory. This is a common enough usage in the profession; for example, Graff writes as follows: "think of literary theory not as a set of systematic principles, necessarily, or as a founding philosophy, but simply as an enquiry into assumptions, premises, and legitimating principles and concepts" (252).[2] But talk about "theory" in general may seem too loose, and so I follow Kathleen McCormick's usage (see her position paper in note 1) and talk in these chapters about "taking a theoretical stance" or "being theoretically aware." First I explore what I sense people meant in practice by "theory" or "taking a theoretical stance." Then I explore the question of what people seemed to mean by it in theory, particularly with regard to epistemology.

A Theoretical Stance in Teaching

I remember hearing discussions about the practical or pedagogical or political implications of this theoretical stance—discussions that took for granted rather than questioned the value of this theoretical awareness. And indeed I sensed this to be one of the great selling points of such an approach to theory, a point everyone appreciated: that we don't have to have interminable or abstract or opaque discussions of theory; we can have discussions of other things—teaching or issues or texts—and make use of a theoretical stance. I think participants agreed that this approach could enliven and sharpen teaching. As Scholes remarks, "I see that teaching and theory are always implicated in one another" (ix).

I've already described a theoretically aware classroom (as the conference participants implied it) when I described what coalition members came to think of as the central activity in a paradigm English class: the process of inviting and affirming multiple readings instead of a right reading and then explicitly reflecting on where those readings come from and where they go, what is at stake in those readings, what premises are implied and interests are served by those readings (see ch. 3, "Difference").

For another concrete picture, I point to the workshop Janet Emig led that I evoked as the epigraph to this chapter. It was a class devoted explicitly to trying to get us to articulate the theories behind all our talk about teaching and learning at the conference. Emig periodically chided us for leaving those theories tacit (for example, in discussions of Hirsch and his list). Her strategy for asking us to be theoretically aware asked us in a cleverly concrete and roundabout way to investigate the relation between what we know and how we represent it on paper. She was helping people to complicate their notion of language and representation and what those notions can signify. She was also following the path that Heath emphasizes, asking people to construct their own theories rather than just discuss "received" or "important" theories. And, finally, I appreciate the Polanyi-like emphasis on trying to exploit tacit knowledge. She asked us to work out explicit and conscious premises about epistemology—but only after we had engaged in concrete acts of representing during which our attention was not at all on epistemological implications. This sequencing of activities led to insight and surprise; people couldn't just espouse epistemological principles they already believed to start with. Her use of experiential and non-self-conscious activities illustrated how one can work on these matters of theory at all levels of schooling.

Shirley Brice Heath gave yet another picture of theory in practice: an elementary classroom where children write on the board as many instances as possible of language uses in which one person asks, orders, suggests, or invites someone to do something. The children then go on to make hypotheses about linguistic forms, language use, and social or role relations between people.

Of course, the coalition proposal for the English major itself is an enactment of what a theoretical stance looks like in the flesh: in effect that paradigm classroom writ large. Readers interested in the major should consult the full report, but it suggests, for example, that English majors should engage in different ways of reading (e.g., aesthetic, biographical, formalist, gender-specific, rhetorical, and political) and understand the premises and modes of arguing of each perspective. Similarly, they should know "something of the critical and historical principles behind the construction of literary and cultural histories" (Lloyd-Jones and Lunsford 35).

For another example of the theoretical stance in teaching, here is Carole Edmonds in her position paper, "Literary Theories and Undergraduate English Classes: Practice Must Be Informed by Theory":

Last year I chose to teach *Their Eyes Were Watching God* by Zora Neale Hurston in a freshman course. It brought a text by a black woman of a different time period and place into my all-white midwestern classroom. That does not take theory to do. The difference theory made was to bridge from text selection—in itself a conscious political act—to classroom practice in new ways that invigorated my reading and teaching and the students' reading and engagement with the text. I not only allowed students to respond to the text but built on their questions and issues to raise feminist issues, racial issues, and educational issues, bringing in reviews, descriptions of educational opportunities for women, commentary on Hurston's stand on integration, information on marriage laws, and anything else that helped us look at the text openly. I also told students that the choice of the text was political, involving a view of the study of literature that suggests that we should see how our thinking has been shaped by our culture as the author's was shaped by hers but also recognizing that Hurston does not "speak" for black women of the 1920s any more than students speak for everyone else in their age group or racial group. A text is an experience in language. The students' papers reflected careful reading of the book, and they raised more questions than they answered. Out of my greater awareness of theoretical perspectives, I believe I opened the text and the classroom experience to allow more critical examination of issues and gave students responsibility for the implications of their views.

Theoretical Implications of Taking a Theoretical Stance

But if the theme is theory, we cannot stay mired in mere practice. I sometimes sensed the following question in the minds of those who weren't trained or skilled in theory: "We seem to be buying the importance of being theoretically aware, but in doing so what theoretical or philosophical position are we buying? I believe in being open about my premises, even about my interests; I don't mean to hide things. But what does this really mean?"

Since the conference ended, I have tried to think about this matter. I've written far more about theory in my notes and exploratory musings and drafts than about any other issue, and I have sought more feedback on it—all the while feeling troubled that perhaps I shouldn't even be messing with it because I'm not qualified and because it wasn't one of the major or explicit focal points of the conference. Yet talk about theory was common at the conference, and theory is a major issue in the profession, and so I end up now with two chapters on it—probably a big mistake. But as I've thought about this matter, I've gotten most interested in the epistemological implications of what it means to say we should be theoretically aware. I see two translations:

1. "We don't affirm any particular theory, premises, interests, or epistemological position. But we urge the importance of looking at premises and interests." This is the smallest claim about epistemology.

2. "We don't affirm any particular theory. But we maintain that to look at everyone's premises is to see that no premise can claim to be universally true." This is not a large epistemological claim, but it is a significant one. Kathleen McCormick seems to be making it in her position paper: "To become theoretically self-aware, therefore, is to recognize the situated nature of our positions and interpretations . . . to see that they are *not universally true* but rather historically situated."

I am interested in what is politically and professionally at stake here. How we translate theoretical awareness bears on the concrete reality of how we live and work with each other in English departments and in the profession. So where did the conference tend to come out on these translations? The answer is not obvious for—and perhaps this is an important fact in itself—there was great tacitness about epistemology. I'm not sure whether the "Rationale" section of the college report that I quoted above implies the first or the second translation. In fact, what interests me is how easy it is for the borderline between these two epistemological positions to become fuzzy. I sense a temptation to hold both positions without realizing that they are at odds with each other.

What's attractive about the first position is that it is so humble. "We argue in favor of no epistemological position—indeed we fight for a hearing for all positions." One can, it seems to me, fairly ask a department or even a profession to adopt this kind of theoretical awareness, and this is really what in the end I think the coalition members were quietly doing. It is this position that helps a community deal better with existing contention: "Of course we disagree. But we must keep listening to each other and make sure no view is allowed a privileged position since we cannot agree on what it would take to make a view privileged or correct." The position is simply a request that we all talk and listen better to each other by being more clear about our positions.

It may seem odd to give a temperamental label like "humble" to an epistemological position, but I am interested in the profiles of theory positions. Perhaps not quite "profiles" as the FBI uses the term, for example, to identify people's epistemology from watching them on line at the United Airlines ticket counter. I am simply making the point made by most people interested in critical theory: to have a position is not just to create a well-formed sentence but to engage in a speech act: the act of doing something to someone. So it is by their speech acts that we shall know them: whether a position really invites increased dialogue or increased separation and nonhearing—whether it has the effect of bringing more people into the conversation or keeping more people out.

But notice how easy it is to slide silently from the first epistemological position to the second one: "We argue for no position and fight for a hearing for all because we know that no position can be objectively or universally true." This seems like a small move, yet in making it one excludes a large portion of the profession: any teacher or scholar who doesn't totally write off the possibility of right interpretations or true knowledge.

This second position is paradoxical or perhaps self-contradictory because while it says that no position can be universally true, it makes that negative or exclusionary claim as universally true (or to put the claim positively, it asserts that all knowledge must be socially constructed). "Universally true" may seem like strong language, but this second position asserts that there are no exceptions.

As an example of how hard it is to keep clear the line between the first and the second epistemological positions—between the "we don't know" stance and a genuine epistemological demand—notice the tendency to create a halfway position between the two. Paul Armstrong, a strong and sophisticated advocate for theoretical awareness at the conference, while not arguing that there is such a thing as *right* interpretation, does suggest in his position paper (and in a *PMLA* essay that won the Parker award in 1983) that there is such a thing as truly wrong interpretation. With this Karl Popper–like move, he is in effect allowing for the existence of a kind of true knowledge. Another example is even the simple kind of thinking Piaget alludes to, that of a child inferring from a father's lathering his face that he is about to shave. When such an inference turns out to be correct, it seems to me an instance of right interpretation or true knowledge. Surely some of our interesting interpretation and knowledge is of this sort—and not just in science but in teaching and learning and even in literature. (Perhaps what this example suggests is that not all interpretation or knowledge is hermeneutic.)

Note that in arguing for the virtues of the first epistemological translation and the problems with the second, I'm not trying to say that we all have to be sweet and pliable or that if we champion theoretical awareness we must agree chameleonlike with everyone else or take a nonpartisan stance. The theoretical stance correctly insists that, after all, everyone has a partisan epistemological theory—if not explicitly, then implicitly—and it's no fair pretending one is theoryless. Nevertheless, I'm arguing that there's a momentous political and professional choice that people must make here: whether or not to fuse one's epistemological position with one's commitment to a theoretical stance; whether or not to say, "If you want to be theoretically aware, you must agree with me about epistemology."

Nor am I trying to pretend that the first epistemological translation is innocent. It has its own ideology and interests: a particular vision of a community. And it is a vision that, because it favors what looks like a naive "fairness" ("Now boys and girls, we all have to take our own turns. Please don't push, please don't raise your voices"), can be accused of favoring the status quo or the powers or privileges already in place. Nevertheless, I urge it as our best hope. If we want to invite people who disagree with us to be theoretically aware, we must be willing to define theory in the first, more open fashion. If we slide into the second epistemological position, we are saying to many colleagues in the profession, "Theory, in itself, shows that you are wrong—by definition," thus ensuring that those colleagues will treat theory as the enemy. It's no fair then to self-righteously blame them for not being interested in "merely looking at premises" or "merely being critically aware" when looking at premises and being critically aware have been preemptively defined to mean "You are troglodytes."

A move from the first to the second epistemological position is particularly problematic when it is performed silently, with premises kept tacit. That is, we sometimes hear cheerful talk about making disagreement the center of our profession, but this talk slips over into, "Of course, no position could be objectively or universally true. How silly to assume otherwise. Of course we know that foundationalist epistemology has been repeatedly demolished. Who doesn't know this?" What's tricky is the "of course" stance. People who talk this way emphasize openly that we cannot have certain knowledge, while keeping tacit their premise that we can in fact have certain knowledge that conservative epistemology is false.

For a long time, people with power and prestige in the field of English have tended to try to show that marginal groups like feminists, reader-response critics, Marxists, and those who did cultural criticism were wrong by definition, beyond the pale. Now these formerly marginal groups have genuine power, and it's tempting to try to show that traditionalists are wrong by definition. Nevertheless, it is precisely this epistemological charity or theoretical humility that the profession badly needs—whether wielded by the previously marginalized or the previously privileged. There is genuine hope of inviting all members of the profession in under the umbrella of theory for a more open dialogue about positions. Theory, defined largely, could help the profession have a better conversation and figure out what it needs to figure out. If defined more narrowly—as in the second epistemological position (and especially if done covertly while pretending to be open)—"theory" just becomes one more party in the tiresome fights that go round and round in the profession of English. Will we welcome full difference or just those kinds of difference that feel comfortable?

When Gerald Graff (professor of English at Northwestern University and author of *Professing Literature*) visited us halfway through the conference, there occurred what I read as an irony of style versus theory on this issue. He introduced his talk by saying he would read us some of what he had read at a Yale conference but would leave out some technical parts that probably wouldn't interest us—and proceeded to read it in a kind of mumbled, offhand way. People's backs went up at what seemed a condescending or elitist manner (see references to him in the "Coalition Blues" [ch. 9] and in "Mother Goose's Coalition Rhymes" [interlude following ch. 12]), though I suspect that shyness played a role here. Yet Graff was the only person I heard at the conference who was really clear and unambiguous in asserting the need for the first epistemological translation of theoretical awareness: that when there is disagreement, a department or institution must organize *around* the disagreement; that the "position" of the department must be that no one wins—must be "We don't know, we can't agree, let's hear more"; that polity must be based on an attempt to maintain a respectful hearing for all positions for the sake of maximum disagreement or intersection of competing positions; that no one must be read out of the polity because of an unfashionable approach; that all are needed.

I want to make it clear that with all my talk in favor of the first epistemological position—seemingly open, wishy-washy, passive, too sweet—I'm not trying to foster mere quiet, passive, relativist spectatorship. I'm emphasizing a crucial distinction between two levels of rhetorical activity: having a particular theory and taking a theoretical stance. That is, of course we are probably trying to persuade others that we are right. But if we are really serious about getting them to listen to us or see it our way—to engage with us so that we can sway them toward our particular theory or ideology—then we must also set up and project a different and larger theory or ideology, a larger set of rules of the game within which to peddle our particular theory.

Perhaps this is putting it too crudely, but I am insisting on the difference between exerting oneself to win a game and exerting oneself nevertheless to stay within the larger rules of the game (without which winning is not possible). This means fighting as hard as one can against the other team yet also struggling to work with them in an act of cooperation or collaboration in following the rules. For example, suppose I want to persuade others that all knowledge is socially constructed, by definition. My efforts will be senseless unless I can entice those who disagree to enter with me into a theoretical stance—unless I can set up a larger ideology or set of rules to play under, a larger community of discourse whose rules say that we don't yet have the criteria to settle the disagreement between us. These larger rules say, in effect, that you are willing to listen seriously to me, but in return I promise to listen to you under the supposition that you may turn out to be right—or persuasive.

In short, it's not a question of choosing between a seemingly unrealistic, wishy-washy first epistemological translation and a seemingly tough-minded realistic stance of sticking up for our own particular theory and interests. Rather, I would insist, both go together: it's not possible to stick up effectively for our own particular theory unless we create that larger set of discourse rules within which to create the possibility of genuine engagement with people who disagree. (See my "Methodological Doubting and Believing: Contraries in Inquiry," which explores ways to induce greater investment and engagement on the part of students.)

To return, then, to my original question: What was the position of the conference on theory? There was no official position, but this is my reading: the spirit of the English Coalition Conference was large and generous, but the language and thinking were not worked out with care. Therefore, much that was said casually and in passing about what it means to be "theoretically aware" or what "theory means" could lead to the narrower or exclusionary stance of the second epistemological translation. Indeed, the very distinction I'm making between the two positions was not clear to me until I went home and took time to reflect and write about my notes—though I did, in fact, feel a kind of itch or discomfort at moments during the conference because of what I feel now as slippage between the first and second positions.

Obviously I have an axe to grind here. I'm trying to create for our profession more of a quality that was happily present at the conference: a spirit where people who disagree deeply even about basic premises can come together in a room and talk and listen—and walk out later seeing things differently (a spirit that Wayne Booth helped make possible in person at the conference and in his *Modern Dogma and the Rhetoric of Assent*). I find arrogance and condescension to be the characteristic sins of our profession—qualities that lead people into not listening, not learning, not changing, and staying stuck in their positions. A commitment to being theoretically aware can help lead to intellectual growth and lessen the tendency of people just to repeat their positions interminably —as I think it helped to do at the conference. But I'm concerned that the injunction to be theoretically aware sometimes has the opposite effect.

This analysis leads naturally to an interesting question: Does an emphasis on theory or theoretical awareness mean more agreement or disagreement? It seems as though there is an obvious association between the foregrounding of theory and disagreement. The importance of theory at the conference and in the profession is surely related to the central fact of deep disagreement in the English profession: what consensus there was has broken down. We no longer just argue about conflicting interpretations of a poem; we can't even agree about what it means to interpret a poem (Graff talks about "the self-consciousness generated when consensus breaks down" [253]). I don't mean to imply that disagreement need be a bad thing or even to imply that there was a good old days (or bad old days) when everyone agreed with everyone else. Academics have always been contentious—English professors at the head of the pack. Nevertheless, it is fair to say that the profession no longer shares some rough but powerful assumptions it once shared: about what literature is, about how to go about reading a work of literature, about what makes a good and a bad reading, and about which works and practices are best and most important and most necessary to teach to students. These deeper disagreements are a benefit, are helping us think; but my point is that they can be associated with an interest in theory theory (whether as cause or effect or both).

Certainly in our family my wife and I have come to recognize a clear relation between theory and disagreement: whenever we focus on the theory or principles involved in some decision we have to make—something as small as what to do for an evening or a week or something as large as where to live—we usually disagree or even fight. Yet whenever we get down to looking at actual instances or examples of things to do or places to live, we agree surprisingly often. This sounds like a warning about the limitations of theory, and indeed I experience it to some extent as such. And yet our act of finally noticing this pattern and learning to finesse some theory discussions was an act of theory making and was very helpful indeed. There are paradoxes here, perhaps stemming from the fact that people sometimes hold tacit theories at variance with their conscious ones.

But there is also an intriguingly harmonious dimension to theory— an irenic effect of taking the theoretical stance—as long as we take it in the first, epistemologically open sense. If the problem of the profession is that we cannot agree on anything, theory will allow us to "make the problem into the solution"—and this was one of the important phrases at the conference. That is, if we simply disagree, we tend to fight— especially if we are academics; but if we disagree and we can look at our quarrel with the magic lens called theory, we can transform "we disagree" to "let's look at the grounds of our different positions and thereby recognize that we can't figure out what is wrong or right."

Graff spoke to us of the need to move from what he called a consensus model of polity to a conflict model. When people assume a consensus model, they assume there *is* an answer, and inevitably the goal becomes to settle the question of what it is. Thus people will fight for what's true, who's right, who gets to occupy or name the consensus. An emphasis on theory, in contrast, helps us move to Graff's conflict model of polity, which suggests that we cannot decide on right answers. This assumption invites people to be more willing to accept differences—and *be* different.

If we finally decide that no one will win, we have a better chance of gathering (if not uniting) to look with more equanimity at the variety of our answers and try to think about the implications or premises and processes behind them. If we can't agree on a product, we can agree on a process: looking at how meaning is made. The specific answer then doesn't matter so much and isn't worth killing each other over. If we agree on taking a theoretical stance—trying to spell out competing premises and interests—we can agree that we all have partisan positions and are all "situated" with respect to our positions in history, culture, class, gender, race, sexual orientation, and so forth. Focusing on theory seems to take the sting out of disagreement. (Paradoxically, what Graff calls a consensus model leads to more fighting, and what he calls a conflict model leads to more concord.)[3]

The relative harmony at the conference was a peculiar and interesting feature, one that bears further thinking. But one important source was an agreement about the centrality of trying to be theoretically aware. For there were plenty of important differences of opinion, approach, and temperament among (remember) sixty people together for three weeks. Participants knew they couldn't agree on many things, and they decided to agree to disagree. But they knew they *did* agree not just about the plight of students, the beleaguered position of many teachers and the teaching profession, the vicissitudes of teaching, and the danger of education being driven by short-answer information and mass testing— but also about the importance of emphasizing how people reach conflicting conclusions as they read and how people write and figure things out differently. Or, to use another piece of jargon, instead of considering the disagreements a problem, people could agree to "problematize" the very processes leading to all those viewpoints.

If this perspective sounds too "theoretical" or "academic"—easy agreement about "mere" theory—there was a practical and political side to this way of looking at things. That is, for this conference—functioning as a microcosm of the profession—theory seemed to invite a friendly and productive dialogue (if not always complete agreement) among the many and sometimes troublesome factions of the profession: literary studies, critical theory, rhetoric and composition, cultural studies, and English education. All these factions came usefully together at Wye around theory, and I am convinced they can do so in the wider world. Or to state it differently, most of the intellectual enterprises that are connected in any way to "English" seem to be happy to think of themselves as engaged in theory: literary theory, critical theory, composition and rhetorical theory, cultural theory, learning theory, reading or reception theory, language or linguistic theory, and cognitive theory. The emphasis on theory itself seems to make people less contentious even if their theories are at complete odds with each other.

Graff went on to argue that if we accept the conflict model, it means that we don't have to take on the job of changing all the colleagues we don't agree with. If we feel we have to wipe out error, it breeds cynicism or hopelessness: after all, the error comes from "impossible old fogeys with tenure who haven't had a new thought in years" or "facile young whippersnappers we'd never have hired if standards hadn't fallen but who now have tenure because publishers now seem to want to publish that nonsense." But we can let all this sniping go, says Graff, and the seeming cacophony of voices will be productive and useful to our students (and of course to ourselves)—and may even build community— so long as we can simply put competing principles and premises out on the table and make the differences public: make them an arena of sharing. In a department built on a conflict model, the opposed voices can lead to thoughtful exploration rather than just underground dissension. When differences remain underground, teachers just talk irritatedly to themselves or their small coteries in tiny separate worlds, and students don't really learn from our differences.

Differences. The single word, central at the conference, points to how theory is somehow about both disagreement and working together. At a number of times during the three weeks I felt I could almost use the words *theory* and *differences* interchangeably. When we translate theory to the human level—and I think this was the main accomplishment of the conference in this realm—it amounts to accepting differences among people and among positions, indeed, sanctioning and rewarding them as good things: celebrating diversity, not trying to get everyone to be the same, framing and taming conflicts.

I sense that we will sabotage ourselves as a discipline if we persist in operating on the premise that some view has to be right and all others wrong, that someone has to win and others lose. I am tempted to see our profession at the forefront of work that the whole academy must soon engage in—indeed, the whole globe, since of course we'll destroy ourselves if we really insist that one side must be right and the others wrong.

Perhaps this account of diversity sounds too sweet, so let me point to an interesting moment that illustrates how nothing is simple—even a theoretical commitment to endorse differences. Near the end of the conference, when we were hearing reports from subgroups, one report spoke of "a sense of common humanity." There were sharply voiced objections to the phrase from people specially committed to theory: the phrase smacks of "essentialism," they argued; that is, it suggests the dangerous notion that we are all the same; it's the kind of language that promotes intolerance of difference. These speakers had argued a number of times during the conference that any talk about something being "essential" can serve as a stick to hit people with, since if we agree about what is essential or about common humanity, then that agreement can serve as a fence to exclude certain people as outside what is essential or common humanity. Yet two members of the subgroup that sponsored the report felt strongly that the phrase needed to be there. What was interesting to me was not just that strong feelings were in the air here, that nerves were being touched; more pointedly, the two who objected to the phrase "common humanity" were white and the two who insisted on keeping it were black—all four being women. No easy answers here. (This was one of the few moments when we fought about final wording of reports. I and others were grateful to the planning committee for setting up things so that we could usually finesse such discussions.)[4]

NOTES

[1]From a position paper by Kathleen McCormick, "Literary Theory in the Undergraduate Curriculum":

> We have no choice of whether or not to have theory in the classroom. Theory is always there—in us and in our undergraduates. We are all always already theorists. We have a choice only of whether or not we and our students will be self-conscious (that is to say, theoretical) about the theories that guide our perceptions. If, for example, I say, "I know that Stephen Dedalus's poem 'Ardent Ways,' in Joyce's *Portrait of the Artist as a Young Man,* is meant to be bad poetry," I am not expressing a purely "subjective" or purely "objective" position. Rather my statement is driven by assumptions derived from a variety of theories—about what good poetry is, about authorial intention, about the status of a reader who can truly know what a text means. These theories are operating whether or not I am self-aware enough to acknowledge their influence on me.
>
> My contention—that we and our students are always already theorists—assumes that literary theories, as a part of our culture's literary (and more general) ideology, organize our systems of belief often without our being aware of their influence on us. One of the exciting aspects of teaching students to theorize their own positions is helping them become aware—often for the first time—that they respond to a text or situation in a particular way because they are influenced by some particular theory. This process relates to the wider educational practice of attempting to get students to become aware of the general ideological constraints and empowerments within which they live. . . .
>
> To become theoretically self-aware, therefore, is to recognize the situated nature of our positions and interpretations, to acknowledge that they come about as a result of certain beliefs, principles, and broader ideologies—to see that they are *not universally true* but rather historically situated. Recognizing the situated nature of our positions should not cause us to despair over either a lost objectivity or subjectivity. For the belief in objectivity or subjectivity is itself situated. This is not to say that our beliefs are any less *real* than we once

might have thought they were: it is in fact our very situatedness or interest-edness that impels us to take up certain positions in the first place. As Terry Eagleton has commented, "There is no possibility of a wholly disinterested discourse. . . . All of our descriptive statements move within an often invisible network of value-categories, and indeed without such categories we would have nothing to say to each other at all. . . . Interests are *constitutive* of our knowledge, not merely prejudices which imperil it" (13–14). . . .

If we teach from a self-consciously theoretical position, we change the function of the classroom from one in which knowledge is disseminated to one in which the principles of the production of knowledge itself are ex-amined and critiqued. Students learn to recognize that they have particular positions or interpretations, to explore the ways in which these positions are culturally situated, and they learn how to develop, articulate, and analyze these positions. In talking about a theoretically self-aware classroom situation, Jeffrey Peck argues: "The classroom . . . becomes a productive rather than a reproductive environment, one in which not only interpretations, but also standards, expectations, and goals are negotiated by the teacher and student" (51).

From a position paper by Paul Armstrong, "The Ethical Importance of Teaching Theory in a Pluralistic Universe":

> Practice in interpreting stories, plays, and poems should alternate at all levels of the college curriculum with theoretical reflections about the assumptions implicit in various modes of reading. Students should not only receive training in how to develop detailed, imaginative, persuasive interpretations; they should also become self-conscious about how the relations they see in a text or between texts depend on their assumptions about literary works and the human world, and they should learn how varying their presuppositions can alter what is open to their view.

Another important source of talk about theory for participants was Robert Scholes's *Textual Power*—one of the most frequently cited books on the suggested reading list. He writes:

> [T]he first job of any teacher of criticism is to bring the assumptions that are in place out in the open for scrutiny. Post-structuralist theory offers an ex-tremely sophisticated and powerful set of procedures for accomplishing pre-cisely this task. That is why it is important.
> . . . Literary theory does not exist in some pure realm of thought but in a world of institutional structures and political forces, which means that theo-reticians must theorize not only over texts themselves but over the role of literary and linguistic study in the development of citizens who will themselves play many institutional roles in their lives, either critically aware or as insen-sitive dupes and victims. (xi)

Despite Scholes's remark about the importance of poststructural theory, I didn't hear (in the groups I was in) much talk about theory that echoes, for example, Paul de Man's more pointedly tropological or rhetorical sense of the term: "the figural structure of language that insures a division variously described as a gap between sign and meaning, between meaning and intent, between the performative and constative functions of lan-guage, and between rhetoric as persuasion and rhetoric as trope" (Culler, "Paul de Man" 275).

²From Joan Hartman (response to draft):

> Naturally I got to puzzling about why we didn't spend much time on particular theories or theories in conflict. I guess we're not foundationalists, looking for the single theory that undergirds and legitimizes all our other theories and practices. We've moved, with various stages of skepticism, from positivism to constructivism. Perhaps, given our place in time (since attention to theory is recent), we're particularly aware of theory as what we have recently made; perhaps this awareness will recede, though something else is bound to supplant it one of these days (how's that for skepticism?). We see most theories as accentuating particular stances—Marxist, feminist, psychoanalytic? Probably the only theory that claims foundational status is deconstruction of the Derrida–de Man–Miller sort.

³From Angela Dorenkamp (response to draft):

> I asked [Graff] after that session about situatedness, which, as you know, includes gender. If Carol Gilligan is near the mark and women's moral code includes peacemaking as a value, what did he think the response of academic women might be to the conflict model? Jean Baker Miller also comments on women's desire to avoid conflict. Graff said they would just have to learn to engage in these set-tos. Another question I had of this model and of your account of it is this: I can't imagine that most academics will not think of it as a game of winning and losing. Maybe it will take another generation, maybe a new human nature. I understood the conflict to be real conflict, since he did say something about untenured faculty perhaps not wanting to come up against a powerful tenured person. I wish he hadn't used a "conflict" model but one that indicates a tracing of theoretical constructs or whatever is up for discussion. I would personally prefer a more collegial model, though I am passionate in my defense of a variety of positions and beliefs!

⁴I myself struggle with this "antiessential" business. On the one hand, the whole debate has sensitized me to notice that I do have a weakness for talking about something being "really" or "essentially" or "naturally" so and so—and how such locutions may hide premises I'd better examine. But, on the other hand, it seems to me that many of the strong antiessentialists themselves fall into the same trap. They like to say that language is essentially social (not willing to admit that there might be marginal or even not so marginal cases where the private dimension of language is just as essential—pronouncing that a sense of language being private is always illusory); or that all knowledge is mediated by language (thereby ruling out any knowledge not in a symbolic form, such as bodily knowledge); or that all language is only about other language. In particular, the phrase "always already," a favorite jargonic tic in theory, seems to me to reveal a hunger for universalizing.

I ask that we look at the premises of such locutions. It seems to me that whenever people say that "all *x* is *y*," they are making an analytic rather than an empirical statement—a move to redefine the keys on the keyboard rather than to type something. Of course, this is fine if you define language as always only being about language—that all typing (discourse) is nothing but redefining keys on the keyboard. But I'm troubled by the move to rule out the possibility of things occasionally or possibly being otherwise.

Changes in the Teaching Conditions between 1957 and 1987

Nancy McHugh
(secondary school section)

*I*FIRST STARTED teaching in 1957 at University High School, part of the Los Angeles unified school district, a large academic high school near UCLA with a heterogeneous population of 4,800 students on double sessions at that time. Since then I have taught at two other academic and comprehensive high schools, both in the San Fernando Valley suburbs, one rural-suburban and barely heterogeneous, one "inner city" with 1,600 students bused in. I have also spent four years in the district office of instruction, where I directed four writing projects and visited schools K–12 as part of my work, including four Catholic schools that were part of my project. There have been many changes in those times in terms of students' home environments, school environments, scope and sequence of curriculum, and collegiality.

Students are different—or are they? They certainly appear different and behave differently. Students in 1957 appeared far more malleable and interested in learning. They may not have been, but they behaved so. They cared about education, and their parents cared. Even in Los Angeles, most students had two parents and were given rather strict rules for behavior, homework, etc. Parents came to school meetings and inquired about their children's work even without prompting from the teachers. Most students did not use drugs or abuse alcohol except on some special occasion such as the prom. Students did homework and were supervised in the doing of it. Few had jobs; those who did did not put the job ahead of school. Students who could not keep up with the postsputnik rigors of curriculum dropped out or went to vocational schools.

During the late 1960s students looked different: they were dressed for the beach or the commune; they had long hair. They argued about homework and assignments and reading, but they did the work. Few used drugs although some were experimenting with substances as they were with ideas like alienation and existentialism. They were still part of family units against which they were rebelling. They read. We opened up the curriculum and procedures for these students, but underneath the poses they did not seem really very different even though their behaviors seemed different superficially.

Today's students seem paradoxically more sophisticated and younger. There is little that they have not experienced in what used to be called the adult world. They take drugs, they drink, and they talk about sex freely. Most of my students work, some because they have to, but many also because they want things: cars, clothes, skis; some contribute one half of the family income. They do not do homework; they do not "have time." They are "into" many things and feel pressured by all of them. Many have little supervision; they belong to one-parent homes, or they live alone. They read as little as possible; their reading skills are poor. They have far shorter attention spans and accept far fewer pressures or strictures than their counterparts in earlier years. But I believe that they are more honest and certainly just as bright. With all the changes in their situations and expectations, they seem today in twelfth grade much as tenth-grade students seemed two decades ago. They appear quite hedonistic, but they are kind to one another. Their peer group is far more important than any adult influence.

Home environments appear to have changed: single-parent homes, less or no supervision, fewer rules, and less instruction in standards and codes of behavior. Parents do not participate much in school activities. They want their children to be "successful," that is, get good grades and get into college (preferably a good one), but they do not seem to be very much involved in "how." It seems as if their children have grown beyond them; life-styles differ, sharing seldom takes place, or else the parents are "peer-pals." Here and there are students who fit the earlier mode, but they seem "out of it" in all but grades!

School environments have changed radically in some ways, not enough in others. Most schools are hopelessly overcrowded, making do with chairs, tables, machines, office space that are hopelessly outmoded. Even books are old. New money for books is just not trickling down. Many schools use textbooks with 1960s dates. Ditto machines have been replaced by xerox machines that break down all too frequently. Classes are far larger: 36.9 students is the norm in Los Angeles, with many classes above 40, usually English and social studies because these do not require space and equipment as do science and shop classes. My present school has 3,400 students, 1,600 bused in, 25 ESL classes, 700 students who have been here fewer than three years, 300 students who have never before been in any school, 46 languages, and 140 faculty members all on a campus designed for 2,000 maximum. The average English classroom has no overhead, no projector of any kind, no computers or word processors, and little access to up-to-date equipment; there is one part-time audiovisual "specialist" (a teacher with one period off who doles out equipment when possible). Libraries are understaffed and understocked, although new detection systems have helped to preserve book stocks. The book room is hopelessly overcrowded. There is no media center, although there are some media capabilities in the "refurbished" library. Teachers have no decent work rooms, lounges, lavatories, offices. There is no professional library. Very little has been done to give faculty members updates in new methods, new philosophies, new machines. Some individuals use computers and word processors, but there is no program toward proficiency for either faculty or students. Buildings are dirty; custodial help is very poor and intermittent (no substitutes). We have no language arts room or auditorium, just a multipurpose room that does little but house large crowds. While these facilities may have seemed adequate for the 1950s and 1960s, they are certainly not adequate now in terms of population or educational needs for the twenty-first century. When this school was new in 1959, it must have held great promise. The promise has not been fulfilled.

It should not be a surprise that the curriculum has changed relatively little. The median age of teachers of English is 54 (down from 56); the curriculum in practice reflects that fact. While some have "heard of" new methods and theories (some through professional conferences and journals, some through writing projects), not very many practice new pedagogy. At least we no longer have to serve all social functions in English classes (selecting careers, learning to use the telephone properly, teaching social behavior of the most mundane kind); but we do serve as the primary testing organ for the school: proficiency tests, basic skills tests, assessment programs—these are just a few that are usually tested (and prepared for) in English classes (because "everyone takes English"). Reading is in poor shape, except perhaps for honors and advanced placement programs. Students do not read outside of class; if they are required to, they use *Cliff's Notes* for novels and plays and refuse or bluff in relation to other materials. If they read in class, they read at such slow rates that lessons become either impossible or three-ring circuses. There is no coordination of student reading from grades 9 to 12, so students may report on the same materials over and over and do. There is no coordinated reading program by grade level. Speaking and listening get very little attention. Critical thinking skills are also slighted, as one might guess.

Because students used to be read to and read, they came to school with both some proficiency and some background. Reading could be assigned as homework and would be done for the next day's classwork. Today most teachers do discrete assignments, things that can be covered in one day. Absenteeism and shifting populations make such schemes, if not mandatory, at least conducive to survival. The most tragic aspect is that teachers seem not to have grasped the new reality and the philosophy that must go with it: "All children can learn; all children deserve success." For today's students that success may take longer and require many different techniques on the part of teachers, but it is possible if teachers truly want to empower students and want to empower each other to help in that process.

Collegiality—we did not use that word in 1957, but we had more of the reality of it then than now. Partly it was a massive effort to compete with Russia postsputnik, and the upgrading that began in math and science filtered down to English. NDEA institutes got teachers together, empowered them, and impelled them to share. Schools worked as teams of people to upgrade instruction. It was a national commitment, and everyone participated to some degree. Teachers taught behind closed doors, and there was no "coaching" (or little), but there was sharing. Today there is little sharing. A number of factors conspire to make teachers more isolated than ever: burnout, low morale, confusion over what to do about today's students and the teaching problems, apathy, resentment over loss of control or lack of control. We do not even have department meetings any more. The principal refuses to make them mandatory in the light of the above disaffection, and the teachers will not attend unless they are mandatory. Crisis reports have indicated that the time for reform is now, but teachers have not experienced much reform and have lost hope in many instances. The changes projected by the Carnegie Forums must come soon if we are to turn things around.

All is not lost. Students have changed, environments are poor, materials are scarce, and collegiality is slim. But a major turnaround can be accomplished with leadership, public affirmation, and will. If we put as much effort and interest into education as we did in 1957, we can turn things around. And we have, I hope, the sense to implement far better methods, philosophies, and materials than we did then.

Learning Logs
for Students

Peggy Swoger
(secondary school section)

*I*N MY NINTH-GRADE classroom the learning log is the garden from which all else grows. Students write every day, sometimes before we read, sometimes as we read, and always after we read. For example, during the study of Faulkner's "The Bear," I asked the students to freewrite on what they thought they had inherited from their families. (The next day one girl brought me a fiction story written by her grandfather that explicitly set out his musical expectations for his granddaughter.) Then, as students read the Faulkner story silently, they stopped often to write in their "double-entry" journals. In one column the reader writes textual notes, but in the other he or she writes personal connections with experiences and other reading, asks questions, speculates, carries on a personal dialogue. Students found that if they delayed writing until they finished reading, many of their thoughts had already escaped. Students discussed the story in small groups, perhaps responding to a teacher-posed or group-posed question. Finally, they wrote about the process and what insights they had gotten from the experience.

All the students experienced a stimulation of thinking. They got up in the middle of the night to write down things. One student said he needed two journals, one for insights when he read and another for the ones that came a week later. It has been the richest involvement with literature I have experienced in my classes. The students were freed to think at their own level, and I was amazed with their level of abstraction. They went far beyond what I would have assigned in a paper. Dixie Dellinger, a high school teacher from Burns High School in North Carolina, introduced me to this technique. Her students reported back from college their disappointment in the intellectual level of their college courses. It was two years before they reached the same thinking level they had left behind in high school.

Learning Logs for Teachers

Susan Stires
(elementary school section)

SCHOOL HAD BEEN out for a week. It had been raining the entire time as I poured over my case-study-student's portfolio and interviews. Although Lisa had achieved success and recognition in writing, and I had learned from her throughout the year, I hadn't yet looked at my material all together. I wrote and realized what I knew about Lisa at this point in her development as a writer. And then I turned to my log and extracted all the references to Lisa, to the group as a whole, as well as any other parts about myself that related.

As I read my entries and the responses of our writing project director, Nancie Atwell, to those entries, I realized how Nancie had helped me focus throughout the year. As I sorted and recombined the entries, I followed the threads of Lisa's writing development and my development as a teacher of writing. When I put all my case-study materials together, I discovered many things. One crucial one was that my constant focus on revision, due to Lisa's frequently incoherent prose, was wrong. Often I hadn't encouraged enough talk or other rehearsal strategies, but I found enough instances where it had been effective. Fortunately, I had another year with Lisa.

Without my log, without my school-based writing project, and without Nancie's expertise, I never would have gotten inside Lisa's writing. Without my understanding of writing development, writing process, and instruction with workshop time, student choice, and conferences, Lisa would not have gotten her ideas, thoughts, and feelings outside to affect her world.

5 | *What Follows from Taking a Theoretical Stance?*

Glimpses from my notebook for the third evening of the conference, 8 July: We've been meeting since early morning and now it's a late meeting after supper. People are grumpy, perhaps anxious. After an affable and cheerful beginning of the conference, with everyone very energetic, the mood goes down; my notes say, "I think the shit is starting to hit the fan. People fear no product, no result. The conference feels desultory. Unfocused, rambling reports so far. Seems like there's no plan." In truth the planning committee has a plan and strategy for a product: to keep a record of all documents, extract something from them, make a record or report or pamphlet. But people don't know this and need to be assured that they can just engage in a conversation—rambling, reflective, not conclusion drawing—and something will be drawn from it.

The group angrily insists on changing the schedule, asking for more time to read position papers. The chair, Jack Maxwell (executive director of NCTE and central to the planning committee), tries to steamroller a refusal and is himself steamrollered: an ominous note. What will come of this?

Toward the end of the long evening meeting one participant is a little tired and manic-punchy; he speaks too long and too often; he launches into a long complaint about the language people are using in their reports of sessions. He refers to highly intellectual, academic discourse; lots of shorthand, undefined abstract or technical or theoretical terms: "I don't understand that language you're using." Seems to me a helpful thing to say, but unfortunately he undermines it by being a bit punchy rather than completely coherent himself, and he turns his statement into a self-deprecating joke. In the end he simply increases everyone's growing dissatisfaction at listening to too many reports of subgroups that are not carefully enough done.

After the evening meeting, it's late and I'm talking with a small group on the dock. Sound of bug zapper zapping bugs. Intensely humid and hot. As we look out over the Wye River in the not quite pitch darkness, faint fog comes in across the surface. Occasional sound of fish jumping. Talk about MLA matters. Eminent literary types who were invited but couldn't come.

Now, putting the light on in bed, it's 1:15. Panicking that I have to write a book—how can I do it? What sense can I make of things? I just wrote a little position paper on testing tonight. Roundly rejected. Got caught up in taking part in the conference and trying to influence it. *How can I be an observer? I need to go over my notes more. Write more.*

I need a notebook. I'm writing on all these sheets of paper. I need my notes in order, with blank facing pages for reflecting on my notes. I need a typewriter. The computers here can't understand my Wordstar *word-processing disks. When I called the company that rented the PCs to the conference, they put me through to their software consultants, who put me on hold while they asked among themselves. Finally a consultant comes back: "No one here can remember* Wordstar."

I must trust that I can write a book. There'll be lots of data, my notes, all the writing. I must have faith I'll find things to write about.

Can I get everyone to do some writing? I'd like to hear the voice of everyone in this book. An excerpt from everyone? Voices.

Starting to go to sleep. Oh no! It's our anniversary. I meant to call my wife. It's too late. And there's no leaving or visitors for three weeks.

IN THIS CHAPTER I explore a few other interesting questions about what follows from taking a theoretical stance or from an interest in theory. Namely:

Does a theoretical stance mean too much abstraction, a neglect of texts and substantive "content"?

Does a theoretical stance mean a neglect of practice?

Does a theoretical stance imply a democratic or an elitist move? Is the effect empowering or exclusionary?

Does a theoretical stance imply a position on the perennial debate about freedom and necessity?

Does a theoretical stance mean too much abstraction, a neglect of texts and substantive "content"? Everyone took the high line here (the low line?), saying that of course it is crucial to avoid the theory sins of hyper-abstraction and no content: studying nothing but theory books, talking only theory doctrine, and teaching in such a way that students end up spouting theory babble. (I attended a talk not long ago where the speaker gave a paper on narrative theory and was asked afterward to illustrate what he was saying by applying it to a particular text—and he couldn't think of one.) The people most interested in and committed to theory worked hard to assure those of us less experienced and perhaps more skittish that they were not for teaching theory as a primary content but rather for teaching what we always teach—texts and writing—and using theory as a lens or guide to how we teach the text or the writing activity:

> In the canonizing method of teaching theory, texts of literary theory are substituted for literature, and theory thus becomes the new canon. Under this approach, teachers clone their students to become literary theorists. This approach involves creating a canon of theory texts, just as in traditional literature teaching there is a canon of literary texts. Both are conceived as objective bodies of knowledge, and the student is encouraged either to master all of this canon or to become a particular kind of theorist. . . . Now phenomenologists or deconstructivists are being made in their mentor's image and likeness. To teach theory in this way is to teach theory without theoretical self-consciousness. Since it lacks an acknowledgment of the situatedness of all theory, this approach discourages critical debate —which should, after all, constitute the major practice of the theorist-teacher. (Kathleen McCormick, position paper)

Yes, of course an interest in theory will make it a content to some degree. We must devote some class time to uncovering the premises or interests in what we read and in the various ways we can read it—and write. But the point is that even though such talk is theory talk, it is still very much talk about the story or about the writing. The emphasis at the conference was on consciously noticing and reflecting on our tacit theories and thus talking about premises. But the important point here is that participants felt strongly that we can engage in a good deal of that noticing and reflecting on the premises behind our writing and reading without thereby taking emphasis away from what we are writing or reading.

On this question of abstraction versus concreteness, I saw some difference between college teachers and the elementary and high school teachers. The college stream was more likely to talk abstractly, and the schoolteachers were more likely to raise the question "What does this mean for our students and for teaching?" But what else is new? The elementary and secondary reports were demonstrably more concrete and specific than the college report.

The question of whether theory undermines "real content" bears on how the conference responded to Hirsch. Hirsch complained that schools have sold their heritage of content for a mess of empty skills. When I contemplate his own history here, I grant him real respect. He was an eminent literary critic who took a deep dive into composition studies. He said, in effect, "If I'm troubled about writing in schools and colleges, I can't just snipe, I've got to commit myself to studying it in depth." He mostly stopped the work he was doing (about theories of interpretation) and immersed himself in the field of language and composition. He communicated his initial conclusions with considerable force in a book, *The Philosophy of Composition*, which argued that we can teach good writing in itself apart from any content—good writing as "readability" or clarity:

> The study of style in literature is a study of the *fusion* of form with content. But learning how to write implies just the opposite assumption; it assumes the *separation* of linguistic form and content. Learning the craft of prose is learning to write the *same* meaning in a different and more effective way. (141)

I also admire his next step: the frankness with which he publicly recanted his position (a rare move) on the basis of further research and argued instead, convincingly enough, that the clarity of a discourse is always a function of its content and of how much the reader already knows about that content. He confessed, that is, that he had committed the sin of focusing on form in the teaching of writing and ignoring the importance of content.

The members of the conference agreed with Hirsch on the need for more focus on content, with less recourse to the exercises, dummy-runs, snippets, and fill-in-the-blanks writing and testing that are so common in the schools (see Applebee). What seems perverse, however, is that while he wraps himself in the flag of content, he's really backsliding into his old sin by completely trivializing content: his entire program consists of asking students to learn long lists of short bits of information—for testing on short-answer tests. Our suspicion of Hirsch, Finn, and the Department of Education was hardly avoidable when Finn simultaneously advocated Hirsch's list curriculum and then chided us for being against content.

Participants insisted that the emphasis on theory at the conference enhanced rather than undermined an emphasis on teaching more substantial pieces of reading, pieces that have purchase on society and on students' lives (and fewer snippets and basal readers with short, watered down excerpts). Similarly, participants favored more writing assignments of full pieces of discourse to real audiences (and fewer writing assignments of short, rhetorically disembodied exercises).

Shirley Brice Heath gave us another example of how a move toward theory need not be a move away from content: she argued persuasively against the current fashion for teaching "critical thinking" and "higher cognitive processes," not because of what those terms stand for if charitably understood, but because they so often lead to exerciselike teaching activities empty of substantive content. She emphasizes terms like *reflection* and *hypothesis making* because they are much more likely to lead to assigning solid, substantive pieces of writing and reading.

Does a theoretical stance mean a neglect of practice? I've been present on two occasions when Stanley Fish rebuffed with evident pleasure the efforts of Kenneth Bruffee and Elaine Maimon (influential writers about writing and collaborative learning), who had invited him to give a keynote paper at a conference in order to enlist the support of his theory for their work on collaborative learning. On both occasions he gave witty papers that said, in effect, "You just keep right on doing what you are doing. It looks dandy to me. But don't make the mistake of thinking that what I'm doing has anything to do with what you are doing." In effect, a "strong theory" position tends to announce that it has nothing to do with practice (Derrida, too, made this point). Fish likes to deride what he calls "theory hope."

I did notice at the conference some tipping away from practice and doing and toward theory and reflecting. That is, I had to resort to some body English in chapter 2 to say that everything the participants cared about depends just as much on a commitment to doing (using language) as on theorizing (analyzing our language use). I think participants were more excited about reflecting than about doing.

Nevertheless, for the most part, participants insisted on a good fit rather than a conflict between theory and practice, between a digging-for-premises approach to education and an activist approach to education. Here is a revealing moment from one of the many occasional pieces written during the conference:

> The sky is clear; the sun is bright. A solitary airplane sails the sky. We have the afternoon free. As I sit and think, I know that some ideas are clear. A theory-centered curriculum is a student-centered curriculum. Practice informs theory as much as theory informs practice. Learning is complex and messy. Learning is constructing meaning through language. (George Shea)

That is, conferees insisted that certain *practices* followed from their interest in theory—in particular from the theory-based principle that we don't have right answers and that therefore all voices must be heard. The most obvious example of a practice that follows from theory is the kind of classroom work I described in the democracy chapter and at the start of this one: a classroom where the emphasis is on exploring multiple readings and the premises and interests that lie behind them rather than on finding best readings. Such an emphasis on theory leads to a strikingly concrete and important practice that, if followed, could deeply change the character of English teaching.

Heath characteristically wouldn't let theory be only a quiet process of sitting outside and above the fray or practice be only an active process working at a lower level inside the fray. Her examples of reflectiveness were always experiential: her standing back was always an active doing, a working out of one's own hypotheses rather than reading the hypotheses of others or listening to those of the teacher. Her fruitful synthesis of theory and practice was a natural fit for elementary teachers; it will be hardest for college teachers, who tend to have more trouble letting students work out their own theories if there are "better" ones to study.

Notice the tempting and pervasive connotations about theory and practice: theory looks up and practice looks down; theory is lofty and practice is grubby; theory keeps your hands clean and practice gets them dirty. Let me point to one place where we ran into this pattern. College English departments have tended to neglect the training and preparation of secondary English teachers as something "low" and "practical," something left for departments or schools of education. (Or at least this has been true in recent decades for departments with pretensions of being "better.") Thus we in the college section pretty much avoided thinking about the preparation of teachers (although a few people, such as John Bordie, tried to raise the issue) until finally, in the last week, these voices got us to think seriously about the fact that English departments have for decades tended at once to complain about English teachers in the schools and yet wash our hands of any responsibility for this practical kind of teaching. Among other things, it was the group's interest in the practical consequences of theory that led the college strand in the end to conclude that teacher preparation is indeed our problem, is central to the mission of college English, and that we must jump into working on it—as English departments, heretical as that sounds. We can't sit back and just kibbitz from a distance about theory as we've done in the past.

But even as we discussed teacher preparation in the final couple of days, we were forced into an interesting moment of healthy dialectic between theory and practice. Participants who had experience in teacher education talked powerfully about how it's not enough just to get prospective teachers into classrooms early for the sake of practice (important as that is). Prospective teachers also need time for sitting back and observing and actively reflecting on what they see as they visit classrooms. As someone said, "Students sit in classrooms all their lives but they don't reflect on it: they don't reflect on the structure of a classroom, the political and social and cognitive implications of how classrooms are structured, and what it means to be in a classroom."

In summary, people concluded that an emphasis on theory leads naturally to an activist interest in changing how we teach and how schools function (for example, to make sure there is a place for views and for students that have previously been marginalized). One might see this activist approach to theory as something bourgeois and American—comparable perhaps to the version of Freud that the United States produced: "Let's take a rich and notably dark European theoretical theory and use it *practically*, to make the world a *nicer* place": a taming or domestication (or to some people a gutting). Perhaps I am just reflecting my own prejudices, but I sense most participants were willing to be bourgeois and American if that means pushing hard for social and educational change.

Does a theoretical stance imply a democratic or an elitist move? Is the effect empowering or exclusionary? I see no logical reason why an emphasis on theory should correlate with the pluralist, democratic, and antielitist mood that was so central to the Coalition Conference. After all, couldn't people who were deeply elitist—who believed they had the truth and wanted to dictate to everyone else what is right—also believe deeply in theory? be committed to looking at the premises and assumptions of their and others' positions? be committed to looking at the historical and ideological structures of society? It might be their interest in theory that leads them to think that the words "always" and "necessarily" should be central to their lexicon and that the opinion of most people should be ignored. Even Plato was a theorist, one preoccupied with exploring premises, and though he wrote a nonexclusionary prose, he was unashamedly absolutist and elitist.

But at the conference people implied a correlation between theory and a democratic, pluralist, and antielitist stance. On reflection the link seems genuine to me. That is, it seems as though when we take a theoretical stance toward a serious dispute and focus on premises and assumptions, "obviously true" and "sensible" and "persuasive" answers seem to rest on premises that are just as shaky as the premises supporting odd or "off-the-wall" readings. Looking at premises seems to cast a mantle of shared fragility over all positions. We see this effect even in Plato. Despite Plato's belief that the process of dialectic will lead to immutable truth, the real effect of Socrates's method of trying to uncover premises and assumptions tends to be to increase doubt. And I sense that was Socrates's goal, whatever Plato was up to, namely, to show that we don't really have sure or solid knowledge and that our only valid intellectual stance is one of humility.

Even in mathematics, looking at premises makes things less self-evident and more open to doubt:

> [M]athematics generally (including geometry and number theory as well as set theory) is from an evidential point of view more like physics and less like logic than was once supposed. On the whole the truths of mathematics can be deduced not from self-evident axioms, but only from hypotheses which, like those of natural science, are to be judged by the plausibility of their consequences. (Quine and Ullian 46)

Thus the effect of theory or interrogating premises seems to *tend* (at least as it's practiced these days) to the conviction that certainty is not available. Everyone must be allowed a say, and no individual or group is in a position to dictate to anyone else. In short, the emphasis on theory points to a democratic, antielitist pluralism. Yes, of course there are better and worse arguments; we need to heed Wayne Booth's lucid and powerful warning against shallow relativism in *Modern Dogma and the Rhetoric of Assent*. But better and worse arguments depend on qualities of reasoning, not on authority or fashion.

Thus the dominant theme of the conference came to be that what are seen as "normal" or "assumed" or "obviously true" views or practices— even "always already" principles—must be recognized to be just as much "special interest" as the views or practices commonly labeled as special interest. Groups in power tend to label smaller groups as special interest, not seeing that they themselves are special interest. As Katherine Cummings put it in her position paper, "Dissent is readily recognizable as political and is so, but no more so than the (insider's) assent to dominant culture or the claim to transcend politics. . . ." Nothing must be taken as normal, neutral, disinterested, inevitable, necessary, objective. People get to take charge of their reading and writing processes and not be told what's right by virtue of authority.

What I described in the democracy chapter as the most concrete outcome of the conference—a classroom that seeks multiple readings and investigates where they came from and what interests they serve rather than seeking a correct or best reading—is clearly an empowering effect of theory. Student perceptions and readings are heard and taken seriously. Students won't so often have that characteristic experience in English classrooms of just listening to the teacher's interpretation in lectures or of just looking for the teacher's interpretation as they engage in discussion or write papers or of feeling that their own perceptions are wrong or irrelevant.

Similarly, there was much talk about how teaching students about theory will help empower them in their transactions with teachers. If students are taught to look for the premises and assumptions and interests behind any view or interpretation, they are less liable to intimidation: they can see that what a teacher says is "a position," not "the answer" or "the truth" but something that can be questioned by analyzing the assumptions and interests implicit in it.[1]

But conferees also acknowledged how an emphasis on theory can be elitist and disempowering when pursued in the wrong way, leaving students more passive—merely disengaged spectators or else dependent on teachers. People alluded to teachers talking fancy theory babble, with students taking it all down in notes and being left passive acceptors of theory. (This sin combines naturally, of course, with the other theory sin of hyperabstraction, where teachers tip away from texts and writing in favor of mostly discussion of theory.)

In fact participants experienced an elitist note at the conference itself. There was, needless to say, a certain amount of theory jargon and high abstraction at the conference, and this felt elitist to some participants and had the effect of making many feel excluded, for a good while anyway. It took a long time for those who experienced it this way to talk about the problem. The door was opened when someone talked about feeling "pistol-whipped by language"—a metaphor that was assented to with some feeling by more than a few people. After all, one of the common effects of difficult language is to make people feel ashamed of not understanding it and therefore reluctant to talk about their sense of being excluded. We all know as teachers that students who don't understand something tend to be reluctant to say so and often sit there silently trying not to look lost.

Characteristically, in the end the matter was resolved amicably. There was some good-natured, tit-for-tat complaining by college-strand members about jargon from elementary and secondary members as comparably exclusionary ("scope and sequence" and the like)—though the criticism of theory talk came from some college members, too. I'd say that some of the songs at the end expressed a mixture of mostly jovial good spirits but also a slight lingering uneasiness ("I'm so situated that I'm [grunt!] constipated, and I don't give a paradigm shift").

It's striking to me that at the very moment when the English profession has been opening up and becoming much more democratized (when the notion of a canon is very much in question; when reader-response, feminist, and cultural criticism seem no longer able to be called fringe activities; when the profession is having to accept composition as a strong and viable branch of the field)—at a moment, that is, when remarkably fewer people are being excluded—along comes a new movement whose most striking effect on many readers, especially teachers from the schools and faculty members with heavy teaching commitments, is to make them feel dumb and excluded. Of course, the effect is seldom consciously intended, but it must be kept in mind that this is going on in a profession with a tradition of making people feel excluded. Note this passage from the published minutes for the college section subgroup working on the major (15 July 1987):

> What about the language of theory? Is it opaque, obscure, obfuscatory, and most of all, intentionally obfuscatory? What are the political implications of this language? How do we deal with the paradox that, on the one hand, theory was intended to demystify, democ-

ratize, and open up the study of literature and, on the other, that
the language for doing it serves to mystify and make that study
arcane, the province of a few? How does the language of theory
function across the range of colleges and universities? How does it
affect our relations with colleagues in elementary and secondary
schools? And with the public?

Sometimes people reply that the difficult language is necessary because
of the inherent difficulty of the thinking—and they sometimes even
appeal to the theory of a seamless indivisibility between thought and
language. But our experience at the conference showed that difficult
and exclusionary language was not necessary in talking about theory.
When experts on theory wrote in their position papers and spoke in
discussions, they were often remarkably clear, inclusive, and noncon-
descending. It was this context of effective and satisfying discourse about
theory that made it more possible for someone to speak out about feeling
"pistol-whipped" about language rather than just remaining silent, as so
often happens in such situations.

We see an interestingly similar shift in the field of writing. At a moment
when many forces have been democratizing the teaching of writing (with
less emphasis on correcting errors, a single standard for what is good
writing, and just pleasing teachers as the only audience—and more emphasis on personal and exploratory writing, writing about topics of
choice, and using peers as audience in addition to teachers), along comes
a movement emphasizing the teaching of academic discourse, whose
effect is often to take students back again to writing for and pleasing
only the teacher and experiencing the results of writing as primarily a
matter of getting it right and wrong (see Sheryl Fontaine for this analysis).

In the end, I see that a theoretical perspective has an inherent potential
for both egalitarian empowerment and elitism. There are certain important questions one must ask about the practice of emphasizing theory.
Is the study of theory an invitation to students and teachers to make
their own hypotheses or to study those of others? Is theory a practice
or a content? Is the pursuit of theory participatory and experiential and
process-oriented—helping students to do their own reflecting back on
premises and assumptions about reading and writing—or is it content-
oriented in the sense of asking students merely to learn and absorb the
theories of others? Does the pursuit of theory invite everyday
language—with teachers using everyday, nonjargon language and students invited to put their investigations into their own language—or
does it invite mostly sanctioned or canonical language and jargon? It
seems to me that the version of theory that came together in the con-

ference was charitable and humane. I hope that in saying that I don't simply disqualify myself as hostile: "You're *great*, Mary—you're not like a girl."

Does a theoretical stance imply a position on the perennial debate about freedom and necessity? I mentioned in chapter 2 that when I read the draft of my sense of a conference consensus out loud on the last day, three or four people had reservations about my summary. They said that when I talk about "making meaning" and "active learning," my language "carried the freight of the free, autonomous subject." I stress too much that students write and not enough that they are written, that we construct and not enough that we are constructed.

This was an interesting moment of the conference. It was the last day, I was reading from a messy text and didn't have copies to put into people's hands, and there wasn't much time for response and debate. I left with two interesting questions I can only speculate about: How deep and thoroughgoing was the objection? How many people agreed with it?

That is, on the one hand, those who objected were rather restrained. I remember Gary Waller and Kathleen McCormick talking as though the problem were only a matter of emphasis and wording and not a central "error in thinking." On the other hand, in objecting to my emphasis on making meaning, they were objecting to the very center of what I was calling a consensus.

I often think to myself that they were simply holding back from a full-scale critique of me as a hopelessly romantic, bourgeois, late-capitalist naïf. They would have had many reasons to hold back: after all, time was short in this session, the conference was almost over, and it wouldn't seem productive to join a deep and possibly divisive disagreement at that point; and the strong majority of the group had already registered what seemed to me a fairly solid and cordial agreement with the main thrust of what I'd read.

Yet I mustn't jump to paranoia either. For they also implied that perhaps it was all right for me to emphasize that the making of meaning implies agency as long as I did justice to the opposite side of the coin: to reflect on how meaning is made is to see the limits of autonomy. McCormick states that "theory exists whenever we become self-conscious about the institutional, conventional, ideological constraints under which we live, think, and read literature" (response to draft, 18 Nov. 1989). Indeed, Waller spoke of "an exciting contradiction we must simply live with" between seeing ourselves as free and as constrained, between "being maker and being made." I think he was even implying that a goal of recognizing our constraints or "chains" is to increase our margin of choice. We can find more moves when we see better the rules of the game, and we are least free when we are blinded by illusions of freedom.[2]

Similarly, Kathleen McCormick stresses on the one hand how our interpretations and positions are a product of our situatedness—our class, gender, interests, culture, and so forth; we don't write, we are written on. Yet on the other hand she stresses how the very study of theory (the process of thinking and knowing and coming to conclusions) also allows us to get some perspective and achieve a view that is not just a product of interests but a product of critical analysis: "only when we glimpse the constraints under which we live, can we begin to work for freedom" (response to draft, 18 Nov. 1989). And she didn't just talk generalities: during numerous discussions she gave concrete and helpful snapshots of her classes, where she clearly used theory to help students fight free of narrowness or stuckness and helped them end up with more choice in reading and action. For example, she talked about getting students to write quick, unpondered "response pieces" to what they read and then getting them to take time to look at these pieces and see what they can learn about how they read and the constraints they tend to work under. To emphasize theory seems to mean stressing that the meanings we end up with grow out of our situatedness but also stressing that meaning is actively negotiated and created—not just found. The same applies for knowledge in general: knowledge is a product of forces acting on us, yet created and not found.

So in the end I agree with Gary and Kathy. (And Chaucer. I feel I learned especially from his treatment of this very issue of freedom versus necessity; see my *Oppositions in Chaucer.*) We are at once free and bound. Like physicists dealing with light as both wave and particle, our task is to find language that does justice to both sides of the contradiction. That's the thoughtful, right answer.

But it's hard to live by the thoughtful, right answers when we're in the midst of things, and I think it is a somewhat tricky question as to whether theory reinforces freedom or lack of freedom. For example, Bob Scholes did an interesting analysis at the conference of poems by John Donne and Emily Dickinson in which he kept talking about the poems as "only the playing out of the central matrix or metaphor—manifestations of language itself at work." In contrast, most of the writing teachers there put more stress on how writing is a matter of an agent making choices and taking responsibility for those choices. I tend to go with this emphasis on agency or taking charge and not being helpless in one's writing. Yet I also try to get students to learn to relinquish control and let language or the story take over. But even here it tends to require an act of autonomous will and of courage to relinquish control and invite the pen to keep moving on its own. Wayne Booth struck a responsive chord when he said that his main goal in teaching literature is to get students to take responsibility for their own readings and not fall back into feeling that the interpretation is being done to them or that the teacher or the text is in charge.

Thus I *think* I heard a bit more emphasis at the conference on agency and making meaning. In reading as in writing, I heard more stress on the idea that it is your choice, your piece: you must take responsibility for your choices; you could have done otherwise than you did. Participants placed more emphasis on analyzing and theory making as processes of active questioning and real leverage, not just on noticing one's situatedness. I am tempted to think that it's a mark of a good teacher to stress agency and responsibility and autonomy, to stress that students can break out of whatever bind or rut or matrix of forces that happen to be pressing in on them.

It's true that students are often naive in their declarations of complete freedom and autonomy, seeming to assume they can do anything. "I'm going to medical school," says the poorly prepared freshman who cannot connect with chemistry or find the self-discipline to study. But despite their pretense of autonomy, when I look more carefully at what they write and how they behave, I see more often a characteristic and sad sense of helplessness. Students are always feeling, "I couldn't do that. I'm not smart enough" or "I'm not brave enough" or "that might give me a lower grade" or "that wouldn't prepare me for the job I want." And teachers too: "I couldn't do that. I would anger my administrators" (or "my colleagues" or "the parents") or "I'd lose my job or not get tenure" or "I'm not smart or brave enough." When students or teachers do something powerful and effective, they tend to experience it as a discovery of choice where formerly they felt they had none. Critical analysis can show us ways in which our thoughts and feelings are written for us by our culture or background. But I'm more interested in the analysis of people like Gandhi and Martin Luther King, Jr., and even the existentialists, who point out the actuality of full choice even in the most constrained circumstances. This reflects my bias, then, but I'm more worried about us and our students thinking we are stuck when in truth we can act.

So in the end? Clearly there has been great complexity and paradox around this issue from the earliest eras of philosophy and theology. I find myself pushing away the strongly determinist position that some poststructuralists take. I try to do justice to the paradox that we are both free and bound, but my heart is more in the position that says, "Let's look for choice, even where it seems as though there's none." And the conference? At the risk of projecting, I think I heard more of that romantic, activist sentiment. The conference was, after all, full of teachers who are working in the midst of an educational system that seems monolithic and impossible to move, that seems to take away autonomy and agency and responsibility from both teachers and students. But these are teachers who refuse to feel constrained or stuck and who are experts at cutting through and helping their students not feel stuck.

An interesting illustration of this issue came up in conversation at the conference. It might seem trivial, but it is important to most public school teachers: the public-address announcement system in all classrooms. With no warning and at all times of the day, often deafening announcements come through and interrupt their teaching. There is usually no way to turn it off or down. It often disrupts hard-won student involvement in a lesson. There's something deeply demeaning about all the teachers in an entire school having simultaneously to stop what they are doing and put all their attention on a loud voice coming through a black box on the wall—all attention forced on an absent person. These announcements enact the principle that the noneducational usually interrupts and takes precedence over the educational. Yet this arrangement is so normal and ubiquitous that most teachers feel there is nothing to be done about it but gripe. But there were two teachers at the conference (separate schools, independent stories) who got together with colleagues and got the practice stopped. I didn't hear in full how they did it, but clearly it was a matter of insisting on something, a matter of effective agency rather than passivity or ineffective protest.

I try to recognize, however, the danger in my bias for tipping the emphasis toward agency. Kathleen McCormick puts it directly: "the ideology of freedom is paradoxically used to bind groups who are not as free as others." She goes on to describe a telling moment from her teaching:

> Some of my students were recently reading Hirsch and were arguing about his assertion that dominant stories of our culture work to reflect universals of human nature. One of these was Lincoln in his log cabin rising to head the country. Students fiercely debated the function of the belief in this country that anyone can possibly become president one day (the myth of the autonomous subject, American individualism, etc.) given the material reality that one needs millions of dollars of backing to run for office. Some students felt that if it weren't for the myth, "the poor" in the country would despair: "at least it gives them some hope." Others argued that the myth gives the poor cause for despair because when they don't succeed (become president) they imagine that it's their fault rather than the fault of the system. Finally a few suggested that if the myth of the freedom to succeed—the myth of American individualism—were actually challenged in our country, we might work to change the system

fundamentally in some way; but so long as it remains uninterrogated, those without money or who support the views antithetical to big business will never be able to be elected to high public offices in the land of the supposedly "free." (response to draft, 18 Nov. 1989)

Enacting a Sophisticated Conception of Theory

People who care about theory often tell us that we should not engage in practice without first figuring out our premises or theory. "Practice without a theory of the nature of language, literacy, and learning is at best a series of lucky hunches, at worst a repetition of the sins of the father" (Daniel, n. pag.). They insist that since we always present an implicit theory of learning and of knowledge and of the world when we teach a writing or literature course, we are intellectually irresponsible if we bumble our way along without first figuring out our premises or theory.

At the conference we seldom started off trying to articulate, much less agree about, our assumptions or premises. It was seldom that someone said, "Hey, wait a minute. Slow down. We've got to be clearer about our assumptions here." Janet Emig said this strongly a number of times but didn't really insist on making us stop to work things out first. Our characteristic procedure was to spend a lot of time talking in a fairly unstructured way about the topic on the agenda but in a freewheeling and digressive fashion. Then at the end of the session or series of sessions we tended to push to figure out or conclude something. But characteristically we didn't spend much time spelling out theory, assumptions, or premises. Don't get me wrong; I'm not saying things were a mess. I sometimes get in trouble because I think of bumbling as one of the highest cognitive forms. The enterprise was well organized. For every session (and there were between six and twelve each day) there was an agenda, a chair, a recorder, and published minutes or a report. The process worked well, I'd say, but it was a process that tended to leave lots of premises unstated and assumptions unclear for much of the time.

To insist that we always start out being clear about premises and theory involves a narrow and misguided idea of theory or what it means to be theoretically aware. It's helpful to bring in the thinking of Polanyi and of Freire here. Polanyi points out that even though theory seems to be prior and more certain than practice—because practice or concrete things depend on or follow from theory (and this is true from the point of view of abstract logic)—in fact, practice or concrete things are prior and more certain, while premises and theory really depend on or follow from them:

Since the process of discovering the logical antecedent from an analysis of its logical derivate cannot fail to introduce a measure of uncertainty, the knowledge of this antecedent will always be less certain than that of its consequent. We do not believe in the existence of facts because of our anterior and securer belief in any explicit logical presuppositions of such a belief; but on the contrary, we believe in certain presuppositions of factuality only because we have discovered that they are implied in our belief in the existence of facts. . . . Indeed, the premises of a skill cannot be discovered focally prior to its performance, nor even understood if explicitly stated by others, before we ourselves have experienced its performance, whether by watching it or by engaging in it ourselves. (162)

That is, theory rests on practices that always imply more than we can know. (This point is illustrated by language use: our language practice always involves more knowledge than we can know theoretically.) Thus our practical or tacit knowledge is always in advance of our theoretical knowledge.

When people insist that we always be clear about premises and theory from the start—before we engage in practice—it leads to various dangers:

It holds things up. I think that many coalition members realized that if we really tried to make all our premises explicit and see where we agreed and disagreed about assumptions, we wouldn't get very far. It would lead to fights that were not necessary.

When people insist that we always be clear about premises and theory before going further, it invites the familiar kind of pressure to exclude or marginalize people with the "wrong" beliefs or theories.

You often cannot trust premises that are worked out ahead of practice: people's premises are often at odds with their practice. It is not by their theories or premises but by their consequences that we know people: how they treat students, colleagues, even texts.

This is not an argument against pursuing theoretical knowledge or uncovering premises and implications. Quite the opposite: it is an argument for a more effective pursuit of theory or premises. By pursuing this kind of knowledge we can bring more of our tacit knowledge-in-practice to conscious theoretical understanding; we can uncover more of our premises. Polanyi urges us to proceed in this fashion. But I want to emphasize his main point here, which is that our success in pursuing and increasing theoretical knowledge usually depends on respecting and trusting practice for a while and afterward interrogating it as a rich source for new theory.

What this means is that we don't have to apologize for bumbling along in our reading, writing, teaching, or discussion—so long as *periodically* we stop to see if we can milk that practice for the potential theory in it. It is not true that we are naive or committing the sins of our predecessors if we don't work out theory first (an approach that rewards only one intellectual temperament). My experience and my temperament and my reading of Polanyi tell me that it is shrewd and sophisticated for teachers to proceed using practical wisdom and even intuition and then to stop and say, "Now what were we doing? What are the premises and consequences of our practices?" (For example, as Heath suggested, to use language in real situations and then to stop and reflect on those uses usually provides a corrective to a naively theoretical grammar.)

This all relates to one of the principles that Freire stresses: we don't know anything—not even a word—except through use or practice. Even though practice without analysis or reflection is empty, analysis or reflection without practice is also empty.

In short, the conference seemed to me to enact a wise theory about theory and a critical awareness about critical awareness. There was a dialectical moving back and forth between premises or underpinnings on the one hand and action, text, and unawareness of premises on the other. Yes, we benefit from self-consciousness, but we also benefit from holidays or time-outs from critical awareness. I think I see this in writing: awareness of theory can help when we are sandbagged by an unproductive way of going about writing. But we don't need writing theory to write well (in fact, some good writers avoid theoretical awareness). We tend to benefit from periodically relinquishing meta-awareness and allowing the words and language to take over—and then stopping, standing back, and looking with a more theoretical eye.

NOTES

[1]This approach might seem to reinforce the cynical view held by many students that being a good student means nothing but figuring out a teacher's prejudices and preferences and "just giving them what they want." But the emphasis on theory can make this cynical stance richer and more thoughtful: "what they want" is not just a quirk of teacher taste or personality but a position and way of interpreting that can be thought through and understood in comparison to other positions and ways of interpreting.

[2]I didn't expect this. Gary isn't one to pull punches or go for "nice" balancing-wire positions. But I look back at his position paper and see that one of the sentences is delicately double-edged in its use of the word *permission*: "We want our students to realize the ways and the permissions by which people make their marks in the world: they do so by the cognitive processes of social structures." This seems to mean, "We want to show you the ways you can make your mark in the world," but also the ways you *can't*.

A Senior English Class

George Shea
(secondary school section)

SAMANTHA ENTERED the room first, as usual, and walked to the file drawer to put a paper in Tom's folder. She had written a response to his paper on why students refuse to break the social barriers in the school. Then she sat down at her desk and started writing as other students arrived.

"Hey, Sammy, where's the paper you promised me?"

"I put it in your folder. I thought you were on a field trip today."

"Okay, thanks. Have you seen Derek? I have a response for him on *The Chocolate War.*"

When the bell rang, students started writing. They responded to a question I had written on the board: "In what ways is the novel you chose to read effective or ineffective in explaining why people were afraid to break through social barriers?" After writing for ten minutes, the students moved into several groups. Some decided they needed response on a piece they were writing. Some decided they needed to read another story on social classes for comparison. Some needed more time to write. Some asked for individual conferences with me. Rachel was one of those students. As soon as I had checked to see that everyone was involved in some activity, Rachel and I sat at a table in the room.

"I'm writing about my P.E. class," she said.

"How's it going?"

"I'm stuck."

"Where? Tell me about it."

"Well, last year I had mono, and when I came back to school, the doctor told me I had to take it easy. So, they put me in this special P.E. class. I didn't know anyone in the class, and I felt weird because they were all druggies, gearheads, or nerds. Three of the girls in there were pregnant and had to take it easy. I don't know why the rest of them were in there. Maybe it was just a class for misfits. The thing is, they all looked at me as if to say, What are you doing in here, Miss Soc [socialite]? I

89

was sort of scared at first, but each day got a little better, and finally I started becoming pretty good friends with Debbie, one of the pregnant girls. When we worked in pairs, Debbie and I worked together. She told me lots of stuff about her parents and her jerky boyfriend—make that ex-boyfriend. The creep that got her pregnant doesn't even want to see her now, and her parents are always giving her a bad time. They want her to quit school and make some money if she's going to have the baby; and, well, there's lots more, but I started thinking about how Debbie and I had sort of broken the social barrier, and I was going to contrast it to that story we read about Holden Caulfield and how he tried to be friends with that nerd Ackley, but then I realized that we hadn't really broken through a barrier. I mean, Debbie and I don't really hang around together or anything."

"You don't?"

"No. You know what my friends would say if I did that, not to mention what *her* friends would say."

"Does that matter?"

"Sure it does. I mean, I know that what I'm saying is terrible, but I know it's true."

"Why do you think that's true?"

"I don't know. I guess we're just chicken."

"Do you want to be her friend?"

"Well, sort of, but I don't know. Maybe it is enough if I just call her sometimes."

"Is that what friendship is?"

"No."

"Do these barriers have anything to do with friendship?"

"I don't know. It seems like they do."

"What?"

"Well, when you're from different crowds, it's hard to be friends. Other friends don't let you do that."

"Don't you let your friends have other friends of their choice?"

"Well, I guess so. I mean, I don't know."

"Why don't you think about that, and think about why Holden tries to be friends with Ackley and why it doesn't really work. Write about it, and we'll talk again after you've had time to sort that out."

"Okay. Hey, thanks, Mr. Shea. I'll see you tomorrow."

"Hey, Mr. Shea, we need you over here. These guys think that my example of those racial fights that happened last week don't have anything to do with this barrier stuff."

"What do you think?"

"I think they do."

"How did you arrive at that conclusion?"

And so it progressed for fifty-five minutes as the students asked questions, discovered problems, and attempted to answer those problems as they read, wrote, talked, and listened. They continually discovered new questions, discovered new books to read, and discovered new problems to explore. The teacher was the facilitator and coach. In the process, the students were reading literature, some of which was suggested by the teacher. They were writing and getting feedback from a variety of sources, and they were making meaning about themselves and their world through language. In other words, they were learning.

Collaborative Teaching

Eleanor Q. Tignor
(college section)

A FINAL EXAMPLE of a course in which I integrate language skills and use comparative texts: the Work, Labor, Business in American Literature course. It is a special thematic course that is part of a liberal arts cluster (Work, Labor, Business in American Society) along with Introduction to Social Science, Freshman Composition I, and The Research Paper. Students take all four courses together. Three teachers (one literature, one social science, and one composition) plan, coordinate, and teach the cluster, reinforcing concepts and demonstrating relationships among areas of knowledge.

An excellent illustration of our collaborative work was a reading unit followed by an essay on women and work. While the social science teacher taught the historical, sociological, economic, political, and psychological aspects of the subject, I had students read Ted Hughes's "Secretary," Molly Jackson's "I Am a Union Woman," Charlotte Perkins Gilman's "Two Callings" and *The Yellow Wallpaper*, and Alice Walker's "Really Doesn't Crime Pay?"

We worked up an essay assignment that we shared with the composition teacher and jointly presented to the students. All three teachers came together in one classroom for the peer editing of the essays, and we coordinated the grading and revisions. The professional and personal compatibility of the three of us who taught the cluster during the winter quarter strongly affected our students' performance. All of us together, teachers and students, created a small learning community that carried over into the spring quarter and continues.

Levels of Language

John J. Joyce

(college section)

I PERCEIVED EARLY on in my life, in junior or senior high school, that I employed one level of language when I was just "with the guys" or in Stepanovich's Bar and Grill, having a beer with friends who had dropped out of school. I used another level when in a classroom entering into a class discussion, a third level when on a date, and another level when at the dinner table with my family. Not only might my tone, diction, and correctness of expression change, but the precision with which I pronounced words did so as well. There is a real sloppiness in employing such distinctions in many of the current undergraduates at my college. This realization was brought home to me recently when a freshman was in my office going over a writing assignment. My radio played softly in the background. At one point the station aired an old Tony Bennett recording, "Because of You." The student suddenly remarked on how clearly the singer on the radio was "pronouncing the words he sang." I am not certain about the effectiveness of my own clarity of diction in advisement at that moment, but I did realize how the lyrics of much current, popular music are lost in performance. . . . I sense in our students today a lessened capacity to identify or even care about identifying the distinctions with which we employ language when addressing varying audiences.

6 | *The Question of Literature*

*P*lenary session. Nellie McKay leads a group mostly of black
participants in role-playing a college class. It takes off from
Maya Angelou's chapter on graduation from I Know Why the Caged Bird Sings. *For
a while there's lots of horseplay, essentially about the tricky authority struggles between
teachers and students, but gradually it evolves into something electric when the "students"
start ruminating on the fact that Angelou's black teachers at her "mere training institute"
were teaching high, hard literature—in particular Shakespeare. They respond with pride
to the W. E. B. Du Bois tradition that all students, even the most underprivileged, should
be taught this high culture. They react against the Booker Washington tradition of focusing
on training for jobs. We resonate to the pride in literature that comes out somewhat
unexpectedly as the role-playing takes its course. The class ends with the students actually
singing the hymn to poetry that the chapter ends with.*

English Studies as Language Arts?

"I've never thought of myself as teaching language arts till this conference." Paul Armstrong, a department chair, made this remark during
one of the final days. We were talking about how college and university
faculty members in English tend to turn up their noses or even sneer
at the term "language arts" as smacking of "education." Paul's new
thought served to remind him that the term comes from Aristotle and
classical rhetoric and the "arts of language." If someone (especially someone highly respected in the college section) had mounted a strong cam-
paign to define the center of English studies as language arts rather than
literature, I suspect he or she might have made good progress. In a
sense the change had already been made implicitly in the consensus I
described in my first chapter (about using and then reflecting on language). There are lots of reasons such a move might be tempting:

1. After all, it's only a recent development for English departments to define themselves as departments of literature. We descend from departments of rhetoric. Perhaps the symbolic first move in the transition from rhetoric to literature came when Francis James Child, the Boylston Professor of Rhetoric and Oratory at Harvard in 1876, grew tired of his job—teaching writing to freshmen—and got leave to teach only literature (Berlin 23).

2. To center on language arts would help bring together teachers of English in the schools with teachers of English in the colleges and universities. For of course I betray my parochial college affiliation by talking about English departments as centered on literature. In elementary school, English doesn't mean literature, it means reading and writing—often with no literature at all:

> [T]he way teachers are educated and the way the curriculum is organized [by basal reading programs] ensures that literature is in no way related to the teaching of reading in American elementary schools. (Bill Teale, position paper)

In junior high school, English means writing as much as it means literature—and often speech. (Also, if we conceive of English as language arts, we link literature not only with reading and writing but also with speech. Interestingly, most members of the college strand wished speech could be brought back to importance, and teachers from the other sections agreed.)

3. To center on language arts would help heal the damaging warfare between literature and writing at the college level—a warfare that looked all the more damaging and silly at the conference because it was so obviously minimal or absent in elementary schools where teachers often comfortably blend literature and writing.

4. To center on language studies would build on the results of a large, important conference on graduate studies in English that the MLA had sponsored the previous April in Wayzata, Minnesota (see Lunsford, Moglen, and Slevin). Representatives of about a hundred graduate programs in English met to ponder the common lack of coherence both within and among graduate programs in English. The Wayzata conference reached no consensus, but there was a remarkably widespread questioning of historical coverage of literature as the defining feature of graduate programs and a lot of searching for alternative centers or sources of coherence. There was some serious exploration of rhetoric as a possible center for English studies, but it didn't really "take." Language arts might be a viable center of gravity that avoids the problems of literature on the one hand and rhetoric on the other.

5. Perhaps this is a parochial concern, but to define English as language studies would be an intriguing move toward bringing together a divided MLA. The organization tends toward being two organizations: a large English wing and a smaller language wing. (Even the combined language sections are much smaller than the English section.) It would be intriguing if the English section proposed unification around the word *language*—the central word in the title of the organization and the word that stands for the side of the organization that sometimes feels overshadowed by English. Such a move would of course reach back to another root of English departments (beside rhetoric): philology.

6. Above all, centering on language studies would help defuse the problem of the literary canon: not solve it but make it less central.

But of course no one *did* stand up and propose "language arts" as the name or even the conceptual center for the profession of English. Even though the consensus I described in the first chapter tends to imply a focus on language arts, and I think the consensus was solid, there was no "grand consensus" to redefine the English enterprise—a superanswer with rockets blazing. What I especially admire, in fact, was how the consensus was a skillful decision to agree on certain activities and themes as important, leaving large definitional questions unaddressed. Despite the emphasis on theory—a "standing back from things"—there was very little standing back and trying to decide the nature or definition or theoretical center of English as a profession.

But What about Literature?

The question of literature was left strikingly moot. Not only was there no consensus, there was a striking avoidance of the issue. It's not that it didn't come up; the question of literature arose recurrently and in various forms:

Is literature the central content of English studies?

Should our profession focus on literature more than on other kinds of texts?

Yes, we need to teach diverse texts, not just the traditional canon—indeed more even than what is commonly called literature—but do we nevertheless have an obligation to make sure our students have some acquaintance with Shakespeare and Milton or with "quality" works?

Probably we need to teach diverse media as "texts"—such as film, TV, video, and speech—but do we nevertheless have an obligation to work at teaching print to make sure our students are skilled and comfortable with it?

Most of all, what makes something literature? Can can we agree on or even talk about "quality" or "better?"

Every time someone raised one of these issues, we had interesting discussions, strongly sparked responses, incipient fights. Yet every time we somehow slid away from the issue into something else. Thus, in the end, even though we reached a strikingly easy and natural agreement on the making or negotiation of meaning as central in English studies, on democracy as a central commitment, and on theory as a central preoccupation and even though we grudgingly worked through to agreement on goals and assessment (see ch. 9)—we never really sustained or worked through the question of literature.

Why? What made us shy away from struggle with what a wag called "the L word"? (Someone had just been speaking at length of literature, all the while avoiding the word itself.) Was it just fear of conflict? I didn't see participants as timid or fearful of argument. My reading is that after getting a sense of how the Department of Education itself is trying to push the curriculum of lists, push teaching as the transmission of small-bore content, and push large-scale testing that will drive the curriculum (trying, that is, to undermine English teachers who want to concentrate on more active learning and the process of enquiry), coalition members tended to reach a position like this: "We could work on the question of literature; we might make some progress; but we'd never reach agreement. However, it's beginning to look like the uncertainty about the nature and role of literature is not our most serious problem. Our more immediate need is to set out a focus or agenda for English that will fight the pressures from a dangerous coalition of people who at best are trying to save money by focusing on efficiency and measurement rather than teaching and at worst are downright hostile toward teachers. We can be a healthy profession even if we can't agree on something as central as our relation to literature, but we can't be a healthy profession—perhaps not even survive—if we are backed into a corner and forced to define English as the learning of information that can be measured on mass exams."

As a result of hearing Finn and Hirsch, participants realized that there was an incipient consensus among us. This agreement became even more clear after Heath gave us a vision and some language that cut through the always troubling conflicts between school and college participants as to jargon, style, and approach. Indeed, I think people sensed a potential consensus in the profession at large about the centrality of the process of making meaning—and sensed that there isn't yet even the makings of a consensus in the profession about literature (even if the sixty of us at Wye had been able to make one on our own). Too much discussion and work and percolation is still needed in the profession before clarity will emerge about literature.[1]

The Dance with Literature

Nevertheless, I see an instructive story to tell about the conference and literature and about the impulses or straws in the wind that emerged over three weeks—steps away from literature but also toward it. Most obvious was the dance away from literature:

1. We heard countless references—indeed, we all got tired of hearing them—to "the breakdown of the canon" and even to the need to get away from the canon. There were many implicit and some explicit invitations for someone to come forward and stick up for the canon. I never heard anyone accept the challenge. There was lots of "maybe we shouldn't go too far" talk but no "wait just a bloody minute" talk. You might say that this speaks to the dearth of truly conservative participants, for of course there are plenty of people in the profession who are happy to say "wait a bloody minute." But there were conservatives among us too. I think what we saw speaks to the remarkable depth of uncertainty in the profession about the notion of a canon of works securely defined as better or more important than other works.

2. A number of participants said they couldn't teach texts in exciting ways and get students involved in them till they stopped calling them "literature" or "literary" and instead called them, say, "texts" or "reading." In *Textual Power*, an important book on our suggested reading list, Robert Scholes writes pointedly: "To put it as directly, and perhaps as brutally, as possible, we must stop 'teaching literature' and start 'studying texts.' Our rebuilt apparatus must be devoted to textual studies, with the consumption and production of texts thoroughly intermingled. Our favorite works of literature need not be lost in this new enterprise, but the exclusivity of literature as a category must be discarded" (16).

3. Women in the profession have pointed out that although most of our students are women, an emphasis on high or classic works of literature seems to lead to teaching works written primarily by men: defining our subject as literature keeps women from being fairly represented.

4. Many coalition members wanted to move away from the emphasis on literature because this has caused the devaluing of writing. When we focus only on high literature, then (as Scholes argues in *Textual Power*) all writing falls to the condition of being merely ancillary to literature.

And thus, looking at political realities, the teaching of writing becomes ditchdigging for the academic underclass. With literature as supreme, writing is never in the same realm as what the profession reads or studies; we cannot ask students to write something that in any way resembles or is in the same mode as what we study. Perhaps worst of all, the elevation of literature has tended to make literature teachers themselves into nonwriters.

5. People noted now and again that even though English has tended to mean literature at the college level, the majority of college English classes in recent years have not been literature classes but writing classes.

6. Given the interest in ways of reading at the conference, it was observed a number of times that our conception of literature tends to derive from our conception of reading—and from the privileging of one kind of reading. But if there is no single, right, or privileged mode of reading, then there is no special role for what has come to be thought of as literature.

7. "But what about Shakespeare?" always emerged as a question. "Mustn't we make sure he is not neglected?" Gerald Graff pointedly asked us not to worry about Shakespeare: his works weren't considered literature when he was writing and putting them on, and it's probably healthier for good popular work not to be privileged.

8. At one point in the conference someone sent around a list asking people to write down the titles of the books they had brought with them to Wye. Most were not literature.

We said and heard plenty of all this at the conference. The subject of our profession should not be literature but rather "reading" or "texts" or "discourse" or "culture" or "interpretation" or "the making of meaning" or "language"—or even "writing" (à la Derrida that is, reading). We saw the obvious advantages in this move away from literature. Above all it's a deprivileging move. It helps us see how literature is not some different special entity but just one among many forms of discourse or language. This mood of the conference made me think of my "Poetry as No Big Deal," and I sensed that the impulse in more than a few of us was to make literature into no big deal. Bigness of deal is not something in the text but something people do to a text—how we treat it, whether we choose to put a frame around it.

Nevertheless, despite the strength of this movement to dethrone or deprivilege literature, I also sensed the presence of the "Old Adam." I continually detected whiffs of the feeling that there *is* something special and precious about literature and that if we don't stick up for it, no one else will. There were certain key moments in the conference that linger in my mind on this matter:

1. Strongest of all was the role-play class built on Maya Angelou's "Graduation," which I sketched as the epigraph to this chapter. I'm focusing here on only one small dimension of this extended role play (most of all it was about difference and the black experience). But some of the greatest involvement for both the players and audience occurred when they happened to evoke the power of high literature. There was even a note sounded of how literature had helped preserve a people from extinction. It was a vivid evocation of the difference between literacy or texts or reading on the one hand and poetry or literature on the other.

2. Participants on a number of occasions ruminated about early experiences that brought them into the profession: more often than not it was a deep personal connection with works of literature.

3. I think most participants assented to Bob Scholes's criticism of basal readers, without perhaps consciously noticing that the premises of his argument tended to privilege literature: he complained that the basal story's genre was mere socialist realism—mere reproducing of reality—as opposed to imaginative literature; and he complained that its "quality" was poor. I also sensed us going along (but perhaps this was naive of me) when he made this point against Hirsch: that Hirsch sees literature as containing information in the same way as any other subject or text does, but what's important about literature is that it gives rise to a different kind of experience from merely understanding the information in it—a literary experience.

4. Interestingly, while many participants at the college level (and some at the high school level) were trying to push literature away from being the defining or paradigm center of the profession, I sensed that most were sympathetic with "one of the big battles in the elementary school . . . to get literature back in the 'basic skills curriculum' " (report of mixed-level session, 16 July 1987).

5. Finally, I saw evidence of our special connection to literature in the way we all responded during one of the last plenary sessions, when Bill Teale read aloud to us the children's story *Three by the Sea* by Edward Marshall. He read as he reads it to his first-grade class—no affectation or performance but great skill. I sensed that the sixty of us were more captured and silent during these twenty minutes of reading than at any other event of the whole three weeks—more focused or concentrated in attention.

But who ever said we have to choose *between* literature and nonliterature? Surely we can do both: read literature but also read what most people call nonliterary texts. Of course. Both. It's such a simple and obvious answer.

But somehow the matter resisted being simple and obvious. Though we continually avoided dealing with literature, literature lurked in the air throughout the conference. It was as though we'd been going steady with literature for all four years of high school and now we were breaking up. Literature says, "Why don't we just be friends." But how can we "just be friends" with this creature with whom we've been so intimate? It's too painful. We must either get very distant or very close. A friendly compromise or middle distance is only possible in relationships where there is not too much passion or deep involvement. Literature (in such a short portion of our history) has gotten into the soul of the English profession. Where relationships involve passion, violence often follows separation. Perhaps that's what distinguishes literature from other texts: literature is what people get passionate about (a weird but interesting way to define what *literary* means). People at the conference talked about getting into the field because of passionate relationships to literature as youngsters. By avoiding working out the literature question, we were avoiding potential violence.

I remember how the students at MIT used to make fun of a pompous public relations phrase about the school being "an institution polarized around science": they called it "an institution paralyzed around science." In the end, I am tempted to say we are a profession both polarized and paralyzed around literature. We see the problems: it unreasonably privileges certain texts and certain kinds of language and certain kinds of reading; it heightens certain destructive political divisions in the profession; it destructively narrows the profession. But in those very problems we cannot help but also see virtues we are reluctant to give up: commitment to special kinds of language, texts, and special ways of reading; quality; stretching ourselves; saying that certain things are good and worthy of prolonged attention. *Moby-Dick is* better to study than Donald Duck—even though Donald Duck will repay sustained inquiry and even though there is something adventitious about the fact that we read *Moby-Dick* differently from the way we read Donald Duck or the back of the cereal package. I think this was a bigger dilemma than we could solve at the conference and that the profession, for the moment, is at an impasse here.

NOTE

[1]Am I describing our process too charitably? My friend Paul Connolly (professor of English at Bard College and director of the Institute for Writing and Thinking) commented after reading one of my drafts: "The whole conference seems so ad hominem, pleased to have been able to coalesce around opposition to Hirsch and Finn—jocularly, glibly glad not to be in that camp. The positive identity of the group does not seem strong. It's almost as if opposition to Hirsch and Finn warded off any threat of exposing the group's own vulnerability to disagreement."

Literature in the Early Grades

Vera E. Milz
(elementary school section)

W HEN I OPENED my local newspaper several days ago, I read that my former third-grade teacher had died at the age of eighty-nine. The words to describe this woman read, "She was primarily a literature instructor and over the years taught the children and grandchildren of some of her first students. . . . Many of them liked to recall such events as the bygone trips to Campbell Library on West Fort, for some of them their first introduction to the world of books. Instilling appreciation of good books was one of her aims, and she frequently read poetry to her classes." I was a child of working-class parents who could not afford many books, yet I received a gift that has lasted me a lifetime. Not only was I taught to read, but I learned to love it! The local public library was a resource that I used continually during my growing-up years.

I followed in my teacher's footsteps and became a teacher myself. Through the years, as various basals, programmed reading, teaching alphabets, and other programs have come and usually disappeared, I have kept that vision given to me by my teacher, Mary McGinnis. In my classroom, I have built a library of over two thousand books so that I have materials that will help children to grow as readers regardless of the level of proficiency with which they enter my classroom. They are introduced to reading by having books read to them. My students are eager both to join in as I am reading and to later read the books themselves after the introductions are made. Eventually they develop tastes for certain authors just as adult readers do. They are not afraid to read a difficult book if it has information they seek. With each attempt comes the growing power that one has as a reader. Writing develops in much the same way, as I encourage my students to engage in the actual process of writing from the first day they enter my classroom. They use spellings that reflect logical, thoughtful decisions as they attempt to communicate their thoughts. The literature selections they have read and heard increase their knowledge of written language and influence their choice of words and use of various forms as they create new pieces of writing. They learn to read and write in a meaning-centered, literature-based, active language learning environment (see Milz).

Current and past research and theory have given considerable support to the meaning-centered, literature-based curriculum found in my class-room and in that of Mary McGinnis many years ago. In 1908, Edmund Huey advised that children always read for meaning and that the learning of real literature should continue uninterrupted. He even hoped that "school readers, especially primers, should largely disappear" (381). In the 1960s, Veatch, Lee and Allen, and Jacobs advocated the use of literature in a classroom reading and writing program. Graves, Goodman, and Smith are but a few of the many recent advocates who maintain that such an approach is superior to isolated skill and drill instruction artic-ulated in many reading programs. The NCTE Commission on Reading expressed concern that "basal readers sometimes preclude children's reading of literature and discourage teachers from developing materials, methods, and techniques better suited to the teaching and learning of reading" (Watson 2). The Commission's report *Becoming a Nation of Readers* states that there is little evidence that most workbook and skill activities are related to reading achievement and suggests that children engage in more independent reading and spend more time writing. Yet the same report also states that basal reading programs account for sev-enty-five to ninety percent of what goes on during reading periods in elementary classrooms, and few children are allowed to write more than a sentence or two. Although I do not believe it is true in my classroom, it is easy to conclude that there is little match between what research and theory support and what actually is practiced in the majority of our elementary schools. Is change possible? Where can we begin?

I again return to my classroom. My students enjoy reading and writing, and over the year will continually grow in proficiency though they are at varying levels of ability. Yet in a discussion with my principal, he informed me that except for me, only a small pocket of teachers with a literature-based program exist in another elementary school and that the majority of principals prefer a basal-organized reading program. These principals believe that the teachers and community are very satisfied with the current programs. Although I receive support from my principal, the district superintendent, and the community, it is obviously easier for most administrators to support a given basal program even if it has components that are not supported by current research and theory. However, as I am asked to give workshops to explain how my children learn to read and write, I am finding that both parents and teachers are attending and are interested in what I have to say even if I do not have a specific program to present to them. More than a few times I have heard the comments, "I wish my child were in your classroom—my son is at another school in your district" or "I wish I could be released from the basal program that is used in our school—I don't have the time to let my children read and write like your students do." Although I may not receive general support, I believe that both parents and teachers are interested in building programs that meet local needs and promote literacy. Even beyond the boundaries of my school, I am aware that there is a movement in the United States where teachers are both seeking information and providing help for each other as they look for new ways of helping their students (see, for instance, *Teachers Networking*). Yet do schools want teachers who take the time to search and read and discover what enables their students to become literate individuals, or do they want teachers able to follow the directions of a mandated program? If we are to have teachers who are able to make professional decisions in their classrooms, I believe that ultimately teachers must become observers and decision makers and that they need administrative support as they seek answers—not a pre-packaged program.

Much can be done as we look into today's classrooms and into the future. I became a teacher-researcher looking at how my students became literate individuals. As I gained insights, I was able to examine my teaching practices, choose the best portions of programs and materials for my children's benefit, and understand when certain materials did not help my students. More teachers need to be empowered in this way. I also maintain close ties with university personnel, as well as with professional groups such as NCTE or IRA, as I long ago realized that I cannot exist in isolation within my classroom.

Thank You, Sister Helen Rose

George Shea
(secondary school section)

I DEMAND YOUR RESPECT." An ominous, thin figure in a black habit, Sister Helen Rose fired these words from the dais at the front of the room on the first day of my senior year in high school. Leaning slightly toward us and pointing her index finger as if it were a weapon, she explained that we need not like her, but we must respect her. A student's liking her was frosting on the arsenic of life. She got little frosting, but she got respect or least order and silence. She ruled her class with an iron hand and a long whip. Everyone dutifully obeyed her commands. When she walked down a crowded hall, she miraculously parted students, as if they were the Red Sea, with a waving of the hand. What power! What control!

Her class was anything but student-centered. She whipped us into shape, her shape, as she lashed out her orders and cracked those who did not conform. She was a machine, coldly dispensing facts. We had long study sheets of facts and objective tests on factual information. "How many sonnets did Shakespeare write? What is a gerund?"

Despite all this, despite the fact that Sister Helen Rose did not allow us to do much thinking and real learning, she was the teacher who first inspired me to be a reader. About once every two weeks, she talked to us about books, about books I'd never heard of, about old books, new books, novels, plays, poems. It was as if she too got tired of her routine. And when she talked books, she "sang." Her voice was melodic. Her words were butterflies, not darts. Her cold, steel blue eyes became warm and soft as she looked not at us, but at the ceiling, through the ceiling. Enraptured by her own words, thoughts, and recollections, her passion showed through, even through the black, heavy cloth of her habit. She talked about *The Brothers Karamazov*, about *King Lear*, about *The Grapes of Wrath*, about *The Stranger*, about *Lord Jim*, about other people and other worlds. She was in love with books and with the world as seen in

105

those books. There was no arsenic there. I was stunned by these performances that seemed to come out of nowhere. That, I thought, must be what literature is *really* about. I hadn't read any of these books, but I wanted to start. I wanted to fall in love with new people and new worlds. I wanted to think about new ideas. Why, I wondered, didn't she talk like that when we read *Macbeth*? Why couldn't we *enjoy* a book instead of *cover* it?

Sister knew I wasn't an avid reader, but I guess she sensed that I liked her book talk. She recommended that I read two books that we were not going to cover in class. And so I followed her suggestions and read *The Catcher in the Rye* and *To Kill a Mockingbird*. I was hooked. Despite everything else she did, Sister Helen Rose's book talk had hooked me. When, one day, Sister Miriam picked up *The Catcher in the Rye* from my desk and asked me why I was reading such trash, I joyfully responded that Sister Helen Rose had recommended it to me.

I did not stay in touch with Sister Helen Rose during college, but after I graduated I went to see her. I wanted to tell her that I was going to teach English. She remembered me, and my news surprised her. Then, she got that special soft look on her face and recalled for me a personal paper I had written for her class. It was the only personal paper we wrote. It had been one of her favorite papers. She even remembered the title: "The Twenty-Four-Hour Job." She smiled as she talked about it. I was ecstatic. Why, though, I wondered, hadn't she told me how much she liked it when I was a student in her class?

Thank you, Sister Helen Rose, for those brief moments of sharing and human feeling. Senior English would have taught me how cold and sterile literature is were it not for those wonderful moments of drama called book talk.

A Change in the Environment in Which We Teach

Carole Edmonds
(college section)

HAVING ASKED STUDENTS to do a paper out of class after developing several in class, I was expecting stronger papers. I thought students would have more time to work on them. My expectations were not met. When I asked the students why they thought that was, they told me it was because they had more time to work in silence and concentrate on their writing when they worked in class. These freshman writing students supported each other in saying that they never had fifty uninterrupted minutes for work outside the classroom.

7 | *What Is English?*

*T*humbnail sketch of an entire session: Thursday, first week, a mixed-level discussion. The planner's agenda asks us to discuss the goals students should achieve in language, writing, and literature. But my notes neglect the question of goals because I get interested in the time we spent digressing to the question of what is English.

Goals. Talk of lists and the temptation on the part of the public to define goals in terms of what is easily testable. Janet Emig says that if we want to make an argument that is persuasive to a public that thinks in terms of test scores and correct information, we need to look at the nature of learning—help people see that learning isn't a matter of pouring material into heads.

Practices. People are talking about how students need to be able to engage in various kinds of reading and writing, and then someone says he learned only one mode of writing, the critical essay—and that he subsequently learned to write in all modes from learning that one mode (transfer of learning). Many of us quarrel: one mode isn't enough, leads to narrowness, and so forth. But Wayne Booth gives us pause by saying that this response sounds in a way like Hirsch: we're not satisfied with one thing in depth, we want a broad list of lots of things—particular domains.

Somehow we get from there to Marie Buncombe asking, "What makes us different? As a discipline? What makes us us?" Various responses. The ability to enter into points of view other than our own, imagination, emotionally charged involvement, play, creative writing, rendering of experience. Before too long, Paul Armstrong interjects, "It's a trap to try to define what English is—or literature."

We start discussing why we got into English. What made a difference to us. It gets a bit personal and digressive. Goes on for quite a while. Some of the stories and experiences are emotional and deeply felt. These stories came to feel to me (and I think to many others too) to be the center of gravity of this session. Stories of adolescent excitement and involvement with grand pieces of literature. But then people also begin to talk about their present reading—and how many of us don't read "great literature" in our free time.

Somehow we get back to What is English? Kathleen McCormick says that English now has the task of critical thinking about all the media. How to be critical about cultural *forces that play on students? It's a moment of meta-awareness in English studies. Move in and out, problematize things, critical theory. Surely this is true. Jeff Golub: "We deal with open texts—texts not finished in one reading." Someone: "We deal with lies."*

Interests me that the question of what's special about English led from attempts to define to lots of personal stories. A dichotomy: defining/distance/analysis versus stories/engagement/involvement.

Janet Emig asks, "Does engagement precede analysis?" Back to What is learning? Back to goals again too. Wayne Booth argues that the overarching goal for students is to take responsibility for their own readings. Even if they get help in arriving at meanings or readings, in the end they need to take responsibility for what they decide on. He made this point powerfully—or at least it resonated with many of us, for I remember hearing participants refer back to it in subsequent sessions.

We are getting to the end of our time. Andrea Lunsford is recorder, and she's feeling the pressure: how to write a report on the results of this digressive session full of stories. "Well now," she says, and sets off a long pause, looking for someone to say something to pull things together: silence. "But look," she says: still silence—people pondering. Like a teacher (the teacher we all are): "What are we going to make of this discussion?" But her tone is very wry—she knows we had a useful time and that the push for "closure" and "time on task" doesn't really make sense, and yet indeed we do need to get somewhere.

We go off on one more tangent, about the nature of learning and engagement or analysis. Finally I suggest that we all write for five minutes—each person trying to sum up what the session was really all about. Seems to work, but people want longer; goes to ten minutes. We only have eight minutes at the end, yet it's time for more than half of us to read what we've written. Seems to me that the quality of discourse is deeper, calmer, more integrative.

IF THE PARTICIPANTS of the English Coalition Conference weren't defining English as language arts or as a profession based on the study of literature, how were we defining it? The answer is that we were not defining it at all. In effect we were saying, we don't have to answer questions like What Is English? and What is our relation to literature? We have other work to do; let's leave those definitional questions vexed and tacit.

Many people say we can't make progress in a discussion till we have defined the main terms, but that's often a formula for holding things up. The surest way to derail a group that is in danger of making progress is to insist that they start by defining the key terms. That will keep them bickering till their time and patience are exhausted. One of the great sources of dull writing is a tyrannical insistence on defining terms first —as with essays that start out with quotations from *Webster's*. In fact our best work often precedes our efforts to clear up the meaning of central terms. Well-defined terms are more likely to be the goal of good discourse, not its precondition (just as getting your thought clear in your mind is often usefully seen as the goal of writing, not its precondition). As C. S. Lewis points out (18), if someone starts by stipulating what a term means, it's usually a sign that he's trying to get it to mean something different from what it actually does mean. In short, at the center of the conference's consensus was an agreement to leave certain disagreements unsettled, even if those disagreements lay right at the center of things.

Nevertheless, I can't resist trying—in this retrospective, exploratory enterprise I'm now engaged in—to carry on by myself with the question What is English? It's not that I'm trying to define an essence. I'm trying to chew on noteworthy chunks that kept turning up in a three-week stew; I'm trying to tell the story of some of the possible ingredients needed for future discussions before the profession can agree on what it's about. (I'm also struck that both books about the Dartmouth Conference try to define English [Dixon; Muller]. At that conference the question seemed to be important and explicit; I guess it took place at a more promising moment for defining the profession, but even so the lesson seems to be that you can't legislate for a profession, since I don't think their definitions "took.")

On the first Thursday evening of the conference (as I sat in my room looking over my notes—notes that I made readable for the epigraph for this chapter), I came up with a category for my notebook that I called "What Is English?" For the rest of the conference I found myself putting more and more notes there and marking more and more passages in my running notes with that label. I was recording not only what people said but also things that popped into my mind about the topic in response to other things people said.

So what is English? Looking back much later at all my musings, what finally strikes me is the diversity of answers—so many different ways of defining English. Perhaps what really characterizes English is that it's the grab-bag, garbage-pail, everything-but-the-kitchen-sink discipline. Or, recasting this with the dignity that English professors love, English is peculiarly rich, complex, and many-faceted. More so, I think, than most other disciplines. We're a *satura* (satire), a mixed bag. This can feel like a problem but is also a peculiar kind of strength. Let me count the ways:

1. As I argued in the previous chapter, we can be characterized by our special link with literature. First we were rhetoric and had no special relation to literature; then we more or less became literature; now we're confused about literature—but still cathected. We're a profession full of people who got excited as adolescents about "deep" works of imaginative literature—but who don't read those pieces for pleasure now as much as we sometimes feel we ought to do. (A remark like that is a good signal

that I had better acknowledge openly what I am doing for much of this chapter: not really reporting on what people said at the conference but rather purposely making risky speculations of my own—often projecting. I permit myself much more of these in this second half of the book.)

2. I sometimes think we get the clearest sense of our discipline every time we introduce ourselves—for example, at a party or on an airplane:

"So what do you do?"

"Actually, I teach English."

(False heartiness) "I guess I better watch how I talk."

From a listener, with an edge of resentment: "I could never figure out why we always had to look for hidden meanings in English."

Most of us have had this experience more often than we wish (thus that faintly defensive "actually" we sometimes fall into). Why is there that peculiar flavor of defensiveness on the part of our listeners too— and not just that but often downright fear or anger that people feel about their English classes? After all, most people found math harder than English and chemistry more boring.

For an explanation we need only look to our tradition. English has tended to stand for two things: the teaching of grammar and the teaching of literature. (When we were rhetoric in the eighteenth and nineteenth centuries, it wasn't literature, but it was belles lettres and elocution to the same effect.)

Grammar and literature may have the potential to create civility, but by the same token they are mechanisms for "civilizing the natives"—the "sivilizin" process that people lit out to the territories in order to avoid. As grammar and literature are taught in schools and colleges, they are characteristically experienced as agents of gentility and good taste or as mechanisms for discriminating—discriminating among linguistic forms, among texts and elements in the text, and also among people: who has taste and sound judgment and who is crude. The teaching of grammar and literature so often makes people feel unwashed or not right—as though there is something wrong with what feels most "them": the way words naturally come out of their mouths and the way they naturally feel about stories and the people in those stories. Students often find they are bored by the details the teacher says are most interesting, that they don't like the person the teacher says is most admirable, and that they miss the details of the story that the teacher says are actually the most important. Somehow, as English teachers, we continue to be defined in the way we want to get away from—as arbiters of good taste. John Goodlad found that in junior and senior high schools around the country, English is the subject that the fewest students rate as interesting (120). I can't resist an analogy in questionable taste to styles of colonialism. Although the French and Spanish colonizers went in for more downright torture—as with math and chemistry—the British somehow always ended up more deeply *hated*. There's something about the tyranny of good taste that rankles at the deepest level.[1]

3. English can also be defined by a peculiar fact that reinforces what I've just been talking about: it's the subject that everyone happens to take *more of* than any other. If we look at anyone we meet—from the corporation president to the homeless person huddling in the bus station—we can pedagogically undress them in our minds and see this one thing they have in common: they've spent more hours with their English teacher than with any other. And not by choice. Thus English teachers are more likely than teachers of other subjects to teach a "prison population" of students forced to take the class. At any moment, more students are in an English class than in any other school or college class. Thus, in this crude but inescapable dimension of things, the general public knows more about English than about any other school or college subject. If we don't like what they know—if we don't like their understanding of what we do as English teachers—we have no one to blame but ourselves.

4. English is ancillary. That is, English has tended to be a "handmaiden" to other disciplines in the humble sense of that metaphor: a "service discipline." We have no content; we "just" teach students to read and write—and perhaps to talk better—and perhaps to think straight. We prepare students for all those other teachers who have solid knowledge to teach—not just "skills." And oh yes, we'll teach them about footnotes and the Library of Congress system. As a "handmaiden" discipline we get to have people from all other disciplines nab us at meetings and parties and say, "My students can't read (write, speak, think). Why aren't you people in English doing your job?" Probably more than any other discipline, English has no "content," no substance to teach.

Insofar as we "just" teach reading and writing, we are the most *amateur* of all disciplines. Everyone knows how to read and write; everyone can tell us what we are doing wrong and how we can do it better. I think of Socrates talking about democracy and morals: it offended him and seemed inherently wrong that everyone should profess to be an expert on democracy and morals—but not on horseshoeing or building beds. Here, I think, is the reason why (at the college level anyway) there is such emphasis on dignity and professionalism in our field, qualities that so easily topple over into pretension and snobbery. In my seven years at MIT, I saw far less pretension, snobbery, showing off, and putting on of airs by faculty members in science and engineering than I see in most college or university English departments. My sense is that those MIT faculty members had an easier time trusting that they were professionals doing important, useful, respected work than many of us have in English.

I wonder if this might not be why at the college level we hold so hard to literature as our primary business: literature is a content, a rich and complicated body of substantive and (above all) professional material. One indication of whether you have a "solid content" to teach is whether you can easily make up exams and grade them—or whether people can easily write a Barnes and Noble or *Cliff's Notes* trot for the course. It's hard to make up and grade exams for reading and writing—and hard to write a *Cliff's Notes* trot; it's much easier with literature. A more pointedly political indication of whether you have a solid content to teach is whether you can apply for grant of any sort from the National Endowment for the Humanities. NEH considers literature a solid and fundable content in the humanities; it won't consider applications in writing. It feels demeaning to have no subject matter to teach, "just" reading and writing. Thus in many universities, the tenured faculty members leave the job of teaching service courses (any nonliterature course, any course that doesn't have a "subject") to people not fully part of the profession: teaching assistants and part-time faculty. This nervousness about having no solid content to teach may also explain why many high school teachers hang on hard to the teaching of grammar since it too is a solid and interesting body of knowledge.

Nevertheless, of course, there are grounds for pride here rather than defensiveness: we are teaching pervasive and universal *practices* rather than just information you can easily summarize, test, and grade for. I don't mean to say that people in physics or history are teaching "mere content" and not "practices." Those disciplines, and most others too, have been helped by recently conceiving their subject as a set of practices. Still, what turns up on tests and in published trots seems to me to show that those other disciplines are more rooted in discrete summarizable information than English is. In short, we English teachers are teaching a process more than a content. Reading and writing are practices that students need (and know they need) for almost everything they do, in and out of school. So perhaps the defensiveness about no content will diminish. Certainly it has diminished mightily in writing, where the more we have explored the practices we are teaching, the less defensive we realize we need to be.

And as Kathleen McCormick and Katherine Cummings and others noted, it can also be said that English in the last few years has become a "handmaiden" in a more elevated sense—perhaps indeed taking over from philosophy the role of "queen of the sciences." For with the burgeoning of literary theory—merging with German sociological critical theory and European hermeneutical theory and French poststructuralist and deconstructive theory—English now feels itself the locus of theory. People in English have some reason to feel proud that ours is the discipline where the most exciting metatheoretical work is going on and where thinkers are attaining the most perspective about representation: the nature of how things mean or stand for things; how texts work and how everything is a text; what discourse is and how everything is discourse. In other disciplines they interpret or make meaning, but English (as practiced by more than a few college and university faculties) has begun to center itself on the study of the processes themselves of interpreting or making meaning. The theory side of English has taken on enormous confidence, advancing enormous claims for universality of provenance, at the very period when philosophy has somehow tended to mute its formerly confident claims for universality. (Those members of our profession trained in rhetoric cannot resist noting, however, that if this current direction really takes, it will be nothing but a return to the central role of rhetoric in the academy.)

So English continues as a service discipline in two senses: as a humble jack of all trades or kicking boy but also as arbiter or theorizer of all knowledge.

5. English seems to be more divided or disunified across levels than other disciplines. That is, in colleges and universities, English tends to mean literature—not speech and often not writing; in elementary school it's the other way round—speech, writing, and reading, but no literature; high school English has all of these but also tends to include a hodgepodge of other things such as values clarification and speech contests about automobile safety. If we put college and school teachers of, say, history (or of math or of biology) in the same room, I suspect they will probably feel more as though they are teaching the same thing than school and college teachers of English.

6. Values clarification reminds us that English could also be defined as the one subject that everything extraneous falls to. Perhaps this is a legacy of the real grammar school of yore: a tradition where the teacher of grammar taught everything that younger children needed to know. But it may just be a product of material conditions: when milk money has to be collected or something needs to get to all students, the job usually falls to English since that's the only subject that all students take. When schools want to work on "thinking," this tends to fall to English. In the aftermath of a racial incident at the University of Massachusetts, the university wanted to do consciousness-raising around race and cultural diversity, and naturally enough the job fell to the writing program: writing is the only course that all students take.

7. Most disciplines are organized around high-level concepts or abstractions. From physics to sociology to linguistics, we see that the shape

of a discipline tends to be determined by a relatively few high-level concepts that serve to organize a virtual infinity of data or instances (for example, entropy in physics, deviance in sociology, grammatical transformation in linguistics; see Bruner, *Process of Education* 17–32). But for that central and perhaps determining part of English that focuses on literature, this situation does not hold. Even though we organize literature around large concepts like satire or the Renaissance, even though there are certain principles that inhere in the notion of satire or Renaissance literature, and even though we see someone as influential as Northrop Frye organizing virtually all of literature around an elegantly few, powerful, superordinate concepts, nevertheless there is still a crucial difference from what we see in most other disciplines. In studying economics or physics, the principles are more important than the instances; in studying satire or Renaissance literature, the instances—the works—are more important than the principles. Many poststructuralists insist that a work about *King Lear* is just as valuable as the play itself, but even that claim is a privileging of a text and not a claim that principles are more important than texts.

In other words, the study of literature is more deeply wedded to the concrete than many other disciplines. (See the section in chapter 5 about how everyone interested in theory still sticks up for the concrete.) Yet another way of saying it is that in literature, the main objects of study are works that don't get outdated. Even "old and wrong" literary theory that most of us don't believe (such as Dryden saying that first we get our thoughts, and then we "clothe" them in poetic language) is much more inherently part of our discipline than a comparable piece of wrong physics. Of course, this point also applies to disciplines like French and art (music being a bit more deeply wedded to principles or overarching concepts.)

8. I'll risk yet another shaky generalization: English is the most personal academic discipline—even more personal than the very discipline that actually focuses on the person and on feelings, namely psychology. The reasons for this odd claim are interesting. For one, most poems and stories that we teach are about personal experiences like love, death, and growing up. English teachers also tend to know their students better than other teachers do, and our students often know us better than they know their other teachers. English teachers simply get more writing from students than any other teachers, and that writing often has a personal dimension; even in their expository or nonexpressive writing, our students often tell us a lot about their lives and feelings. As teachers and students discuss stories and poems in class, it is common for both parties to bring personal experiences to bear. English teachers are also more likely to reveal something personal about themselves than other teachers: partly because of this context where the stories and student responses

and student writing are so often personal and partly because so many English teachers simply turn out to be people who chose the field because they were attracted to this most personal of subjects. (My point may apply less to college professors than to English teachers in schools.)

9. Let me point to a different sense in which English is a peculiarly personal discipline: English trains its members' sensibilities as much as their minds. Our sensibilities and feelings are central tools in our work, not just extra and perhaps unpredictable mental appendages. Psychoanalysts and therapists are explicitly trained to pay respectful attention to their feelings about their patients as a source of evidence about what's going on—evidence they might well miss if they only attend to their thinking. In English (not just literature but writing too), we may not be trained to attend to our feelings, but most of us learn that in trying to figure out how texts function, our feelings and intuition are as important as our analytic reason. On the one hand, this is a virtue. English is a discipline that has traditionally taught and valued the ability to yoke reason and imagination together into the same train of thought or in the same piece of prose. This leads, in my opinion, to a happy result. The best work in English has a peculiarly rich quality of mind: it is personal and imaginative without any loss of controlled and driving rationality. (I'm not talking about elegance, which may be the besetting weakness of the profession.)

But, on the other hand, this focus on sensibility and imagination has its tricky side. It means that we get our *selves* more than usually tangled up with our thinking. I am not trying to deny ego investment in other disciplines (as illustrated, say, in Watson and Crick's *Double Helix*), but in most other disciplines it is a bit easier to find a difference between someone's ideas or conclusions and their sensibility or voice or personality. In English, if you disagree with my interpretation of a work of literature or find my writing ineffective or even if you just disagree with my proposal about the graduate program, you are not just disagreeing with a thought of mine; I tend to experience you (often correctly) as disagreeing with my very sensibility, my self. (I remember a teacher of mine from another discipline getting ready to explain what was wrong with my essay saying, "I want to start out by making it clear that I'm criticizing your writing, not you." This is harder to pull off in English.) This central role of sensibility in English leads to a characteristic touchiness and even acrimony or bad feeling in our college and university departments. I have been a faculty member at many and diverse institutions and visited dozens of other campuses and departments (and not just for a one-hour talk but usually for extended time and interaction), and I believe I see college and university English departments as more often rancorous or grumpy than other departments.

I also fear that this potentially wonderful emphasis on sensibility as a central tool in our work also leads to that snobbish, patronizing, and condescending tone that is so unfortunately characteristic of professors of English (if not school English teachers). I know I'm making a risky subjective generalization here; I know there are many exceptions; and I stick by my previous point that students are more likely to share something personal or private with an English teacher than with teachers from other disciplines. But before you dismiss my perception of snobbishness and condescension, check it out with colleagues from other college or university departments and also with students who have wide experience with a range of teachers. I would be happy to be proved wrong (or, rather, depressed).

So what do all these conflicting characterizations of English amount to? Shall we question whether we are a discipline? On the last day of the conference, Phyllis Franklin asked, "Is English studies a discipline?" and the overwhelming response was "Yes," despite everyone's awareness of how difficult it is to characterize. (But perhaps some readers in English will be skeptical of this response because people also said that they thought education was a discipline too. "I wouldn't have said so two weeks ago," said one participant.)

It's hard to draw a conclusion. The only one seems to be that we are more of a grab-bag, hodgepodge, amateur discipline than most others —with less of a clear and definite professional content. And that's that. Perhaps understandably, colleges and universities have tried to find grand unifying theories or methodologies for the profession (such as New Criticism and now some of the postmodern theories), whereas high schools have for various reasons more often reflected the pluralistic and pragmatic ethos of the profession as a whole. If we don't like this everything-but-the-kitchen-sink quality of our profession, we'll have to lump it. I hope we can like it because I sense that much of the defensive and snobbish behavior on the part of English teachers comes from trying to compensate for the inherently mixed, messy, unprofessional quality of our profession.[2]

When I look around at the profession and ask if we have a center, it seems to me that the strongest center remains the traditional one that doesn't easily let go: English as the profession of grammar and literature, correctness and good taste. But when I turn back from these wide and dangerous speculations and look at the Coalition Conference and ask what *it* suggests about a possible emerging center, I come up with this: perhaps we will gradually get a new cohesive focus on the *productive* dimensions of language. The conference stressed how we are producers when we make meaning (in both writing and reading) and also when we analyze that process and the scene and the forces that act on us when we make meaning. Perhaps English can end up being a discipline that is, above all, about making knowledge rather than about studying already existing knowledge.

NOTES

[1]Paul Armstrong made this comment in response to an earlier draft:

> [A] large part of my resistance to privileging "literature" or defining it mono- lithically comes from how put off I was as a student by New Critic teachers who saw themselves as "cultural priests" and us as the unwashed. They knew what "literature" was and what it meant and what its values were—and those who didn't weren't anointed. The egalitarian implications of theory's chal- lenge to New Critical assumptions have a lot to do with the need or desire many of us feel to attack that attitude.

Joan Hartman offers this comment:

> But how and why did we escape being made to feel crude and unwashed? Or were we made to feel crude and unwashed and loved it because we're all masochists? A friend of mine in graduate school—in psychology—said she (and others like her who were children of immigrant parents) stayed away from specializing in literature because it wasn't their culture and they always felt uncomfortable, not smart enough, in literature classes. That gave me pause. Although not the child of immigrants, I was, like her, the first in my family to go to college. Yet I was powerfully attracted by literature. When I met people who'd grown up in cultivated families, I was impressed (probably I still am) and also led to wonder what it would have been like at least knowing about the things I discovered with such excitement in literature classes in college. I suspect familiarity would have diminished my excitement.

[2]Lack of definition is not a new problem in our discipline. Fred Newton Scott pointed to it 1900: "[T]he most characteristic thing about English teaching at the present time is its unsettledness. It is fuller of unsolved problems than any other subject that can be mentioned. It is a kind of pedagogical porcupine" (qtd. in Stewart 199). Applebee, in his recent history of the discipline, talks about

> the uneasiness which teachers of English have traditionally felt about the definition of their subject matter. The Committee of Ten [1893–94] in effect brought together a number of disparate subjects, each with its own body of rules and formal subject matter, and called them "English." Beyond the cliché that each of these studies deals with language, they have no real unity *as a subject matter*; attempts to interrelate them have been artificial, and, for the most part, short-lived. Whether the model for the educational process has been growth in language, the four basic skills (reading, writing, listening, speaking), or the three basic disciplines (language, literature, and composi- tion), some aspect of what teachers considered to be important has been lost, reemerging to assert its own values and undercut the basis of the reconcili- ation. Inevitably, the edges of the subject have blurred and wavered, creating for the teacher of English a perpetual crisis of identity. (Applebee 145–46)

Teaching Writing: Motivating Inquiry

Larry R. Johannessen
(secondary school section)

WE DISAGREE WITH Carol's group," Dan said. "What this woman did doesn't go beyond the limits of freedom of speech."

"Could you explain why?" I asked. This was the second day of an activity designed to teach eleventh-grade "regular" students some of the thinking strategies involved in writing extended definition essays. They had worked in small groups most of the previous day trying to determine whether twelve different incidents involving freedom of speech should be allowed under this right. Now, we were discussing the incidents as a class and using them to develop a set of criteria to define freedom of speech.

"Well," Dan began, "an airport is a public place, and freedom of speech guarantees a person the right to say what he wants in public as long as he doesn't like cause people to riot or harm anyone and—"

"But this woman says she has guns and explosives. She could blow up the plane!" Kim shouted at Dan. "I'd say that could cause a little harm!"

"All right, Kim. Let him explain," I said.

"It says she 'jokes about hijacking her plane using the submachine gun and the grenades in her purse,' and 'her purse is tiny.' There is no way she could be doing anything but telling a joke. She couldn't get all that stuff in her purse."

"Yeah," Sharon quickly added, "and we also thought just because you don't like what somebody says doesn't mean you can arrest them. Freedom of speech means you have a right to speak your mind even if other people don't like it."

"But this is different," Kim said. "We're talking about a situation where people's lives are at stake. You can't take chances with people's lives."

"I don't know, Kim," Steve chimed in. "If this woman was really going to hijack the plane, I don't think she would announce it as she goes through the security check. It's just a joke. She doesn't even have any weapons. That's why we thought people have the right to say whatever they want in public as long as they don't hurt or intend to hurt other people."

"I hadn't thought about the fact that she doesn't really have the guns and stuff," Kim said. "But I wonder whether they really have time to think about if she has explosives or not . . . if someone could be killed. . . ."

Two periods later, I found myself running a very different kind of discussion with another eleventh-grade "regular" class. They were also studying definition. The previous day they had read about the importance of defining, discussed their reactions to the reading, and then worked in small groups defining five terms. Here is an excerpt from that discussion.

"Let's move on to the term *freedom*. Any volunteers?" After a pause, I said, "Somebody from group one. What did you come up with for freedom and how did you distinguish it from harmful criminal behavior and economic freedom?"

"Which one?" Bill asked.

"Freedom," I replied.

"Freedom is being able to think whatever you want," Bill said.

"Do you all agree?" I asked, looking around the room. "Does anyone have something different?" After a long silence, "Group two, what did you decide?"

"We had the same thing," Andy said.

"Okay, group three," I said.

"We said that it is being able to do what you want and go where you want as long as you don't break the law," Jenny said.

"Does anyone have any comments about their definition?" I asked. Silence. "Is there anything they left out?" After a long silence, "Group four, what did you come up with for freedom?"

"Being able to say whatever you want, go where you want, and do whatever you want," Jill said. "But you can't commit a crime that hurts other people."

"And how did you distinguish freedom from economic freedom?" I asked.

"Well, we sort of thought they were the same thing," Jill said.

Why is there such a difference between these two discussions, and what does the difference say about what approaches help or hinder students' learning? First, what happened in each discussion? In the first excerpt, students went through a sequence of defining steps. Dan offers a criterion for the incident: freedom of speech allows people the right to freedom of expression. Students then measure the example against this criterion. Kim points out that the right should not allow people to harm others. Students then consider intent and conclude that this incident does not go beyond the limits of freedom of speech because the woman did not intend to harm others. Finally, Kim points out that an immediate potential danger justifies immediate action.

In the second discussion, Bill gives one feature of freedom: being able to do as one pleases. He does not try to distinguish freedom from harmful criminal behavior or economic freedom. Even with urging, students do not challenge Dan's definition. Andy adds nothing, and Jenny offers two characteristics of freedom and an attempt to distinguish freedom from breaking a law. No one challenges anything she says, even with my considerable urging. Finally, Jill gives three features of the term and distinguishes freedom from harmful criminal behavior. The class seems to be unaware of all of this. When I question her about how freedom is different from economic freedom, she doesn't see how the two terms are different. It seems no one else in the class does either. Clearly, this class has made little if any progress in understanding definition or the process of defining.

One important reason for the differences between the two classes may be that the first class was given concrete data, while the second class only read about the importance of defining and then worked on defining five abstract terms. The difficulty the second class has distinguishing the term from other related concepts does not necessarily mean that the first class is smarter than the second. It may mean that instruction involving concrete data set up with problems that engage and involve students enables them to learn thinking strategies involved in writing.

In the first class, the incidents students discussed were purposely made arguable. With no easy answers students found themselves, sometimes despite themselves, embroiled in debate with their peers. Notice that their audience is not primarily the teacher but one another. In the second class, even though I made every attempt to encourage students to talk with one another, there was virtually no student interaction. Nothing is built into the activity to ensure engagement or to push students beyond a superficial "answer."

Small group work appears to be important. The high level of interaction in the first class can be partly attributable to students first discussing the incidents in small groups. Students came to the class discussion with a stake in what their group produced and were more willing to share their ideas. However, just putting students in small groups is no guarantee they will interact or learn, as the second excerpt illustrates.

The first class practices key strategies for defining: comparing examples of the definiendum with examples of similar but different concepts to determine essential distinctions and stipulating criteria for making distinctions. These strategies are key not only for the assignment I will give them in a few days but also for other defining problems they may encounter. In the second class, students merely imitate the features of a formal written definition with abstract terms. Freedom and economic freedom remain abstract terms, without meaning. As the two excerpts illustrate, it is the students in the first class who are learning the skills involved in defining.

My experience and research indicate that teaching students to write is most effective when instruction focuses on inquiry. This approach utilizes concrete data, involves students in solving problems that require them to practice and use the thinking strategies inherent in various writing tasks, involves problems that are student-centered (small group and whole class), and encourages high levels of student interaction with a minimim of teacher lecture. A growing body of research indicates that engaging students in inquiry, the approach described here, results in highly significant gains in student writing over other approaches (see Hillocks, "Mode and Focus," *Research on Written Composition*, and "What Works"; Hillocks et al.; and Johannessen et al.).

Nello Carlini

Brooke Workman
(secondary school section)

NELLO CARLINI WAS a dynamo. And he broke nearly every rule in the Book of Common Pedagogy. He swore at the kids—of course, he swore at everybody. In fact, I overheard our principal at Munich American High School once tell a disturbed parent that she should worry when Nello didn't swear at a student. (Strangely, she didn't protest, nor did any other of the students' parents. Maybe it was because it was an overseas Department of Defense school with parents who could live with honest profanity.)

Nello also played a role in every play his Thespians performed at Munich American High School, and when he accidentally fell off the stage when he played the Grand Inquisitor during a performance of *St. Joan*, he said with obvious delight, "Did you notice? Nobody broke a line! I love those kids." He was right about the acting. And nobody laughed in the audience.

One late November day, I went to the faculty room for a cup of coffee, and there was Nello on the sofa lying in the posture of a deceased saint. Suddenly I remembered that this was not his prep period. Good God, I thought, remembering my Iowa high school principal's adage ("Never leave your rooms unattended!"), Nello is not in his class!

So I asked, "Nello, don't you have a class this period?"

His pencil mustache twitched and his eyes opened ever so slightly as he snarled, "I'm mad at those little bastards! They aren't doing their work. They are not thinking. They are just copying from books."

"How long has this been going on?" I asked.

"Two weeks."

"TWO WEEKS! But . . . what are they doing now?" I asked.

"Go look for yourself," he said, closing his eyes.

So I did. I walked up to room 205 and peeked in the small window slit of the classroom door. There was Nello's gilded throne chair that he bought at some antique shop in Munich. And there they were, kids in groups, some alone, writing or talking, books around them, obviously engaged in Nello's American literature course. One of the students in

Nello's class was Sophie Rosenkowski, who was in my Enriched English class.

The next period was Enriched English class, and I inquired of Sophie just what was going on.

"Oh," she said sorrowfully, "Mr. Carlini is mad at us. We kind of sluffed off, but now we're trying to get him back."

And they did about two days later.

It's a story about high expectations from a teacher who believed in students, collaboration, an understanding principal, and supportive parents.

A Moment

Paul Armstrong
(college section)

ONE DAY A STUDENT came to my office and announced she was looking for the previous occupant, who had been her English teacher two years ago. I informed her that he was no longer in the department (he hadn't gotten tenure), and she looked at me with evident despair. I asked her what was the matter, and she explained: "Professor X taught us this story in his class (I forget the name of the story), and he told us what it meant, and now I have the same story in another class and I've forgotten what its interpretation is. I need to find him so he'll tell me, because this other teacher won't."

She asked me if I knew the story, and she was a bit disgusted when I didn't. I told her that she should try to think for herself about what the story might mean, but this lame advice clearly demonstrated to her that the wrong person had been fired.

We need to teach with learner-oriented methods that encourage students to become producers of their own readings of texts.

8 | *The Question of Writing: The Wars in My Head*

*I*n a plenary session toward the end of the conference, Bill Teale captured the whole conference more than anyone else did, I think, by reading a children's book to us as though we were his first-grade class. He read Three by the Sea (Marshall), from which I quote the following lines (from "Sam's Story," which is a story within the story):

> "My, my," said the rat. "What a pretty cat. And I have never had a cat."
> "I will buy that cat and have a friend," he said.
> And he went into the shop.
> "I want a cat," he said.
> "Are you sure you want a cat?" asked the owner.
> "I am sure," said the rat. "And I want that one."
> "That will be ten cents," said the man. "If you are sure."
> "I am sure," said the rat. "Here is my last dime. Give me my cat."
> The rat and the cat left the shop.
> "We will be friends," said the rat.
> "Do you think so?" said the cat. "Well, we'll see."
> The rat and the cat sat in the sun.
> "What do you do for fun?" asked the rat.
> "I like to catch things," said the cat.
> "That's nice," said the rat.
> "I am hungry," said the cat. "How about lunch?"
> "A fine idea," said the rat. "What is your favorite dish?"
> "I do not want to say," said the cat.
> "You can tell me," said the rat. "We are friends."
> "Are you sure you want to know?" said the cat.
> "I am sure," said the rat. "Tell me what you like to eat."
> "I will tell you," said the cat. "But let us go where we can be alone."
> "Fine with me," said the rat.
> The cat and the rat went to the beach.

126

"I know," said the rat. "Fish. You like to eat fish."
"Not at all," said the cat. "It's much better than fish."
"Tell me," said the rat. "I just have to know."
"Come closer," said the cat. "And I will tell you."
"Yes?" said the rat.
"What I like," said the cat, "is . . ." [pregnant page turn]
". . . CHEESE! I love cheese!"
"So do I," said the rat. "And I have some here."
"Hooray!" said the cat. "And now we are friends."
So they sat on the beach and ate the cheese.
And that was that.
> *[end of "Sam's Story"]*
"Very sweet," said Lolly.
Spider looked cross.
"I did not like the end," he said. "It was dumb."
"Then you tell a story," said Sam.
"Easy as pie," said Spider.

AS I WAS TRYING to work out this book, it struck me that perhaps I could tell the story of the ugly relations between writing[1] and literature—a professional, disciplinary, political relation—by telling the personal story of how it wasn't a problem at the conference. It ends up being a story of a fight we didn't have and a story of my two loyalties: to writing and to literature.

Though I was trained in literature and still consider myself a literature person as much as a writing person, my primary identification in the last decade or more has been with writing, and I came to the English Coalition Conference prepared to fight the dirty rats in literature. In fact, that was probably the determining factor that overcame my reluctance to give up three weeks of a difficult summer: it felt like my duty to come and stick up for writing at what promised to be an important forum—especially when I and others discovered how few writing people were invited. Out of sixty participants, only a small handful of us could be called specialists or especially loyal to writing.

Why this mentality of having to fight literature? The answer is that we in writing (at least at the university level) feel badly treated by literature. Ever since I switched from a specialization in Chaucer to one in writing, I've felt my former "profession" treat me as less serious, intellectual, and scholarly—indeed, less a member of the profession—than before. In meetings to decide who teaches a writing course and who teaches a literature course, I often discover decisions being made on the premise that someone must be smarter to teach literature than to teach writing. Now that I'm sensitive to that premise, I see it often. Thus people often assume that only advanced and experienced graduate students should teach literature but that raw, first-year students are ready to teach writing. In discussion groups called to explore the interesting relations that have been emerging in recent years between literary theory and composition theory, I've often encountered the assumption that of course all the learning will proceed in one direction.

Like most university teachers of writing, I have seen departments routinely grant contract renewals, promotions, or tenure to literature faculty members on the basis of perfectly ordinary or run-of-the-mill scholarship—sometimes even shoddy—yet deny renewals, promotions, or tenure to writing faculty members on the basis of scholarship that was just as good or better but didn't look to them as "serious" or "scholarly." Literature faculty members often see scholarship as "not solid" if it is tainted with pedagogy or social science methodology. I was on a departmental council where literature faculty members ruled against someone in writing because they mistakenly questioned the methodological validity of a kind of quantitative research in which they had no experience at all and which they didn't understand. We in writing are not able to apply to the National Endowment for the Humanities for grants or fellowships for our work because the agency doesn't consider writing part of the humanities.

Perhaps this attitude has led to the striking difference in material conditions for teachers of writing and literature—or perhaps the conditions have led to the attitude (see Slevin). But people who teach writing at colleges and universities are usually paid far less and teach far more—under worse working conditions—than people who teach literature. People who teach writing are more apt to be teaching assistants or non-tenure-track lecturers or adjunct part-timers who have no contracts and who must often piece together enough money to live on by taking jobs at two or three institutions—sometimes four or five. The pay is often less than $1,000 per course, with no benefits. These writing teachers often don't know if they'll be hired till a month or a week before the term begins—sometimes, in fact, only a day or an hour before the first class. I pass over how this damages the departments themselves and the whole profession (see Wayne Booth's presidential address to the MLA). Here I'm just viewing the situation from the partisan position of writing teachers. In short, English departments often "live off" writing teachers in an arrangement where literature faculty members have comparatively smaller classes and lighter loads paid for by the larger loads of adjuncts and teaching assistants teaching writing. As director of writing programs at Stony Brook, I couldn't get colleagues in the English department (with very few exceptions) to teach writing, even with the chair trying to support me. It is common for tenured literature professors to refuse to teach writing and to condescend to it as a low order of work and yet criticize how it's done by those who do it. Virtually every writing administrator has had the experience of getting more financial and moral support from other departments and from the administration than from the English department. James Slevin lays out these conditions with more detail and backing while also making an interesting argument about the relations between literature and writing.[2] Some people in composition want us to break off and form our own departments (see Hairston), leaving English departments to shrink to the size of French or classics departments. But for me, though I'm sympathetic with this impulse, it doesn't feel like an option: I experience myself and the enterprise of writing as part of English and literature.

There is an instructive parallel between how literature is treating writing and how it has treated education. I've found it difficult, for instance, to get a literature-based English department even to consider the possibility of hiring someone with a PhD in English education, even if that person is well qualified for the job. I sense here an odd instinct to exclude fields that are really the root systems of the profession: education and English education train the teachers of English; writing helps students learn the mother tongue, the main medium of the profession. There is a parallel story in how departments of literature have treated rhetoric and speech.

I have had an interesting glimpse at how the literature profession somehow encourages its members to internalize an attitude of ironic condescension toward writing. When I teach a practicum or any graduate course in writing, I ask students to write case studies of themselves as writers: to look back through their lives at what they've written and to figure out as much as they can about how they went about writing and what was going on—all the forces at play. I've noticed a striking feature that is common in English PhD students that I don't much see in graduate students from other disciplines in my course: a wry and sometimes witty but always condescending tone they take toward their younger selves, who were usually excited with writing and eager to be great writers. Behind this urbanity, I often see a good deal of disappointment and even pain at not being able to keep on writing those stories and poems that were so exciting to write. But instead of acknowledging this disappointment, these students tend to betray a frightening lack of kindness or charity—most of all a lack of *understanding*—toward that younger self who wanted to grow up to be Yeats. Instead, I see either amused condescension or downright ridicule at their former idealism and visionary zeal. My point is that people cannot continue to engage in writing without granting themselves some vision and idealism and even naive grandstanding—yet these literature students, now that they see themselves on the path to being professors of literature, seem to need to squelch that side of themselves, however urbanely.

In short, I arrived at Wye on guard, indeed loaded for bear. But it turned out there were no bear, no dirty rats, no one to fight. It's not that everyone said how wonderful writing is and sympathized at the bad treatment or even that everyone was so knowledgeable or interested in the teaching of writing. In fact, I was mildly disappointed at how little direct discussion there was about writing and the writing process. There were talks and presentations about at least a dozen topics or issues but none about writing. (Perhaps Janet Emig's workshop could be described as about writing, but it seemed to me more about the nature of language and representation. I describe it at the head of chapter 4, "Taking a Theoretical Stance.") The "problem" was that everyone seemed to have an enlightened attitude: they simply took for granted what we in writing so often cannot get people in literature to grant—that writing, the teaching of writing, and research about writing are just as important, dignified, scholarly, and integral to our field as literature. (Of course, the majority of conference participants were elementary and secondary school teachers, who comfortably combine writing and literature: the problem I'm talking about is in higher education. And also we were only in Maryland for a visit: we didn't have to fight over salaries, teaching loads, teaching schedules, offices, and who would teach what.)

Indeed, one of the major accomplishments of the conference was a movement of writing and literature toward each other. This movement was most powerfully enacted in the first of three recommendations in the college section report: "Freshman Writing and Reading." This is a recommendation for a full-year course that is neither writing nor literature but something that integrates the two and speaks to their interdependency.

In short, as I listened and looked around and talked during the conference, gradually I had to let down my dukes. I began to realize that the condition of writing was not a problem in the context of this conference. There were plenty of problems, but they seemed to be problems in literature or in the profession as a whole. And so a surprising category began to take shape in my mind sometime late in the first week: "Writing Leads the Way," it says grandly across the top of the page in one section of my notebook. I began to record there things that struck me as problems for literature or the profession that we in writing seem to be handling better. Instead of feeling defensive and ready to fight, I began to toy with feeling smug. I am not trying to imply in what follows that everyone in writing is enlightened and that everyone in literature is doing badly. We probably have an equal amount of bad teaching and weak scholarship in both areas. My point is that whereas literary studies have tended in recent history to be the paradigm for the English profession, I suddenly began to sense that writing could serve as a paradigm for

English—a paradigm that offers help on some of the important problems in the profession.[3]

The Problem of How to Teach the Making of Meaning

Participants at the conference often discussed the difficulty of teaching students to understand meaning as constructed: the difficulty of getting them to feel the meaning of a literary text (or any text) as actively created and negotiated, not just found as an inert right answer sitting there hidden in the text or in the teacher's mind or in a work of authoritative criticism. Yes, there may be constraints on an interpretation, and not any interpretation may be acceptable; but still the resulting meaning is something that people have to build. This lesson is all the harder to teach because of the ever-present Charybdis of "Well this is what *I* think the poem means, and nothing you can say will change my mind. Literature is just a matter of personal opinion."

Writing seems to have an obvious advantage here. Writing is cognitively complex on the *outside*: students can often see themselves and others constructing and changing meaning as they write and get feedback and revise; and, as most writing classes are now set up, they can often see written meaning being constructed through a process of social negotiation with peers and teachers. Reading, however, is cognitively complicated on the *inside* where, for the most part, students often don't see the making of meaning. It's worth noticing that this "obvious advantage" wasn't there a few years ago. Teachers and textbooks and even theorists commonly described writing as a matter of encoding or transmitting thoughts already fully formed in the mind of the writer. If you were having trouble, it was because you hadn't first got your meaning clear—and that wasn't writing, that was thinking. The field of composition has brought about a major change in how we conceive of the act of writing. Most people agree that we cannot separate writing from thinking. In short, if making meaning and analyzing how meaning is made constitutes the central process that people in English want to focus on, writing is now an enormously helpful paradigmatic activity. (Thus Derrida calls reading "writing.")

Similarly, because the reading process is more hidden—and also quicker—it seems less fraught with struggle for someone who is good at it. Therefore literature teachers often fail to experience themselves in the same boat or engaged in the same process as their weak students. When it comes to writing, however, almost all teachers experience the common bond of struggle or even anxiety, no matter how good they are. Writing is a leveler.

Students could come to see reading as an obvious process of cognitive and social construction if there were only a tradition in literature, as there is in writing, of teachers and researchers sharing what we might call "rough drafts of reading": showing or talking about their actual reading process from the beginning. For example, teachers could work with colleagues or students on pieces they have not seen before or give a protocol or an accurate account of the mental events that go on in one's mind while engaged in creating meaning from a text. (For a discussion of these "movies of the reader's mind," see Elbow, *Writing with Power* 237–78.) If there were more widespread attention to and sharing of our own reading processes, we'd spend more time talking to our colleagues and to our students about how of course we misread and misunderstand an enormous number of words and phrases and sections of a text as we engage in even the most *skilled* reading. That is, the mysterious innerness of reading doesn't just stem from good readers "revising" and correcting themselves so quickly and often subliminally; it also stems from the lack of any tradition of revealing misreadings and wrong takes (like sharing early drafts). Where the writing tradition of the last two decades shows teachers how to write with students and share what they produce in its raw, crummy state, the literary tradition tells literature teachers that it would be wrong to teach a class on a text that they have not carefully studied beforehand and that it would be odd to have a discussion with colleagues about a text they've never seen before. (Obviously, there are exceptions. As Elizabeth Wallace of Western Oregon State University reports, "In lower-division survey or general education courses, I regularly teach texts I just managed to read for the first time the previous day—and those are usually the best classes. The students see all kinds of things I didn't see, and they see me learning from them and see the delight it gives me" [response to draft].) Students and colleagues would benefit enormously from exactly this kind of workshop class where participants reveal early rough readings in process and show how these are adjusted and transformed over time and by means of negotiation through comparison with readings by others. One of the virtues of reader-response criticism is that if people really engage in it honestly and empirically, it tends to make them braver about the kind of exploring I've just described. It promotes professionalism in the good sense (nondefensive thinking together) and undermines professionalism in the bad sense (trying to hide your struggles and to erase bonds with the unwashed).

Thus the teaching of literature is more liable to be stuck in the right-answer trap, with many students thinking that teachers just want the correct interpretation and many teachers unfortunately reinforcing that mentality. Of course, there is no shortage of writing teachers who do the comparable thing—who want every essay to have the same five-paragraph or "funnel" structure or every paragraph to start with a "topic sentence," or who just teach grammar and parts of speech exercises. But there is a kind of consensus in the writing profession that this is not the way to teach writing—whereas I see no comparable consensus in the literature profession that teaching right interpretations is not teaching literature.

This matter is pointedly illustrated when we look at testing. In the field of writing we have managed to convince schools and colleges to insist that testing means testing a practice or a performance, not a content: that if they want to find out how well students write, they've got to get them to write (despite budgetary pressures and the blandishments of cheaper, sophisticatedly predictive tests of grammar and usage from the Educational Testing Service). In the case of literature, however, virtually every school, college, and university in the country accedes to ETS and ACT testing of literature and reading by means of multiple-choice machine-graded tests—many of them tests of correct information. We see some of the same thing if we look at the testing that goes on in courses: it has come to feel peculiar if the final exam in a writing course asks mostly for recall of information, whereas that does not seem peculiar for a final exam in a literature course.[4]

Because students in a writing class usually have to revise the drafts they get feedback on, self-interest leads them to see how useful it is to get accurate movies of readers' minds: "I need to know the story of your thoughts and feelings as you read my piece, especially those thoughts and feelings that occurred when you began to resist me or misunderstand me and the nature of your resistance or misunderstanding. I have to figure out how to revise this piece." In literature classes teachers often have a harder time showing students the practical value of the reader-response exercise, especially because of pressure from two directions: the temptation to slide off entirely into readers' stories that don't throw light back onto the text and the pull toward interpretations that the teacher thinks are better. (Can it be that reader-response processes are more alive in writing classrooms and research than in literature classrooms and research?)[5]

In the teaching of writing we've learned to use the whole class to teach this process of writing as socially negotiated meaning, but I'm thinking in particular about the use of small peer groups in writing classrooms for the purposes of sharing drafts and discovering readings. We have slowly built up enough experience and wisdom (and courage) that it is now impossible for teachers to say, as only recently they used to say, "Groups can't work—it's just the blind leading the blind." There are too many teachers who are making them work. It's important to note too that these are teachers of widely different style, approach, and temperament—not just "free spirits." (Indeed, free spirits often have the hardest time with groups. For a powerful nonfree spirit who illustrates the uses of carefully focused peer groups, see Hillocks, *Research on Written Composition*.)

The Problem of Working Together as a Discipline or a Community

I didn't see people at the conference downhearted about the remarkable lack of consensus in the profession of English. Partly it was a matter of strong theoretical arguments by Graff and conference participants themselves that disagreement is healthy rather than cause for alarm; partly it was a matter of experience or practice: we discovered that even though the sixty of us seemed to reflect most of the divisions in the profession, we also seemed to be able to work together productively. Nevertheless, I sensed a little more edginess about the fact that we seem to have a serious problem about that prominent issue in our profession, literature. One of the main reasons we avoided real work on the question of literature (what is it? what place should it have?) is that the profession lacks effective working agreements for how to deal with the issue. Part of what fuels people like Hirsch and Finn is that the English profession is in pretty thorough disarray about what students should know about literature (whether they are nonmajors or even majors): Should they be acquainted with certain important authors or works (or experience them or love them)? Which ones? Should they understand certain principles in the study of literature (say, about structure, genre, plot, character)? Possess certain historical knowledge? Be able to engage in close reading? Be able to interpret? Do cultural criticism? The only thing the field agrees on is the one thing that the most senior members deny with their behavior: the importance of teaching students to write.

Perhaps people in the field of writing have more of a shared consensus than those in literature because we have tended to be a smaller, more beleaguered community; as we get less beleaguered, we generate more disagreement. Stephen North wrote an interesting book that claims *no* consensus in the field. And writing is surely a broader, more interdisciplinary, and more methodologically diverse field than literature (stretching from classical rhetoric to cognitive science to ethnographic research, etc.). But our quarrels are against a backdrop of theory, research, teaching, and practice that all tend to converge on certain shared premises and principles: that writing is the creating or constructing of meaning, not the transmission of meaning already worked out; that we need to work in whole discourse, not in bits and pieces progressing from word to sentence to paragraph to longer pieces, and that we need not start by learning grammar; that it's an essentially rhetorical enterprise such that we cannot put all emphasis on message and leave out audience and stance or voice; that we need to get students to write to more audiences than just to the teacher—for which it's helpful for them often to share their work with each other in small groups; indeed, that the construction of meaning tends to be a social enterprise as much as if not more than an individual one.

The Problem of a Conflict between Teaching and Research

There wasn't much talk at the conference about this problem, and much of what there was consisted of people insisting that it is a nonproblem —that there is *no* conflict between teaching and research. (Graff in particular made a strong pitch on this score.) But I think the problem is real, and I would insist that holding this view does not make me an enemy of scholarship or professionalism or a comforter of anti-intellectuals. I am in favor of research and professionalism, but I don't see any good in denying the fact that most university and many college faculty members (particularly when untenured) tend to feel more pressure from the institution and the profession to invest themselves heavily in their research than in their teaching. As Nellie McKay writes:

> In the struggle to achieve tenure, we are encouraged to concentrate, not on how best to help students to learn, but on individual research and publishing. Thus, by the time we have achieved that goal (and six years is a long time for such socialization), we have almost forgotten that the reason we were attracted to the profession in the first place was a love of literature, and the wish to bring young people to love it too. [See the interlude preceding ch. 1.]

In the field of writing, however, there seems to be a stronger link between research and teaching than we see in the field of literature. Faculty members in literature seem to have a harder time than faculty members in writing at bringing their teaching to bear on their research and vice versa (except in graduate seminars). I don't want to exaggerate; of course there are exceptions (indeed, I have even heard writing researchers sound a kind of superior note while saying, "This research has *nothing* to do with teaching"). Paul Armstrong writes this in response to an earlier draft:

> My research on literature informs and is informed by all of my teaching. Even my freshman-sophomore Introduction to the Novel course has given me lots of ideas for my books and articles about narrative, and my work on those projects has given me ideas to test and discuss in class.

Nevertheless, a cursory examination of scholarly books and articles in the two fields reveals a definite tradition of omitting from literary scholarship consideration of pedagogy and a tradition of inviting pedagogy into composition scholarship.

I see no inherent or logical reason why pedagogy should be more closely linked with composition scholarship than literary scholarship, but this connection exists strongly in people's minds. I remember having polite conversation with the chair of a large university English department and being unable to understand what he was saying until I finally figured out that he was using the word *pedagogy* when he meant *composition*. If anything, the linkage is just as natural the other way around. That is, reading literature is probably a more school-based activity than writing: few jobs require that people read literature, but most jobs require writing. Thus research about literature ought by rights to be linked more closely with teaching. Of course, there are obvious historical reasons for the linkage we actually see between composition scholarship and pedagogy: the recent interest in writing in higher education has grown from the needs of teaching writing. But since there is no inherent reason for the tradition of excluding from literary research the scholarly consideration of the processes by which texts are studied or taught, it seems to me that literary scholarship could usefully learn from the contrasting tradition in composition scholarship.

The Problem of Noncommunication across Levels

An important problem forced itself on our attention at the conference because it wasn't there: the problem of noncommunication and bad relations between English teachers in the schools and English faculty members in colleges and universities. Somehow we escaped at Wye the pervasive tradition of strained relations: condescension and lack of respect on the part of college faculties, suspicion and defensiveness on the part of school teachers. (Bill Teale evoked this tradition with his elegant zinger that I used as an epigraph to chapter 1.) In the last fifteen years the field of writing or composition has seen remarkable progress in overcoming these strained relations. It is a process that could be emulated.

The notion of a process approach to writing has become an abused cliché, but the fact remains that when professionals commit themselves to figuring out what actually happens as people write, they become braver about engaging in certain humbling activities: talking honestly about what happens when *they* write, actually writing together in workshops, sharing early raw drafts to compare notes about what happens, and relying on each other for honest feedback even on early drafts. These activities make it harder for people to be pretentious and put on airs. Whenever I am in a writing workshop with school and college teachers, I always notice (as do most of the other college teachers) that the college teachers often don't write as well as some of the school teachers. People may be doing different kinds of writing and come from different school levels, and some may be far more skilled than others, yet it soon becomes clear that everyone is dealing with similar kinds of struggle.

The writing tradition has produced a flowering of conferences and workshops in writing that are unlike most of those I know in literature for bringing together people from all academic levels. At these conferences people from the different levels have learned to talk collegially to each other. In addition to conferences by the National Council of Teachers of English and the Conference on College Composition and Communication, the so-called Bay Area Writing Projects deserve special credit for helping create this community (and so does James Gray for having started it all). These projects have been operating around the country for seventeen years now, and this year there are more than 150 projects that bring together twenty-five to seventy-five teachers from all levels of schooling for four to six weeks of sharing their writing and their teaching. (There are also a number of comparable summer workshops not officially connected with the Bay Area network.) Lynn White, visiting our conference from NEH, wondered if there could be literature projects analogous to the writing projects—and indeed, a number of such summer literature projects have sprung up (such as at the University of California, Santa Barbara) that are consciously based on the Bay Area model: not university faculty members bringing light to the heathen but school and college teachers working collaboratively together.

In the end a kind of metaphor or allegory took shape in my mind. The field of English is a big old house that's been around for a long time—lots of wear and tear. We in the writing wing have been fixing up the small, run-down quarters with sweat equity for two decades or so and have been living amid the mess. We find ourselves mad at all the money they put into expensive antiques in the rest of the house and at paying double oil bills because their furnace doesn't work and because they have so many leaks around their doors and windows. But they are only just discovering that their furnace is on its last legs and that their foundation and beams have been heavily eaten away by termites and dry rot. As we've been busy fixing up our wing, surface and foundation, they've cocked a sardonic eyebrow at our taste because we've used plasterboard instead of real plaster over lath, double-paned windows with fake muntins, and (here there were stage-whispered ironic jokes) aluminum siding over the clapboards. But the winters are cold here and the winds fierce, and now we have something that keeps us warm and doesn't shake when the kids jump. (No jumping allowed in their part of the house.) Of course some literary groups are abandoning the old manse itself and creating spiffy new outbuildings of their own (as for example at Carnegie Mellon and Syracuse). The architecture of English is getting complicated.

But at the Coalition Conference I didn't see any of the raised eyebrows or whispered jokes, only a sense of alarm and occasional dismay at the state of the grand old manse. And more than that, our consensus about what's central to English reflected another consensus: that writing and literature need each other. This benign situation on a bay in eastern Maryland doesn't mean that the old inequities will go away. After the conference, we all returned to the political and ideological world where the study and teaching of literature are privileged and people who study and teach writing are treated shabbily, both materially and ideologically. But being at the conference helped me let my dukes down long enough to stop defending myself against those teachers in the literary enterprise and see instead how much they could use us—and not just to support them. But of course (perhaps unfortunately for this chapter), when I'm not benignly ensconced at Wye, my dukes seem to go up again.

NOTES

[1] Of the various terms for the field, it is important to me to use the most blunt, common term: *writing*. *Composition* and *rhetoric* are of course frequently used terms, and they have obvious advantages. *Rhetoric* emphasizes the ancient, venerable lineage for our field; *composition* has come to be associated with the exciting renaissance of the field in the last twenty-five years; and *writing* is sometimes confused with handwriting or the mere physical act of inscribing words on paper. Nevertheless, the plain, common term seems to me the one to use because *writing* is what grown-ups and professionals do. Only children and students (and musical composers) say "I'm going in the other room to write a composition," and only political speech writers and advertising copywriters say "the deadline for my rhetoric has been put off a week" (except when people are being wry about their writing). Grown-ups or professionals call their serious writing *writing*. Part of the difficulty we have in teaching writing in schools—and some of the unfortunate things that go on in this enterprise—comes from labeling the activity with a word that's only used in school. It might even be harder for people in literature to mistreat people in "composition" and think of them as dumber or having less discriminating taste or doing a lower order of intellectual work if their enterprise were always called *writing* rather than composition.

[2] Here is some of the information from Slevin's essay—all derived from surveys and other information gathered by the MLA:

> MLA statistics indicate that roughly 70% of the postsecondary English classes or sections taught in this country are composition classes; in terms of number of sections, composition represents at least two-thirds of what we do as a profession. But the curriculum conceals these courses; they are all crammed within one or two different titles; one official description usually serves for

all sections. . . . These sections are usually and miraculously taught by that most ubiquitous of teachers, "Professor Staff". . . . Literature courses [are] "authored" and writing courses [are] "anonymous." . . .

We know that half the teachers at two-year colleges are part-time. We know that over one-quarter of the faculty at four-year colleges—one in four—is part-time, and that of those three full-time faculty it is certain that one will have only a temporary, non-tenure-track appointment. And we know that even at our most distinguished departments, those 139 elite schools (6% of the total) offering the Ph.D., over half of those teaching are part-timers, TAs, and temporary appointments. Almost always, it is composition that gets taught by those faculty in the least privileged positions.

Fully one-third of the "English professoriate" hold positions such as those I have just described.

We are often told, however, that this policy of relying on part-time faculty to teach composition is the result of economic problems beyond our control. . . . [But] the ADE survey indicates, for example, that the English Major is doing surprisingly well; only 20% of the institutions note a decline in the major, while in nearly twice as many (around 35%) the major has grown. (The other 45% are stable.) . . . [N]early 70% of the graduate literature programs are doing either as well as or better than they were in the past three years.

These figures are from 1983 to 1986. Things have been going even better since then; the MLA has no figures for the earlier years.

³I wasn't the only person to have this reaction. Here is the first half or so of the minutes from a mixed-levels session (16 July 1987) at which I was not present:

Why do people feel that there have been greater strides made in reforming the teaching of writing during the past decade than there have been in reforming the teaching of reading? One reason: the Bay Area Writing Project (now the National Writing Project) has had great impact on secondary and elementary teachers at the local school district level. Nancy McHugh gave a historical overview of the evolution of the BAWP/NWP. Key reasons for the success of the project:

Empowers teachers to believe they have control, value. Confidence to try various things. Not rely on gimmicks, but theory.

Gets teachers to regard themselves as writers, to engage in the writing process themselves. (Writing-project classrooms are models of how teachers should teach writing in their classrooms.)

In more recent years a variety of subject area teachers *and school administrators* were included in the project.

Provisions are made for continuity beyond the actual five weeks of the course itself (continued meetings or writing groups, in-service).

Not top-down imposed.

There are variations, both positive and negative, in how writing projects have actually been implemented across the country. Also, there is not a great deal of hard evidence to indicate that the practices recommended by writing-project philosophy have significant effects on student writing abilities.

Literature. There was agreement with the assertion that the kind of change effected in writing at the tertiary level in the past decade could not easily be replicated with literature because literature, as it has been defined, is hierarchical, top-down (that is, there is a canon from which selections are made by the instructor, there is a reverential attitude, the notion of great books or great souls, the great speaking to the ungreat). Some things qualify as literature (Literature); others don't. For example, *Uncle Tom's Cabin* is usually regarded as propaganda, not literature. Also, it would be harder to convert the literature classroom from a product to a process orientation because of the tremendous amount of information taught in the literature. . . .

If we accept that the general shift from product to process in the writing area has been good, would a comparable shift in the literature area be good? Should we shift from literature to reading at the secondary and tertiary levels?

[4]But there's an interesting exception here. When people say, "There is no right way to read," they mean that there is no right way to go about reading *and* that there is no right result. But when they say "there is no right way to write," they usually only mean the first half. They happily assert that there is no single right way to get things written or to teach writing, but they usually aren't so comfortable saying that there is no right result of the writing process—no right kind or discourse for writing. But I sense some percolation on this issue these days: just as we don't have absolute standards for what a right interpretation is, so we don't have absolute standards for what the right kind of language or discourse is for communicating and publishing that interpretation. And it is clear that the flourishing of the theory movement over the last decade or two has led to a striking expansion of kinds of discourse judged publishable by the profession.

[5]As I understand the tides and currents in our profession, the interest in reader-response criticism has tended to fade because of a sense that it focuses too much on what is individual and psychological and not enough on what is social, historical, cultural, and ideological. I see the force of the objection, yet I wonder whether this development hasn't served to free us from a helpful pressure that reader-response criticism was starting to bring to bear: to try to uncover and talk honestly with one another and with our students about what actually happens in our minds when we read. For surely if we want to understand and illustrate those important dimensions of reading (social, historical, cultural, ideological), we have to be able to see them in the context of individual acts of reading. I look back at the moment when literary theorists were interested in reader-response criticism and can't help seeing it as an interlude when they were tempted to engage in the reading process from a stance that was more collaborative with students and colleagues across academic levels—but then the temptation passed.

Scott's Gift

Peggy A. Swoger
(secondary school section)

*T*HE URGE TO COMMUNICATE must be as basic a need for humans as hunger and sex. I remember once a small, friendly girl approaching me on the sidewalk, smiling and gesturing to me. The child was mute, and I could see in the urgency of expression how desperately she wanted me to understand. Finally she tugged me down to her level and touched my necklace. "Oh, you like my necklace," I said. She smiled with delight at having communicated her thought and returned, contented, to her play.

Scott must have felt the same joy when he wrote on his self-evaluation after several weeks of writing workshop, "I feel good when I write." Scott was one of several learning-disabled students in my basic English class. Generally, I taught advanced and regular ninth-grade students, but this year I wanted to see how effective writing workshop would be for the basic writers. I set up the same class structure for my three gifted classes and the basic class, hoping it would work equally well for all ability levels; for, if so, I could demonstrate that tracking of students is not necessary.

From the first day, I had outside visitors to these classes, especially to Scott's first-period class. Nancie Atwell says in her book *In the Middle*, "Close your door and try it; open your door and share it" (25). Well, my door never closed, and the students and I never tired of sharing our joy of writing.

Scott's Writing

That first day all fourteen of the students wrote on their own topics, but two of them needed extra prompting from me. When I said, "Now write three topics of your own on your topics list," Scott hunched over his clean paper and looked up helplessly at me. He is a tall, broad-shouldered boy, sixteen years old and going out for football. It is also his first year out of special-education classes, and he feels the pressure of "making it." His special-education teacher said that last year Scott became so depressed and withdrawn that they considered special counseling for him. He rarely tried to communicate; in fact, Scott's problems had always been complicated by his language and speech difficulties. He seemed not to be able to generate sentences, even orally.

Scott's mother told me about his efforts to cultivate friends. He invited a boy from his special-education class to go home with him after school. Scott offered his friend everything he could think of in the kitchen: "You want Coke? You want potato chips?" But after that, neither boy could think of anything to say. They sat around the living room in embarrassed silence, thinking of nothing to do. Will Scott ever be able to talk with people? the mother wanted to know; will Scott's progress this year continue? I could not answer her questions because this was my first time around the track, my first experience with the learning disabled.

Perhaps that was a blessing because I just accepted whatever they could do and praised it. If they did not perform, I waited, but I revisited each desk every day. "Tell me about your story," I would say while looking with interest into their eyes at the person somewhere within. Scott was shy, but his soft brown eyes said that he liked my visits to his desk. He stumbled over each word and started over repeatedly. After three days he had written three sentences (fig. 1).

After three weeks he had finished this story (fig. 2), which he punched into the computer one painful letter at a time. The importance of this first story was not that, with help, he corrected most of the spelling and put periods in the right places. Instead, Scott, visualizing and reliving this experience of his earlier years, had touched a deep pool of emotions. Probably this had been his first realization of death and his first painful awareness of love. His special-education teachers were surprised and delighted at this expression of emotion, something they had never seen from him before.

With his first story published on the bulletin board, Scott was cooking. "What's your next story?" I asked. "Snow skiing," he announced, while already hunched over his paper and writing. As he read the first draft to me, he thoughtfully went back to his sentence: "I was real afraid of the mountain." He said, "I was real afraid of the *steep* mountain." Scott had entered the world of revision.

These two stories and a first draft of a visit to his grandmother's at the beach comprised his first nine-weeks' work. Both Kellogg Hunt's T-Unit

Fig. 1. Hambone.

When I first got Hambone, I was only 6 years old. I was so excited when I got him. He was a Dalamiun dog.

Fig. 2. Hambone.

When I first got Hambone, I was only 6 years old. I was so exicted when I got him. He was a Dalamiun dog with spots un him. He weuld always slept in the dinning room. Then he got old and sick. One day we took him to the vect. We came home. Got him some medican at the vect. Then he jus went off. We couldn't find him anywhere, and we looked everywhere. The neibhurs looked everywhere but they didn't find him. This went on for one week.

Some kids found him and came to us. They found him neer this fence. He was lying dead with flys flying around him. He looked pretty gross. We lifted him up to the fence. I was pretty scared.

So then we got a shvle and dig a good hole for him very deep. Then we buiried him. It was a little sad. We knew he would die sometime. So we buirded him in that hole and we covered it up, Tom and me. We were pretty sad.

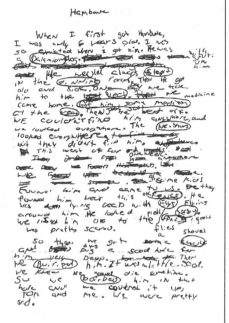

analysis and Fry's readability level suggest that Scott's first published story equaled that of an average first grader. Carol Avery, a first-grade teacher visiting my classes, had made that comment about several of the papers on our bulletin board. "This is about what my first graders can do by the end of the year," she said. Carol observed Scott at work in the computer room. He was capitalizing every word, and she, a wonderful observer of children's learning, asked him why. "She told me to capitalize all the important words," he said as he gestured toward the aide in the computer room who had been helping him with the title of his story. "Every word was important to Scott," Carol commented.

It is interesting to me that although Scott seldom used language, he had language. It's like those millions of seeds and deep roots lying dormant until the rains come. Scott's desert began to bloom. I first noted changes in his choice of words. He wrote *obnoxious*, his first three-syllable word, when describing his two new puppies (fig. 3). No doubt he had picked up some of his mother's vocabulary in relation to those dogs.

One day, later in the year, he came to my desk and asked if there were two meanings of the word *hospital*. He wrote: "The friend's sister had a lot of people over to celebrate Mardi Gras. I met lot of them and they were very hospitable." Scott seemed to be noticing words. He needed words; he was a writer.

He also needed details. "Scott notices everything," his mother told me. His writing began to show this attention to detail. He wrote: "It was the first time I ate crawfish. You suck the inside of the head and eat the tail. It was very spicy." These details were certain to entertain his class-mates.

By March, his syntactic structures and vocabulary indicated a growth of nearly three years. The only activity that will produce syntactic growth, critics of sentence combining said, was intellectual development. My teacher instincts told me that Scott's growth was intellectual; the more complex his thinking, the more complex grammatical structures he required to carry his message.

Scott's Reading

But what was happening with Scott's reading was even more phenomenal. Even Scott commented that his reading had improved. Each week he had time for two periods of sustained, silent reading in English class, and he had five periods a week in reading class. Scott read slowly, agonizing over the fact that he couldn't pass a simple five-question computer quiz on the books he finished. About a week before Christmas holidays, Scott finished *The Outsiders*. He loved it but, again, could not pass the multiple-choice quiz. He asked if he could write to me about the book. For the first time, with events organized for him already, he wrote with abandon. "Cutting loose," someone has called it. In two class periods Scott wrote three pages of readable prose. He enjoyed himself immensely.

His classmates suggested that he should read *Where the Red Fern Grows* because they wanted Scott to name his two new puppies Dan and Ann after those in the book. Scott selected three books to take home for the holidays. His mother exclaimed to me later, when she and I cried over his reading scores, "He was really reading all those books he carried up to his room!" In just eight months Scott's reading growth, measured by the Stanford Reading Diagnostic Test (Brown Level) moved from 2.8 to 7.3—over four years' growth!

As unbelievable as these scores were, they were not the best in the class. Scott's reading growth was fourth from the bottom of the class, and his syntactic growth was about the same as that of his peers. The length of Scott's pieces doubled in words, but many of his classmates tripled their output. The top student, with an IQ of 100, moved from approxi-

Fig. 3. *Retriever*

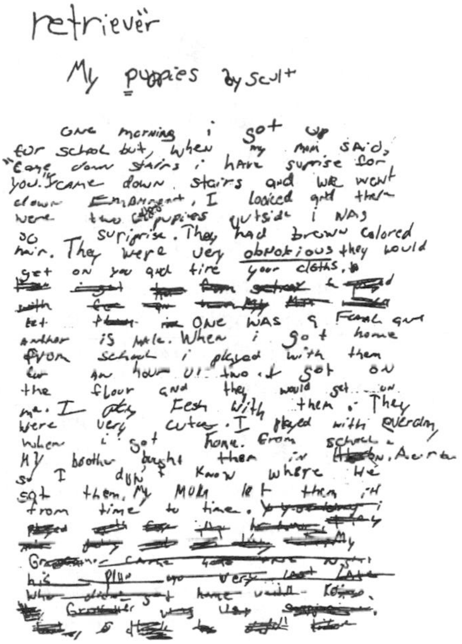

My puppies by Scott
  One morning i got up for school but, when my mom said, "Come down stairs i have suprise for you." I came down stairs and we went down in bhment. I looked and there were two pupies outside i was so suriprise. They had brown colored hair. They were very obnoxious they would get on you and tire your cloths. One was a femal and another is male. When i got home from school i played with them for an hour or two. I got on the flour and they would get on me. I play fesh with them. They were very cute. I played with everyday when i got home. from school. My brother bought them in Aura so I don't know where he got them. My mom let them in time to time.

mately the fifth to the ninth stanine in reading and from 9.8 to 11.0 in syntactic maturity. His first story was 98 words and his final one 716. On an average, the class members increased their essay length by 100 words. But none of them had as much to overcome as Scott.

Scott's disability had been diagnosed as Attention Deficit Disorder (ADD) with hyperactivity and speech difficulties. Paired with an IQ of 74, these are terrible hurdles. Scott could not have struggled harder if he had been wrestling Grendel's mother.

Scott's Growth: Some Lessons for Teachers

The question is, Why? What was happening here that had not happened before for these students? It is as though something clicked and suddenly written language made sense. The students made giant leaps, first in writing and then in reading, greater than I had ever seen before in my fifteen years of teaching. My instinct told me that the workshop approach worked because the students had the time and the freedom to work out of their own mental constructs. There were no assignments, no tests, no homework, nothing that the students had to see *my* way.

Scott was telling his own story in his own way from what he knew. His mind was learning to "go around," to cope with the learning disability. Special-education teachers tell me there is no cure for a disability; the kid just learns to live with it.

Scott's efforts and successes surely must inspire us all. I would like to say to him the words of Beethoven: You, Scott, like all humankind, were "born with a divine spark; you deserve to be free." The fact that language was your liberator makes me realize as never before the importance of my job, of being called an English teacher. You have unknowingly been both the writer and the teacher, showing us a way into your world, into your intellectual world. Your lesson is a rich tapestry, written as much by the patient silences between us as by your written and spoken words.

I know that you are ready to step out. Your mother told me, in a worried way, that for some time now you have been going to your room to stand in front of your mirror and talk to the person you see there. She seemed to think you do this out of loneliness, that your reflection is a kind of imaginary friend. She thought you might be "cracking up." But I think you are practicing as children do when they learn a new skill. You are using your own language, listening to your voice, observing the movements of your lips as you form words. You are working on your speech, a speech that has always embarrassed you, to make it sound normal. You are practicing to enter that wonderful social whirl of the high school hallway with the strutting jocks and the pretty girls; you are practicing to say "yes" the next time a girl asks you to a lead-out.

Some lessons seem obvious to me from Scott's experience. First, our students, even most of the handicapped, are little learning machines when, as Frank Smith says, they are learning what *they* need to know. Writing seems to be a catalyst, an ignition system to start up these learning machines. Scott and his classmates wrote every day in both English language class and reading class. Having school time to write and read in a community of learners is essential.

Next, we must, as language teachers, take advantage of the social purpose of language itself. Who taught language to the grunting cave dweller? We know that out of that basic drive to communicate, human beings have created language, our greatest invention. It happened naturally, out of daily needs and daily give-and-take. Language growth happens in a social context, and that is the only way it happens. If literacy is our goal, students need to be working and interacting purposefully in pairs and small groups.

Finally, perhaps no other children in our schools have had learning dissected into such small pieces as much as the learning disabled. We feed them like feeding crumbs to birds. Their natural learning has been stymied by contrived assignments, worksheets, and writing formulas. We must understand that the mind works naturally with whole pieces of discourse.

Let us sit at the feet of the learners and let them guide us into their worlds; let us trust and celebrate their potential by focusing on what they can do. Like Scott, these children have gifts to give us if we can learn to receive.[1]

NOTE

[1]Reprinted with permission from the *English Journal*, March 1989. Copyright 1989 by the National Council of Teachers of English.

An "As If" Artist

Joe Lostracco
(college section)

A STUDENT AT our college recently noted how an English teacher assigns a short story that she has never read. Then the teacher and students work together exchanging ideas and interpretations. By grappling with the unfamiliar, she shows her students how to do the same thing. The student described this teacher as an "as if" artist: "She acts *as if* there is a new meaning, a new interpretation lurking behind every sentence that crawls or leaps from her students' mouths."

9 | *Goals and Testing*

A *moment from the next-to-last evening of the conference. A performance by Jim-Bob Jumpback and the Dips—a small, lowdown, and funky chorus line in costume and makeup—to the tune of "Faded Love":*

The Coalition Country Blues

by Joe Lostracco

As I read the list that Hirsch has compiled
As the names and phrases I peruse,
I feel myself getting more and more riled
And I wonder, "O, what is the use?"

CHORUS:

I've been so situated
that I'm constipated
and I'm sure that
Elbow gets my drift.
Though the canon exploded
and lit'racy eroded
I don't give a paradigm shift.

Now after Hirsch left us to contextualize,
I enjoyed the next week and a half;
But then something happened that brought tears to my eyes—
They decided to foreground Gerald Graff.

CHORUS

The end draws near with each passing hour;
Phyllis says that we must take a stand.
But the only words with textual power
Are the ones of "So's your old man."

CHORUS

149

THE FIRST main agenda item for all groups at the conference was goals: to talk about learning goals and to work out a list of goals for each level of education. An obvious place to start: if we're setting out on a journey, we might as well figure out our destination. So we all got busy in our various groups discussing and listing. I and a few others volunteered as a subcommittee to collate and clean up all these lists into one. Toward the end of the first week, then, our little committee worked late into the night and came up with our master list.

The next morning everyone looked at our list and said, "Yuck!" "No, that's not what we meant at all. This is terrible." Voices were raised. People were angry. The written report by one of the groups declared, "Scrap the goals statement." In my notes for that time I ask, "Why is the search for goals such a disaster?"

Perhaps the anger arose because some of us on the subcommittee tried to defend our work and show people (what I think was true) that this list was nothing but a summary of what they themselves had come up with in the past two days on their separate lists. The goals hadn't sounded so bad in each little subgroup; but, pulled together and neatened up into a long list, they looked repellent to many participants. Perhaps they were awful; I'm not sure. At one point I said, "Maybe we should come out with a final report that says, 'Skip goals and tests. Just leave us alone and let us teach.' " This drew the biggest laugh of the day—not without rue and a touch of bitterness. Elementary and secondary people laughed most; some of the college people didn't see the joke.

Anyway, people weren't just saying we had the wrong goals or conceived them wrong. Many were saying, in effect, "I don't care what we said yesterday; I don't care if goals are on the planning committee's agenda. Let's not specify goals." Someone put it this way: "Making nicer goals statements is just putting a Band-Aid on something rotten." (Gerald Graff accused us of being too harmonious, not fighting enough. But this episode shows that people were perfectly willing to fight openly right from the start.)

I confess I'd gotten invested in the issue, and I defended the full list. This was perhaps partly because I'd worked on it, and we were just collating what the groups came up with. But it was also because I had spent three years on a research team looking at "competence-based" experiments in higher education where I'd grown intrigued with this business of trying to articulate what one is trying to achieve in one's teaching. After all, if we as teachers don't state our goals, we are insisting, in effect, on our right to refuse to let anyone decide whether we are successful at what we are attempting—and our right to refuse to announce publicly what our grades mean. In addition, if we don't work out goals that testers can test for, then those testers (or legislators) will formulate their own goals and make us teach to ones we can see are wrong. In addition, I was struck with the remarkable arrogance on the part of many faculty members in higher education about refusing to state their learning goals. (This was tangled up with a snobbish sense of being "above" matters of "pedagogy" and "educationese.") And yet, of course, I had to admit that I often find myself not wanting or not able to figure out my goals ahead of time. I love teaching as an adventure into the unknown. (For my exploration of this perplexity, see my "Trying to Teach While Thinking about the End.")

But in the end—though this took some time—participants came up with a statement of learning goals that everyone could approve of or at least live with. It was the elementary section that took the lead in finding a way to formulate goals that made sense to people, and the crucial move they made was to change things from statements of skills or abilities to the description of a person. At the end of the conference their statement of goals was endorsed by the secondary and college sections. It's worth inserting an extended excerpt here:

The Person We Would Like to See Emerge from the Elementary School Classroom

Our hope is that when children leave the elementary school, they will be well on their way to full participation as citizens. We hope that as individuals, they will be caring and compassionate, respectful and understanding of social and cultural diversity. . . . In more specific terms . . .

That they *be* readers and writers, individuals who find pleasure and satisfaction in reading and writing and who make those activities an important part of their everyday lives, voluntarily engaging in reading and writing for their intrinsic social and personal values.

That they use language to understand themselves and others and to make sense of their world, and as a means of reflecting on their lives; that they engage in such activities as telling and hearing stories, reading novels and poetry, and keeping journals. . . .

That they leave the classrooms as individuals who know how to read, write, speak, and listen effectively. As competent language users they will: . . .

respond personally to texts
comprehend the literal messages in texts
read and listen interpretively
read and listen critically
be able to write in a wide variety of forms for a wide variety of purposes and audiences
be able to read varied types of texts, including poems, essays, stories, and expository texts in both print and electronic media

> make connections within texts and among texts
> use other readers' experiences with, responses to, and interpre-
>   tations of texts
> be able to hear literature, appreciating its sounds and cadences
>
> That they recognize when language is being used to manipulate,
> coerce, or control them, and that they use language as an effective
> response to such attempts.
> That they become language theorists, understanding how they and
> others around them use oral and written language, and learning how
> to describe these uses in terms of grammar, syntax, and rhetoric. . . .
> In reading, they notice and monitor their own reading processes
> and their purposes for reading. Self-evaluation is a key component
> of their oral and written language activities, one that leads to a sense
> of ownership of their language. . . . (Lloyd-Jones and Lunsford 3–4)

Why did we have this struggle about goals? How can one be against starting a journey by saying where you're going? against starting an enterprise by thinking about what one is trying to do? against being *rational*? But of course I escalate the argument with that final word, for one of the things at stake here is a definition of rationality. Notice that crucial move the elementary section made in their rearticulating of goals: from disembodied skills to a vision of a person. Teachers can resent an emphasis on goals because they are so often specified in terms of disembodied skills and divorced from the actual people we teach. "The focus and source of all curricular development and assessment must be on the individual learner," writes the elementary section (Lloyd-Jones and Lunsford 6).

Most of all, however, there is a historical and cultural context to this reaction against "rationality." That is, in the last three or more decades of educational policy and administration, there had grown to be an obsession with goals, outcomes, and objectives. This has been the era of MBOs (management by objectives) and MDI (measurement-drive in-struction) and BOs (behavioral objectives) and the lesson-plan mania. Educational technocrats have hit teachers over the head with goals in reductive and trivialized forms, and many of the bad things that have been done in education have been done in the name of goals and "ra-tionalization." "Never do anything unplanned, always have everything worked out in advance" is the constant message to teachers in the schools. This ubiquitous approach emphasizes instrumental thinking and prac-ticality as the highest good and gives no space for learning for its own sake, for play, for serendipity, or for "mere growth."[1]

Worse yet, although goal setting is usually praised as a way to gain more control over one's teaching, the goals-and-objectives movement has tended to function to undermine the authority and control and professionalism of teachers. That is, the goals are as often as not worked out by an "expert" and handed down for teachers to follow—all in a spirit of distrust of teachers. This leads to the most damaging situation of all for teachers: the teacher as follower of orders, as production-line worker (and, of course, it is the same management-by-objectives movement that has tried to "rationalize" the rest of the work force). Even when teachers are invited to work out their own goals, they are often obliged to put them in reductive or behavioral form and to get them approved by the "manager" or "expert"—or at least to have a rigid lesson plan for each day. (See the last chapter of Langer and Applebee for research that undermines arguments for a management or industrial model of education. Their research supports the idea that open-ended assignments work better.)

Reductive goals and lesson plans are inimical to the main emphasis at the conference on the student as active learner and maker of knowledge rather than receiver of already existing prepackaged knowledge and to the emphasis on the knowing process rather than the knowledge product. If we emphasize these things in our teaching, we don't necessarily know ahead of time exactly what the student is going to learn or exactly where we are going in our teaching. Our emphasis at the conference on knowledge as created and on the experiential dimension of learning makes for an inherent element of messiness and unpredictability in teaching. With full specification of goals and objectives and lesson plans, there is little room for the unexpected digression. If something especially interesting happens in the world or the community, if some student falls on unexpected tragedy or good fortune, or if there is an unexpected chance for a good field trip, there is no time for building one's teaching around it. Yet such teaching that connects to what is impinging on students tends to produce most learning and, better still, helps students build connections between school learning and what they see as the "real world." The best teachers do a lot that is serendipitous, depending on where the class is and how it responds to previous activity. Teachers who remain alive and interesting manage to get into their teaching a quality of responsive conversation or dialogue: an interaction with the students, with the world, and even with the teaching process itself.

During my three years' observation of competence-based programs in higher education, even I (with my interest in the uses of chaos) learned to be a bit more goal-oriented in my teaching. Like writing, teaching is often best when it is a process of discovery of what is not yet known. But if I actually decide that this experience of discovery is a goal, that decision helps me plan certain structures and activities that increase the chances of it happening—structures and activities where I purposely don't know the outcome. People who push goals often don't realize that having a goal is not the same as having every activity planned out in advance for each fifteen minutes or each day or even each week. If we choose certain goals—for example, the development of curiosity and independence in students—it follows that we should avoid having all our time preprogrammed, in order to leave some time open for activities that students or emergent activities suggest. In sum, the goals movement in education has tended to be reductive.

There is something curious here. That is, an emphasis on goals ought to provide the most dignity and professionalism for teachers. It seems to be an emphasis on ends rather than means—telling teachers what outcomes are needed, not how they must go about achieving them. After all, society gets to tell us, "Teach our children to read and write"; by making its request thus in terms of goals, it is not butting in and telling us how to teach but simply telling us what end results it needs from us. But of course it hasn't worked out that way. The entire thrust of the goals movement has been in exactly the opposite direction. It's been a movement in revolt against large vague goals like reading and writing and in favor of breaking things down. Thus in practice, the emphasis on goals has almost invariably involved telling teachers how to teach—for example, what order to take things in.

A final note about goals: It is important to note the differences between the culture of the schools and that of the colleges and universities. Few people in the college section got worked up about the goals issue: few of us have been touched by this teaching-by-objectives obsession.[2] Many of us might even benefit from having our feet held to the fire just a bit to spell out more explicitly what we are trying to accomplish and how we think our particular teaching and testing activities are likely to accomplish those goals. Most primary and secondary teachers, however, need some relief from this fire that does not always refine: they need an invitation to take on more of the approach of so many college and university teachers of focusing entirely on the subject matter itself—for its own sake or for its inherent importance in the world—rather than focusing so much on learning and teaching goals. (The recent calls for prospective teachers to major in a traditional discipline rather than in education seem related to this thought.)

Assessment

Above all, however, the fight about goals had to do with assessment: all the testing and especially the mass standardized testing that has become so influential in K–12 education. The huge growth in assessment seems to me the most important development in education in the last thirty or so years—crescendoing in the accountability movement dating from the

1970s. Chester Finn told us that the Department of Education spends more on the National Assessment of Education Progress (huge nation-wide assessments) than on any other item. More money for testing clearly means less money for teaching in most education budgets, some of which are actually shrinking. It's often easier these days to get money out of administrations, school boards, towns, states, and the federal government for testing than for teaching.[3]

In an interesting newer development, assessment has expanded massively in the last decade from elementary and secondary education into higher education. Almost seventy percent of colleges and universities currently use assessments other than teacher grades—more often community colleges than others; the majority of the testing is for basic skills, but many institutions are looking to assessment of long-term outcomes among graduates—one in four already doing so, half planning it (these figures are from a survey conducted by the American Council on Education; see El-Khawas). At least one state, Missouri, requires public universities to give tests of general knowledge to entering freshmen and to give similar follow-up tests to graduates to determine how much the students have learned (Blumenstyk).

> [A] new report by the National Governor's Association . . . says 24 states now require assessment and another 12 are debating whether to follow. It cites Florida and Tennessee as two states that have seen student test scores rise as a result of assessment programs. . . . (Blumenstyk)

This growth of testing has bred, in response, an interesting movement of skeptical inquiry into assessment. In higher education in particular, many people find themselves saying what boils down to this (my summary is unfair to some teachers, but it's still true): "It's okay to barge into the classrooms of our colleagues in elementary and secondary schools and force their students to take standardized, multiple-choice tests that they have no say over choosing or scoring—with no outcome but a computer printout of two- and three-digit scores in the mail four to eight weeks later. It's okay to try to compute the educational output of one school teacher compared with another and to let those tests dictate what they must teach and how they should teach it. But now that you're trying to make *my* students take tests that I have no say over and try to measure how much my students have learned from me compared to how much my colleagues' students have learned from them—perhaps I better look into this assessment business and think hard about it." We used to feel we were exempt: that we could close our doors and do what we wanted—to choose what to teach and how to teach and how to test. Most of all, if we said someone passed or failed, they passed or failed. Meddling with our professional evaluations was grounds for litigation. But now structures like that found in Florida are not uncommon: the decision as to whether a sophomore graduates to junior status in English is determined not by the grades of English faculty members but by a statewide writing test.

It's true that the Florida test asks for an actual writing sample; sometimes such tests rely entirely on machine-scored multiple-choice questions. But this writing sample is usually a short five-paragraph argumentative essay on a topic about which the student has had no chance to think in advance. Such a state-mandated, high-stakes test puts powerful pressure on teachers (especially untenured or adjunct or graduate instructors—and most especially those at two-year colleges where there's enormous pressure to graduate students into four-year institutions) to focus their writing courses on the narrow and limited kinds of writing tasks demanded by the test: to produce short essays on topics sprung without warning and without any opportunity for reading or discussion or exploratory writing—or sharing of drafts or substantive revising. In short, what even the more expensive tests ask for is a kind of parody of what most thoughtful teachers think of as writing.

The growth of state-mandated assessment in higher education has attracted a lot of thoughtful attention. One of the most effective forums for this attention has been an ambitious series of annual conferences on assessment sponsored by the American Association of Higher Education. More than a thousand people from around the country came to the first one in 1986—far more than the planners expected—and each one since has been planned bigger but still has attracted overflows. Most of the participants are involved in assessment programs on their campuses—sometimes committed to them, sometimes feeling stuck with them. I went to two of these conferences after the Coalition Conference and was interested to hear plenary talks with passages like the following by Linda Darling-Hammond of the Rand Corporation:

> Over the last twelve to fifteen years in elementary and secondary education, assessment has become, first, narrower in form and content with each successive state mandate; second, used for more purposes than those for which it was originally designed; and, third, tied in its results to greater and greater stakes with each successive refinement of state policy.
>
> The same is likely to occur in higher education unless a new view of assessment is born and spread throughout this country.

The K–12 Experience: High-Stakes Assessment

> . . . In the early 1970's, accountability legislation [for K–12 education] was passed in a great number of states, and it looked very much like the legislation that you're encountering today [she is speaking to a higher education audience]. . . .

Five or six years later, by the late 1970's, those methods had proved to be insufficient for policy makers' goals: Minimum competency tests were instituted. First, they were used as the criteria for graduating seniors. Later, the mandates were extended throughout the grades—with testing in grades 3, 5, 7, 9, and 12 in many states. A requirement that they be nationally-normed standardized tests became widespread. By then, the tests were to be used not only for graduation but for promotion, tracking, and sometimes (but not always) remediation of students. None of this provided what policy makers considered sufficient accountability.

And so, in the mid-1980's the states began to mandate curriculum guidelines that were heavily specified and aligned with the test. So, the current rage is curriculum alignment. The tests themselves didn't produce the outcomes desired, so now curricula are being redefined and mandated to match the test.

Part of the reason for this trend is the increased use of test results and their higher stakes. For example, standardized tests are now used as the basis for decisions about even such things as students' graduation from kindergarten in states like Georgia. They're used for decisions about remediation, tracking, placement in gifted and talented programs, and a variety of other things—things that these particular tests were not created or designed to do. In some states, they're now used as the basis for decisions about school funding. (We see that in the higher education realm in a few places.) Mandated tests are now used in elementary and secondary education as the basis for evaluating teachers for promotion, for career-ladder status, for salary, even for tenure and retention. They're used in some places for evaluating administrators.

We see in this brief account of the K–12 experience that three things tend to happen when assessment measures are introduced. First, once a measure gains currency, policy makers have a tendency to use it for purposes and decisions not originally intended, as they arise, and regardless of whether the measure is intended for or suited to that purpose. Second, quantitative, comparative data tend, over time, to override or overwhelm other forms of information, especially for people who are not expert in that area or enterprise. The tendency is to turn quickly and unskeptically to numbers, because, although we can't decipher all the other information about the quality of your physics program, we all know that a 42 is better than a 38. Third, there's a tendency to forget what the number represents—if that was known to begin with. Robert Sternberg, a noted testing expert at Yale, makes the point that "the appearance of precision is no substitute for the fact of validity." Try telling that to a legislator who doesn't care to examine the disjuncture between the goals of your international studies program and the material on the ACT-COMP. . . .

[If the stakes are high], then teachers will teach to the test. This is easy enough to understand. High-stakes tests, it is argued, can, on the positive side, focus instruction, giving students and teachers specific goals to attain. Unfortunately, because such tests are indirect measures of the actual learning we care about, it's possible to do all kinds of things, quite successfully, to raise the test scores without actually increasing the amount of learning taking place. In fact, much recent research on the effects of high-stakes testing has shown that as scores on the instrument being used for assessment increase, scores on the other measures tend to decline because of the shift in emphasis to that which is being measured. This has been studied and found to be so across tests, across settings, and in a number of countries. Studies of the effect of examinations on learning in Australia, India, Japan, Ireland, and England all turn up the same kind of result: that teaching to the test correlates with a de-emphasis on other forms of learning. . . .

[T]eachers pay particular attention to the form of the questions on a high-stakes test—multiple choice, short answer, essay—and they adjust their instruction accordingly. . . . In fact, in most places now, particularly in large cities across this country, reading instruction has come to resemble the practice of taking a reading test. In reading class, students use commercial materials to decode short paragraphs about which they then answer multiple-choice questions. The teaching materials have evolved to resemble the tests the students will take. And tests dictate both the content of instruction and the teaching methods. (6–8)

Surveys have shown us that during the time state policy makers began to institute test-oriented accountability measures (between 1972 and 1980), the use of teaching methods appropriate to the teaching of higher-order skills declined in American public schools. There was a decline in methods such as student-centered discussions, writing essays or themes, and project or laboratory work. (11)

At the same conference in June 1988, Alexander Astin, a kind of dean in the field of assessment, spoke of the problems with norm-referenced multiple-choice tests:

Our old friend the multiple-choice test is still by far the most popular approach [to assessment]. Multiple-choice tests are popular for at least two reasons: They can be administered and scored very cheaply in large groups, and they naturally yield quantitative scores that make it easy to differentiate among students. Aside from the many technical criticisms that one can make against this multiple-choice methodology, I have several concerns that are more value-oriented.

First is the way multiple-choice tests are *scored*. Typically, the number of right answers (or a weighted combination of rights minus wrongs) is converted into some type of *normed* score, either a percentile or a standard score. Now what do we really do when we make such a conversion? We have lost the basic information about how many items (and which ones) the student got right and wrong, and replaced this information with a score indicating only how well the student performs *in relation to other students*. . . . [T]hese relativistic and competitively scored tests . . . make it virtually impossible to determine how much a student has actually changed or improved over time [what he or she knows or doesn't know]. All we can say is that the student's performance has increased or decreased in relation to other students.

There is another, perhaps even more subtle problem with normative assessment . . . : When we choose to assess performance using a normed instrument, we create what the economists would call a "scarce good." Only so many students can be at the top of their class and only so many students can score above the 90th percentile. . . . Normative assessment, in other words, automatically constrains how much "excellence" you can have. The important thing to realize is that this shortage is a completely *artificial* one, rather than something inherent in the trait being assessed. The shortage, in other words, is something created by the assessment method itself.

As with any scarce good, the scarcity itself tends to exaggerate the importance of being at the top, so that below average or even average performance is often viewed as failure. Normative scoring, in other words, guarantees that a substantial number of students, if not the majority, will view themselves as failures. . . .

[T]here is something that we in the assessment field can do to overcome the negative consequences of most norm-referenced tests. Very simply, we can insist that the testing companies give us back the raw score results and, ideally, the results from *individual test questions*. Raw scores provide a way to measure how much each individual student is actually learning or improving over time, without requiring any competitive comparisons with other students. Furthermore, results from individual test questions can be useful to individual students in understanding their particular strengths and weaknesses. Item results aggregated across students can be very useful in curriculum planning and course evaluation. I feel strongly that all of us who utilize any type of standardized test in our assessment work should begin insisting that the testmakers give us this kind of feedback.

My second concern about multiple-choice tests is the artificiality of the task itself. After students finish their formal education, the ability to find a correct answer from a predetermined set of alternatives has a very limited usefulness. How often in real life is any of us presented with a prepackaged set of possible answers to a question, only one of which is correct? And how often are we required to read the question and find the answer under intense time pressure? How often do life's problems take such a bizarre form?

And what about the myriad real-life problems that call for *creative* solutions? My point here is that the ability to perform well on such tasks is so highly specialized and so foreign to the kinds of real-life problems that we normally confront that I really wonder if we ed-ucators have been wise to make such liberal and uncritical use of the multiple-choice test. The testmakers might respond that such tests have "predictive validity," and indeed they do. But in such validity studies the outcome being predicted is almost always school or col-lege grades or simply another test constructed in the same manner! (12–14)

In June 1989 I heard Rexford Brown give a plenary talk exploring assessment as "the Vietnam of education." He spoke of assessment re-flecting a hubristic, promethean impulse to rationalize education through technology—reflecting the ideal that planning can finally make instruction neat and rational and completely under control. The assess-ment movement has reinforced a conception of education as manage-ment and encouraged the appointment of superintendents and principals who are managers rather than educators. It has fueled the dream of at last getting rid of the waste and the messy personal dimen-sion in teaching. Classroom teachers over the last fifteen years have had to devote more and more time to administering local, state, and national tests.[4] Even the head of Educational Testing Service, Greg Anrig, has recently tried to persuade the state of Georgia not to use a mass statewide test for graduation from kindergarten—and failed. He is arguing against mass testing for higher education and not having much success (Anrig).

But of course assessment will not go away whatever we do or say—not even in higher education. I think of the shadowed flavor of the laughter in response to my comment that perhaps we should come out with a report that says, "Skip goals and tests. Just leave us alone and let us teach." This is how education used to be. Society used to hand its children over to elementary and secondary teachers (as it still often does to college and university teachers) and say, "You take it from there." All teachers got to do what they thought best behind a closed door—and just came out at the end of the term and gave their verdict about each student. That was it. (This difference in autonomy between school teach-ers and college faculty is one of the sources of tension between them.)

This loss of faith may be sad, but it is understandable. If society no longer trusts the evaluation of its most authoritative professionals—no longer lets a doctor say, "Trust me; don't look over my shoulder; just let me close my door and reach my verdict by myself"—and insists instead on second opinions and other kinds of checks, can we expect parents and legislators to have faith in the evaluation of a lone teacher? Not even we have that faith, since we know that many of the grades of our colleagues are wild. Indeed, we know that some of our colleagues are incompetent and do serious harm to students. We seem to have got past the days when teacher unions tried to prevent the removal of harmful teachers.

Thus participants at the Coalition Conference recognized that some assessment other than that carried out by the lone teacher is not only politically necessary but desirable: "Certainly, some form of assessment is unavoidable in the interests of accountability. And if carried out with moderation and sophistication, assessment can help students learn and teachers teach" (Lloyd-Jones and Lunsford 41). Here are some of the arguments I heard at the conference that lie behind the rather short conference statement on assessment.

Accountability. This was the magic word the report used to summarize the need for assessment. Teachers, especially those in elementary and secondary education, live close to the taxpaying process. Not just the size of their salaries but their very jobs often depend on yearly tax votes by citizens. Many teachers are laid off each spring and only rehired in the fall if the voters back the schools. Unless citizens have some faith in teachers and schools, they will not come up with support, and of course, dwindling support is common now. Teachers realize they cannot just say, "Trust us, give us the money." They need to show good-faith willingness for the public to look over their shoulders at how they teach and at results. For most people, "results" means numbers on state or national tests. The same kind of thing is starting to happen in higher education.

Fairness. Teachers recognize that smart kids are often labeled dumb by teachers who find them difficult or unpleasant or even just different and that good grades often reflect docility (which of course means, literally, "teachableness"). Standardized tests have often served to identify talented students who would otherwise have been passed over. For a striking large-scale example, there is every reason to think that SAT exams were instrumental in opening up higher education to Jews in the decades before World War II—not that discriminatory quotas and exclusionary clauses were finished even as late as 1950 (Riesman 123–36, 225–70).

Feedback. It's nice to be trusted, but teaching is a mysterious business, and most teachers want help in knowing how they are doing: What are students really learning? What techniques seem to be effective? How are we and our students doing in comparison to colleagues using different approaches? We can find out a certain amount with our own tests, but one tends to feel in the dark. When we are experimenting with an approach that is new or controversial, we may be particularly eager for this kind of outside feedback. As Peggy Swoger's story indicates (see "Scott's Gift" in the interlude preceding this chapter), because her colleagues thought she was not "really teaching" by giving her students so much autonomy in how they read and wrote, she needed outside evidence from standardized tests that her teaching in fact produced remarkable gains (even on tests of crude, quantitative criteria). At one point during the conference, Janet Emig said, "Just give us *fair* testing so we can show that holistic methods work—reading and writing whole texts."

Helpful pressure on curriculum. Testing drives curriculum—it's the tail wagging the dog. But if you like the tail, you may like the new motion in the dog. For example, the biggest force helping to get actual writing into the English curriculum (rather than the teaching of grammar and drills and exercises and discussions of good and bad writing) has probably been the growth of state and national assessments that ask for writing rather than just answers on multiple-choice questions.

So the real question, coalition participants recognized, is not *whether* to have assessments other than teacher grades but rather what *kind* to have. But before looking at kinds of testing, it's also just as important to ask how tests are used. For of course, purposes often determine what kind of tests are needed. I won't go into the relatively straightforward and explicit purposes for tests (such as diagnostic versus final testing or student evaluation versus program evaluation); instead let's look at what is more important to explore here, namely, the implicit and hidden agendas behind the movement toward assessment.

Are tests used to gatekeep or to open doors? Do they keep people out of school and in low tracks or bring more people in and help those who are already in? Diagnostic testing can help identify those students who are at risk and thus ensure that they get the support they need instead of just flunking out. The truly massive, systemwide City University of New York testing program was instituted as a way to help the open admissions effort, but some now wonder whether it is being used to help disadvantaged students or to get rid of them:

> Now that I am an administrator, I have become very cynical (very rapidly), and I now believe that almost all forms of large-scale assessment serve only one purpose—"gatekeeping." CUNY and other large systems used to provide extensive and appropriate support for students who failed the tests (at entry, junior, and exit levels), but this has been dramatically reduced—at most schools. Now, instead of raising their admissions criteria, large universities use placement or minimum competency tests to revolve out those students whom senior faculty (and administrators) never wanted and still do not

want. The only reason I ever supported testing was because it forced schools to provide something for students who failed ("my" students—the basic writing and ESL students who matter most to me). But if this is no longer going to happen, then I will give up on testing and fight for something else.

Karen Greenberg wrote these words in an informal letter rather than a considered essay for publication, and perhaps she's not so discouraged every day of the week (but she had no hesitation about letting me quote her). But she is someone worth listening to. Besides being on the Hunter College faculty, she is chief reader for the huge CUNY Writing Skills Assessment Test and also director of the influential organization, the National Testing Network in Writing. She is a notable example of someone in the recent assessment movement.

What kind of learning theory lies behind the call for testing and behind the tests used? Does the push toward assessment reinforce a simplistic view that education means taking in chunks of information and that studying means memorizing? Reliance on large-scale testing leads to an emphasis on what can be tested on these instruments: memory, facts, information. Hirsch's list is ideal for mass testing. It's hard to use large-scale assessment for "measuring" interpretative imagination or the ability to make meaning or even just plain skill at explaining. Students, parents, and even teachers can too easily succumb to overly simple assumptions that learning means memory and right-wrong answers. It turns out that the publishers of major school literature textbooks often provide teachers with electronically graded "scantron" multiple-choice tests keyed to the literature in their anthologies—thereby, of course, reinforcing the message that thinking about literature means deciding right and wrong short answers. When a state legislature decides to test all public college and university students at entrance and exit to compare the "value added" by different colleges in the state (as some states are doing), will they be willing to pay for a test that measures anything other than informational recall?

Similarly, what kind of theory of intelligence drives the call for assessment? Is there recognition that there are different kinds of intelligence and different modes and styles of demonstrating what you know (see Gardner; Allen) and different paths of development (see Belenky et al.)? Much assessment seems to be driven by a hunger to rank all students along a single numerical scale. This fosters a peculiarly unrealistic model of competition even if you take competition as your model for learning. That is, conventional scoring along a single continuum implies that all of school and learning is just one kind of race, say the hundred-yard dash, rather than a whole track meet. In the hundred-yard dash everyone can validly be given a score on the same scale; but in a track meet, different competitors come out very differently in different events, such as one-mile and five-mile races and hurdles and long jumping and high jumping and throwing javelins. (Interestingly, the size of the test is not an issue here: small-scale testing and grading can just as easily imply that there is only one kind of intelligence or knowing or mode for demonstrating knowledge.)

Is the call for assessment driven by a distrust of teachers? Is it driven by a feeling that "we've got to take control away from them and decide what they should teach and how they should teach it"? This is common. We see this when teachers are not consulted about what tests to use or what things to test or how to use the results. We insist on second opinions from doctors, but that doesn't mean that we need to treat them as non-professionals or functionaries. The growth of goal- and test-driven education over the last fifteen to twenty years has not just "gone along with" an enormous decline in the prestige of teaching as a profession but has often reflected a genuine distrust and devaluation of teachers and a desire not to treat them as professionals.

Is the call for testing driven by the conviction that it will save money? Teachers' salaries may be low, but those salaries are a huge part of the education budget. "If we could just spell out more clearly what needs to be learned and gear it precisely to tests, much less teaching would be required. We could get rid of all that time wasting that teachers engage in." (Meanwhile some of the same people want to prolong the school year!) This was one of the underlying goals in the competency-based programs we investigated in the three-year study. A number of the programs were set up so that students could even learn without teaching since they were told clearly what the tests would ask for. It's an appealing vision (and surely students should have the chance to demonstrate and get credit for what they know without always having to undergo teaching), but none of the competence-based programs saved money. Far from it. Testing is always expensive. I suspect that if, in those districts and states where there is a large testing budget, they took half that budget and put it into assessment processes that really help teachers do a better job—and even into non-assessment activities such as workshops and grants for teachers to learn new ways of teaching and to work on their own professional development—and the rest into teaching, we might get better progress than from trying to "measure" teacher output. It's also common to cut back on teaching and then say, "Gee, the students don't seem to know enough—we need tougher gatekeeping assessment" (see the story of Stony Brook's testing in the interlude following this chapter).

Does the assessment imply teachers as enemy to be checked up on or as ally? Does it imply students as enemy? Even when the goal of evaluation is accountability—to make sure that the teacher is doing a good job and that the student is learning something—powerful things can happen when teachers and students are asked to be *allies* in the testing process rather than adversaries. Of teachers we can ask questions like this: "What are you trying to teach? What are some of the various ways your students can best demonstrate what they are learning?" Of students we can ask this kind of question: "What are you trying to learn? What do you see this course trying to teach you? What are some of the ways you could demonstrate what you are learning? What criteria do you think it makes most sense to evaluate you on?" Or, even more pointedly, "We need some assurance that you are learning things this semester. What are some ways you think you could demonstrate to us that you have learned?" This approach to evaluation is obviously messier and less "careful," but it tends to produce more learning by enlisting the cooperation of the two most important parties in the transaction.

When assessment treats teachers as adversaries, they often sabotage the assessment in various ways, for example, by producing good scores but not really getting students to learn deeply or care about learning. Students can sabotage assessment more directly. Many assessments are used to test programs or school districts or colleges, and students have no incentive to try very hard. Evidently there are cases where students actually try to trash the test—for example, when they realize that the test results determine funding for a school or district or college for which they feel resentment. Much more common, surely, is simply a lack of caring and investment as they take the test. Albert Shanker quotes an eleventh grader's answer on a National Assessment of Educational Progress test—a letter of application for a job:

> I would like to work in a restuarant [sic], or a store. I have worked in restuarants before and it was fun. I also think that it would be fun to be a salesperson, because I'm good with people. I want a fun job, because I'm the type of person that does well in a certain thing, when I like what I'm doing and I'd like to do well in my job.

Without minimizing how dismal this writing is, I would argue that the test isn't giving us a very good picture of how skilled or unskilled the writer is. The main thing I see in a test answer like this is an eleventh grader who is writing but not giving a damn. Imagine for a moment this student's situation as one of the myriad eleventh graders in a lower or bottom track who not only is beyond caring about the usual round of quizzes and tests but is also asked a couple of times a year to take some big, glossy, statewide or nationwide test. Imagine the scene of writing. The student knows all too well that school has defined him or her as dumb, therefore providing the worst teachers and physical resources. "Now pick up your pencils. Be sure to give this test your *very* best effort! Do not turn over your test booklets till I start the stopwatch." These tests go on as many as two or three times a year, and some are so comprehensive as to last a week. Yet for the student there are no important consequences to this test—just a computer number sent to the school and perhaps sent home. Yet the student senses that the results *do* matter to the teacher and to the principal. Imagine what kind of letter of application for a job this student is going to write. My point is that the mania for this kind of mass test is fueling the very problem we see here: making students and teachers feel as though education consists of going through extensive bureaucratic motions and therefore making them tend to withdraw their investment.

These are the kinds of questions that were asked by those members of the Coalition Conference who were interested in testing. Peggy Swoger, for example, is a founding member of the National Board for Professional Teaching Standards—a group originally supported by the Carnegie Foundation that brought teachers, teacher unions, and administrators and policy makers together to try to work out standards and useful ways to assess skill in teaching (see appendix C for more about this enterprise). Two other members of the coalition are involved in that enterprise, Mary Krogness and Joe Tsujimoto. On the basis of questions like these, people around the country have recently begun to develop forms of assessment that are more interesting and useful than large, normed, multiple-choice tests: not people with advanced degrees in psychometrics or assessment but teachers and administrators who are trying to rethink assessment. For a description of many new and creative kinds of assessment that are being tried out, see a helpful small book published by the National Association of Secondary School Principals in 1988, *Beyond Standardized Testing: Assessing Authentic Academic Achievement in the Secondary School*, by Doug A. Archbald and Fred M. Newmann. In short, new people in testing are asking, "How can we create assessment processes that reinforce good teaching and learning rather than undermine them and that treat teachers as autonomous professionals? How can we avoid assessment that sends the message that learning is all a matter of right and wrong answers or memorizing information and that tempts teachers to teach to the test?"

A prime example is evaluation that centers on a portfolio of a student's work. Notice how the assessment statement in the report of the elementary section zeros in on portfolios:

> The focus and source of all curricular development and assessment must be on the individual learner. Because they are necessarily con-

structed for mass use, externally developed tests and programs are often of considerably less value to literacy development than those created within the community of teachers and students in particular situations.

Standardized tests constitute only a part of the whole assessment process and are generally more useful for examining programs rather than individuals. Individual assessment must be based on the principles and assumptions about learning theory that support literacy development as described in this document. The ultimate aim of any assessment program . . . is to provide a better instructional program for the learner. Because we desire able language learners and users, our assessment strategies and instruments need to focus on literacy development. Our proposed model would consist of a portfolio of the child's work—collected, viewed, and assessed periodically, passed from grade to grade, and used to make instructional decisions and reports to parents. Included in the portfolio would be teacher observations, reading records, writing samples, art samples, varied responses to literature, and other pertinent work samples. (Lloyd-Jones and Lunsford 6–7)

Portfolios are particularly useful for assessment because they avoid the problem of trying to measure a complex skill like writing or reading (much less intelligence or aptitude) by means of seeing how well a student performs under exam conditions on one particular day. The results are particularly problematic if the instrument is a multiple-choice, standardized test. We have the same problem even with more sophisticated writing exams that ask for a writing sample that is graded by careful holistic scoring. It's still a question of how students perform under test conditions on only one morning or afternoon on only one kind of writing, usually on a surprise topic with no chance for reflection, discussion, feedback, or revision: a poor guide to what the student actually knows or can do under nontest conditions. (Of course, if all you are trying to measure is test-taking skills, then test conditions are ideal.)

Portfolio assessment helps the learning climate because it reinforces continuing effort and improvement: it encourages students to try to revise and improve poor work rather than to feel punished or to give up because of the poor work they start with. It gets away from a "putting in time" model for learning and instead makes for a more forward-pointing dynamic of "building toward your best." It reinforces good teaching by bringing into play the best parts of a writing process: discussion with others of what one is writing about, peer feedback, teacher feedback, and above all, revision. In a writing course, portfolios invite students to invest themselves and try for what's exciting rather than play it safe with "acceptable" writing, writing defensively.

> You will be interested to know that the Education Department of
> California recently established the ruling that mathematics teachers
> should not rely simply on tests to measure students' knowledge.
> Portfolios or files of students must contain at least two other types
> of evidence than that given by standardized or criterion-referenced
> tests, since they cannot adequately indicate students' understanding
> of concepts, ability to identify problems, and capability for handling
> alternative manipulations of mathematical notions. How ironic that
> the field the public thinks of as the most fixed would be the first to
> say that students' abilities to reflect on information, connect concepts,
> and put them into action make the difference. (Heath, response to
> draft, 24 Jan. 1989)

For an example of another interesting approach to assessment, Astin
speaks of the good use that some schools and colleges are making of
observing and/or videotaping students on representative occasions or performances when they are actually doing what we want them to do—rather
than just working on exam problems. For evaluating a method of teaching
or a whole department or program or school, this and other kinds of
ethnographic and descriptive evaluation can be as educationally useful and
trustworthy as collecting scores on quantitative norm-referenced tests. Traditional quantitative assessment is usually built on a positivist model that
implies we can control all the variables, which clearly we cannot do: people
look at scores and make unwarranted inferences. Careful and thoughtful
observations of classes and students working and of portfolios of a selective
sample of students' work can be cheaper than mass testing and are usually
more supportive of good teaching and learning.

Another interesting venture in assessment: There are eighteen colleges and universities that have been experimenting with integrative ways
to evaluate students on their whole college major—trying out comprehensive exams, comprehensive interviews, outside examiners, and special "capstone courses." As these experimenting faculty members (none
of them professionals in assessment) try out different methods, their
main finding is how typically incoherent and unintegrated is the collection of courses that most students have taken for the major—and, understandably, how incoherent is most students' understanding of the
field they have allegedly majored in. What especially interested these
faculty members was how the evaluative procedure itself helps students
bring more intellectual coherence to their major. (The Association of
American Colleges has been supporting this experiment and has published an interesting report on its study of the major.)[5]

In the end, the Coalition Conference worked its way to a sound position about assessment, and Richard Lloyd-Jones, a leader in the field

of writing evaluation, was a central figure in drawing up a strong report: tough warnings about the dangers and prudent realism about the benefits. Here is a substantial excerpt:

> In recent years, the increased call for assessment of student learning has often resulted in a curriculum that is test- and assessment-driven. That is, what students learn and how they learn it is now, at least in part, determined by the various assessments that have been imposed on elementary and secondary schools and sometimes on colleges. Often those directly concerned with the education of students have little or no say in determining what will be tested, how, why, when, or under what circumstances. . . .
>
> Therefore, we set down the following thoughts about assessment at all levels of education.
>
> First, English teachers are the professionals most qualified to specify what is important in English studies: what are the understandings —and more important, the *ways of knowing and doing*—that our students should achieve. As professionals, we must insist that *at all levels* assessment should be based on our highest standards of learning rather than on mere memory. . . .
>
> The recent shift in the field of writing from multiple-choice tests to holistically scored tests of extended writing represents a move in the right direction. But it represents only a step, because even these holistic tests usually fail to allow for or measure certain skills that we hold as crucial in writing: sustained reflection before writing; exploratory prewriting; sharing drafts with peers for the sake of feedback and discussion; and revising on the basis of this social interaction. . . .
>
> In the area of reading and the study of literature, we badly need to state learning goals in ways that reflect the complex, highly constructive processes of reading, and that can serve as the basis for tests which enhance good teaching of reading and interpreting texts. At present, most tests undermine good teaching by stressing mere recognition or "decoding" and by implying that reading is a largely passive process of getting "right" answers. . . .

Assessment devices must recognize the role of "instructional pluralism" by allowing classroom teachers the means for developing and organizing curriculum and instruction based on local needs and conditions.

New types of activities and fewer time constraints in testing situations are necessary for measuring reading and writing skills in interactive classrooms.

We must encourage, through the blending of research and pedagogical practice, new approaches to testing which will further improve learning.

It can be misleading and dangerous to compare test results on a state-by-state, region-by-region, or school-by-school basis. (Lloyd-Jones and Lunsford 41–43)

Finally, somewhat by way of summary, I call attention to the process by which conference participants dealt with goals and testing. At first there was a concerned and dutiful listing of many goals. Then people angrily rejected these lists when they saw them all neatly spelled out and sensed how much they played into the assessment mania. Then, after walking away and giving it time, some participants rearticulated goals in such a way as to serve the realistic pedagogical and political needs. Finally, a committee came up with solid and sophisticated statements on both goals and assessment. And by the end of the conference it all became no big deal. (But as the length of this chapter might imply, assessment persists as a big deal for me. I can't resist exploring and kibbitzing further in appendix C, "Evaluation, Grading, and the Hunger to Rank People.")

It is interesting, further, to look at how the conference dealt with this issue in comparison with how it dealt with other difficult and important issues. With regard to the main consensus (the "remarkable consensus" about making meaning as central to English), we had no ambivalence or difficulty: when Shirley Brice Heath gave us the right language or way of conceiving things, we pretty much all felt a click of agreement. With regard to the large question of theory, I felt people developing fairly early a sense of a shared view, but much here was tacit and unexamined among those participants not knowledgeable about theory. With regard to the role of literature in our profession, we weren't just ambivalent; we slid away from the question whenever we started to engage it in any depth and made no progress at all. With regard to the subject of this chapter, the processes of goal setting and assessment, most of us were ambivalent or even resentful, yet we worked our way through to a clear and workable position.

NOTES

[1]President Bush's behavior in the first few months of 1990 is typical of the goals mentality: he feels that he has done the job if he can articulate and endorse a set of important goals for education—and doesn't have to provide any material aid for schools or teachers.

> [Mr. Fernandez, chancellor of the New York City schools] might consider taking Mr. Bush and a few governors into a classroom of 34 pupils working at 60-year-old desks, being led by a teacher who cannot introduce new books because the school cannot afford them—nor even duplicate texts because there are only two photocopying machines for a faculty of 300.
>
> Then the politicians can explain to the teacher and the class how the problem with public education is a lack of standards, not resources. (Freedman)

[2]From Paul Armstrong (response to draft, 4 Oct. 1989):

> The college people felt solidarity, I think, with the K–12 teachers but couldn't see this problem from the inside—at least that's how I recall feeling. The solidarity was sincere but abstract, unlike the surprising immediate bond I and other college teachers felt with elementary teachers when we talked about what we are trying to do in the classroom.

[3]This situation leads many of us to the expedient of trying to figure out innovative forms of testing to help address the teaching deficit. People devise writing exams that help students explore and think about the writing process—for example, a placement test that builds in not just exploratory writing but also sharing drafts with peers and revising or a proficiency exam that helps students think about genre and audience by having them write, say, a letter, a story, and an essay all about the same material. It is helpful, finally, to realize that a test can still function as a good test—and also as teaching—even if we don't evaluate every activity and piece of writing in it (see Grant and Kohli).

[4]From Carol Avery (position paper):

> Unfortunately, in many classrooms today, more and more of the environment is not established by the teacher, but by a reading program. The "teacher-proof" curriculum materials that most teachers are asked to use do not help teachers teach well or effectively. Teachers are burdened with "covering" a multitude of "skills" to be measured on "mastery" tests. The results are questionable. We may be producing children who *can* read—at least decode—but who *do not read* and certainly do not bring to a text a questioning mind willing to analyze, reflect, and ask, "What does this mean to me? How does this connect with my world as I know it?"

[5]England and Wales are now putting in place an ambitious national curriculum in virtually all subjects for all elementary and secondary school students ages five to sixteen. The 1988 Education Act creates a curriculum of common goals ("attainment targets") that are assessed at different levels in interesting and varied ways—often, for example, by means of focused observations by the students' own teachers.

Classroom Environments for Teaching English

Julie Jensen

(elementary school section)

*T*EN YEARS AGO, a sixth-grade class at Highland Park Elementary School in Austin, Texas, phoned an astronaut. Any witness to their preparations could have predicted a personable and businesslike transaction. The telephone call was one part of a study of space science, during which teacher and students read school and public library materials, ordered documents from the Johnson Space Center, viewed films about the United States space program, requested and filed application papers to obtain a moon rock, invited a geologist to be a guest speaker, contacted the phone company about long-distance costs and equipment, wrote a letter to the astronaut making arrangements to phone, developed interview questions based on the goals of their study, evaluated and refined the questions, role-played the interview, invited other classes to the interview, placed the phone call, wrote a thank-you letter, debriefed using an audiotape of the call, added the tape to the school library, and prepared an article about the experience for the school newspaper.

Supporting this classroom-based study were schoolwide resources and projects: a library in each classroom as well as a central open-access library; a literature-based reading program; a photography darkroom fashioned from a storeroom; a portable oven on wheels; lessons on computer programming; music experiences with guitar, piano, recorder, and synthesizer; a developmental gymnastics program; a popcorn business with profits invested in the stock market; oceanography, space-science, human-anatomy, and birding projects; a greenhouse; regular creative drama sessions; a world newspaper collection; a weather station; special-interest groups for chess, knitting, macramé, model building, lapidary, and stamp collecting; all-school events such as paper drives, a Halloween carnival, a science fair, and a track meet; and experiences that took students off the school campus, including visits to geologic formations, historical sights, and businesses.

Ten years later, in September 1986, third graders at Oasis Elementary School in Austin, Texas, were studying for the TEAMS[1] tests (see fig. 1).

Practice exercise for TEAMS Writing

Match the word to its sound spelling:

a.	(ə gō')	ago
b.	(änt)	away
c.	(ə nuth' ər)	again
d.	(ôl' wāz)	aunt
e.	(ə gen')	always
f.	(âl' so)	another
g.	(āt)	ate
h.	(ə wā')	also
i.	(an'ə məl)	animal

Sample item for TEAMS Reading

Choose the word that sounds the same as the make-believe word in the box. Mark your answer.

kraydl

- ⊂⊃ crocodile
- ⊂⊃ crawl
- ⊂⊃ knelt
- ⊂⊃ cradle

Fig. 1

Today the curriculum in many Austin, Texas, classrooms approximates the length, breadth, and depth of the state-mandated skills tests. Directives to teachers from the superintendent begin:

Teachers will know the TEAMS objectives appropriate to their grade levels, thoroughly.

All teachers will teach the TEAMS objectives and/or prerequisite skills.

Given sample items and instructions on formatting items and measurement specifications, teachers will advise sample practice items that match.

Teachers will be inserviced on Dr. Popham's strategies for improving students' performance on the TEAMS.[2] . . .

The superintendent is abetted by a bandwagonful of pushers—publishers who have been Pophamized so well that they have not only formatted, but fonted, with exactness. As a special bonus for lucky Texas teachers, they have even buried within the growing heaps of practice test questions exercises on overcoming test anxiety.

The Signs of the Times

Isolating, separating, and fragmenting are in; integrating, synthesizing, and relating are out.

"Getting it right" is in; experimenting, exploring, and diverging are out.

Language study is in; language experience, involvement, and use are out.

Skills, independent of content, are in; talk, reading, and writing to serve children's purposes are out.

Decision making by texts and tests is in; professional authority in the classroom is out.

The Power of Good Examples

Highland Park Elementary School, 1977, is neither a metaphor for educational excellence nor a symbol for a golden age. Then, as now, some faculty members kept the ditto machine hot and children's faces in textbooks because they were unable to see the promise of a teleconference, an oven, a weather station, a greenhouse, or other riches in the school environment as tools for learning science or math, to say nothing of language. But ten years ago the *professionals* on that faculty were free to design a language-learning environment. Their environment was based on the simplest of assumptions: both teachers and students are competent, both are questioners and researchers, both are readers and writers, both are learners, and both need to listen, speak, read, and write about *something*. Knowing that rich experiences in a rich environment are the source from which language springs, they guided a study of space science that required the integrated, purposeful, enthusiastic, and memorable use of all the language arts.

Those who are absorbed in today's passion for imposing test-driven oral language, reading, and writing programs on children and teachers in elementary classrooms might, more productively, identify teachers whose classrooms are positive language communities; listen to and observe the kinds of talk, reading, and writing that go on; and document what these teachers know and what they can do. Clearly, such a guide to educational improvement requires more than the usual trust in the practical wisdom of competent teachers.

NOTES

[1]The Texas Educational Assessment of Minimal Skills tests in math, reading, and writing are administered in grades 1, 3, 5, 7, 9, and 11. With the exception of a writing sample at grades 3, 5, 7, and 9, the format of these criterion-referenced measures is multiple-choice.

[2]Those who have been "inserviced" know, for example, that "teachers must teach the skills measured by the TEAMS exactly in the way the skills are formatted on the test."

Writing Assessment at SUNY Stony Brook

Peter Elbow
(college section)

*T*HE STORY OF writing assessment at Stony Brook is worth telling as a paradigm. It used to be that Stony Brook's writing requirement was satisfied by a two-semester freshman composition course taught mostly by faculty members. Then in the late 1960s the requirement was reduced to a one-semester course. Then the university expanded and the course began to be taught largely by graduate students. Before long, the limit of twenty students per section was raised to twenty-five. During this period it's unlikely that the writing skills of entering freshmen were improving.

Throughout this period, the determining evaluative decision about proficiency in writing was in the hands of individual teachers—first faculty members, then graduate instructors. It was assumed that teachers would not pass students who were not proficient—who could not write well enough for college. In the mid 1970s, however, faculty members from around the university began to complain about students in their classes who had passed the required writing course but who nevertheless were unable to write acceptably. No doubt these complaints were not new— since such complaints can in fact be found in previous decades and even centuries (see Daniels)—but they had a new bite because these "problem teachers" were no longer other faculty members who could fight back but graduate students. For we found consistently that faculty members gave higher grades (more A's and fewer failures) than graduate instructors.

In response the faculty senate instituted a proficiency exam: passing English 101 no longer satisfied the writing requirement; the new requirement was to pass the exam. With this change, the determining decision about proficiency in writing was taken out of the hands of the individual teacher and given to examiners who did not know the student. The legislation said the exam should be given to students on entrance as a placement instrument—allowing students who passed it on entrance to skip taking the freshman writing course.

Till the time of the proficiency exam virtually all students took freshman English, and thus the English department and the university were always in the position of saying, "What a lot of freshmen there are; it's a struggle to find enough instructors." But the exam invited the English department and the university into a crucially different stance: "Some of these freshmen write rather well; I guess we can exempt them"—sliding before long to, "Money is really tight this year; you'd better exempt a few more freshmen." Thus, though the exam was instituted as a move toward rigor, it functioned as a way to cut back on instruction. The year I arrived to direct the writing program, 40% of freshmen were exempted.

I really see two stories embedded here. The first is a story about distrust of teachers leading to assessment: "What's the matter with these teachers? They're not teaching what they are supposed to teach—and then they don't have the guts to fail those who don't learn." But beneath this is a story about cutting back on teaching and how this spurs distrust of those teachers left holding the bag. For there probably wouldn't have been any need for this assessment if the university still provided two semesters of instruction. But then the resulting assessment procedures somehow invite further cutbacks in teaching—further accelerating the distrust of teachers. Yet all this was done in good faith. No conspiracies or malice here. The story also shows, by the way, that it doesn't require meddling legislators to get mass assessment into higher education. Every year most freshmen took the exam twice (once as placement and the next time as proficiency)—a few exempted ones taking it only once and more than a few taking it three and four times.

I hope that the rest of the story might turn out to be paradigmatic too. My colleague Pat Belanoff and I didn't like the kind of testing we found at Stony Brook, but at first we felt stuck. We didn't know anything about this enormously technical field. As we looked into it, however, we found that even though there is a vast expertise in psychometrics about reliability and validity, in truth when we ask about any test, "Does this test really give us an accurate picture of what the student knows or can do?" the answer is always dubious or at least debatable. The professionals have not settled things with their usual precision, and there is lots of room for experimentation by amateurs. (Many if not most of the people in higher-education assessment are not trained in evaluation or psychometrics.) It may be that the need to assess writing has helped highlight the limitations of testing in general. That is, a test of math or history seems simple—a matter of clear facts. But when we try to test writing and see that we are testing not a fact but a performance with many dimensions, we might be led to speculate: "Maybe we should think of testing in math or history as testing a complex performance rather than a fact."

We knew we couldn't just persuade the university to give up the proficiency exam. Distrust of teachers was too great. We needed some kind of test—some form of quality control—but one that would reinforce good teaching rather than undermine it. (For, of course, the proficiency exam was like most exams: a test of impromptu writing on a new topic in only one mode with no time for talk or sharing or responding and little time for revising. The situation tempted teachers to make their classes into prep sessions for the exam. The five-paragraph, don't-take-too-many-risks essay is the most reliable path toward a passing exam. When students got really interested and invested in a topic, they sometimes got in trouble and wrote failing exams.)

What we came up with was a portfolio procedure as assessment or quality control: all students in the writing course produce a portfolio, and students cannot get a satisfactory grade in the course unless their portfolios are judged satisfactory not only by their own teachers but also by one other teacher who, of course, doesn't know them. This is a way to get assessment to underline and reward processes that are central to a writing course rather than peripheral: students discussing topics with each other, writing rough drafts, getting feedback, and revising; and teachers working together in groups to decide on what they mean by "satisfactory" and what makes a satisfactory portfolio. (For more on port-folios, see Elbow and Belanoff; Belanoff and Dickson.)

10 | *Questioning Two Assumptions of the Profession*

WE ENGAGED IN activities at the conference that call into question two ruling assumptions in English studies. We didn't do these things all the time, and we didn't walk around saying, "Look at us going against ruling assumptions! Aren't those assumptions just awful!" That, however, is what I want to say in this chapter.

Writing to Respond or Writing to Initiate

The English Coalition Conference began with writing rather than reading. Our first participation in the conference was to sit at home in May and June and nervously write an essay to be distributed to the other fifty-nine colleagues we had for the most part never met. We got in the mail a list of nineteen questions and were asked to name our first three choices to write about—so the planners could end up with three people writing on each question, one person each from the elementary, secondary, and college levels. These papers were to be distributed to all participants by mail beforehand. I ended up answering this question: "What methods, in your experience, work best to encourage student motivation in language, writing, or literary studies?" (Examples of other questions: "How, in your experience, have students changed over the past ten to fifteen years [similar questions for curriculum, for textbooks and teaching materials]? What types of problems do students have in relation to English/language arts studies? What are some of the positive [negative] aspects of cultural literacy as described by E. D. Hirsch, Jr.? How do you think television has affected student behavior and motivation in the English/language arts classroom?")

Yes, we were sent a tiny description of the conference plan and a bibliography of suggested reading (included in the coalition report), but the first real and obligatory activity was for each of us to put our experience and thinking down on paper for strangers—most of whom taught at a different level from our own.

We got many of these essays in the mail before the conference began. It was interesting to sit at home and read them and try to infer who these writers were. The rest we got on the opening day or two of the conference (we are no better than our students at meeting deadlines). Writing one's own piece and reading the pieces written by other participants got us more invested in the issues and connected to each other than anything else—and so, I believe, did more than anything else to determine the community spirit of inquiry at the conference.

Then sometime toward the end of the first week, participants grew restive and rebellious about the fact that we weren't being given enough time in the schedule to discuss these interesting papers that people had worked hard on. We felt we were missing the benefit of a valuable resource. Adjustments were made.

I want to meditate on the importance of writing to initiate—writing to start a conversation—and how, in an educational setting, writing is almost universally assumed to be for responding. It would feel peculiar to most teachers to start out having students write papers before they read or listen to other authoritative voices. By beginning with writing, the conference planners ran counter to the basic model for instruction in schools and universities: that input precedes output. Almost invariably we ask students to start with input—to start by reading important or authoritative texts or listening to lectures—and only then to write. Notice what this standard practice is implicitly saying:

Don't speak until spoken to.

Writing *means* responding to authority—authority outside the self.

Don't write your own ideas till you prove that you can reproduce correctly the ideas and information of others.

But this peculiar activity of writing before reading is exactly what is going on in many classrooms of teachers at the conference and in those of other teachers around the country. The practice is most striking at the inaugural level in the kindergarten and first-grade classrooms of children who are just encountering reading and writing for the first time (see Avery). Teachers have discovered that writing is more useful than reading as the entrance into literacy. Young children turn out to be able to write much more than they can read—can indeed write *anything* they can say—if they are given just a little help and encouragement, for example, by being shown how to use invented or shorthand spelling. Even the youngest children can often "write" anything by just scribbling. And they'll call it writing and "read" back to you what they've "written." In many classrooms around the country kindergartners and first graders are not just writing stories but "publishing" little books. Teachers and helpers type up their writing in conventional spelling, the child adds illustrations, and then these books are bound with cloth covers and become texts for reading.

Of course, the effect of this approach is obvious once people like Don Graves had the sense to figure it out: students are much more excited and competent when they read what they and their classmates have written than when they read published books from the outside (especially basal readers). They learn reading faster; they have a healthier stance toward reading—a stance that recognizes, "Hey, these things called books are things we write. Let's read books to see what other people like us have written." No longer do children think of books as something written by a corporate, faceless "they"—like arithmetic workbooks. (There is a story making the rounds of a reporter visiting one of these classrooms where the first graders eagerly offer to show some of their books. "Have you really written a book?" the reporter asks one child with a tone of condescending surprise. "Haven't you?" replies the child.)

Shirley Brice Heath had graduate students in linguistics analyze stories written in this way by young children, and they discovered that such stories were usually at a higher level of development and sophistication than the stories the children could read. Thus, interestingly, output precedes input—and prepares the way for input.

The conference was a place where participants could hear about this happening at all levels. Brooke Workman has his junior high school students write about their own strong experiences—such as sudden experiences of shock—and then move on to poetry by Emily Dickinson. Some college teachers do the same thing. (See Charles Moran's early classic essay "Teaching Writing/Teaching Literature.") When I had trouble with students failing to connect with Shakespeare or putting his text "under glass," I learned from Moran to start with writing as the initiatory act. (For example, after having difficulties teaching *The Tempest*, where Prospero seems both hallowed yet unattractive, I learned to ask students to write about some grudge they've had for many years—before any reading of the play. When we move on to Shakespeare, I find students more invested and skilled in dealing with this difficult character and play. Of course, I don't let my writing suggestion determine our whole reading of the play.)

Just as one of the principal reading texts for many first graders now is the writing that they and their classmates have started off by writing and publishing, so goes it also for some high school and college students in writing courses. The same benefits accrue. (It is not so uncommon any more to build a lab fee into a course—indeed into a universitywide writing program—to pay for the publication and distribution of student writing numerous times throughout the semester.) Some teachers at the conference talked about how it is easier to get students involved in what they are studying when they start by writing rather than reading. One of the main emphases in the powerful writing-across-the-curriculum movement is on helping students use writing not just for demonstrating what they have learned but also for the process of learning itself. Indeed, many people call this the writing-to-learn movement.

But notice *how* I find myself arguing for the usefulness of writing as an initiating act: that it benefits reading. When an assumption is a ruling one, even one's efforts to fight it tend to reinforce it: that the goal of writing is to serve reading. For in the assumption that reading comes first and writing is for the sake of responding to a text, schools and colleges are really privileging reading over writing.

Thus schooling tends to act out the originary story that input precedes output—that we hear and read before we speak and write. This seems a natural story: babies and children seem to hear before they can speak—to listen before they answer. But it's not so simple. Yes, children wouldn't speak unless they grew up in the presence of other speakers, and of course babies and children often answer when spoken to. But careful observation of children shows that just as often it works the other way round: the reason that children get input—hear language—is that they initiate the "conversation." Even when a baby gives as little as a gurgle or a goo, the parent often takes it as the initiation of discourse (which it sometimes is) and responds. I'll settle for a fifty-fifty deal here between initiating and replying, but my hunch is that children's initiation of conversation is more crucial for learning to talk than their responding to the initiation of others. That is, the adult's enabling act is as much listening and understanding and answering as it is initiating a conversation. At one point in the conference, when we were talking about what made us teachers and scholars, Janet Emig said, "The reason we are here is because someone important once listened to us. Not because someone told us something." Her statement rang true for many—and I heard it often repeated. Thus the most productive and generative act by a teacher or parent is often to listen.

If we think about how schools and universities work, we see that the governing metaphor is that learning is input—taking things in, putting things inside us. Too many people think of the root activities in school as listening and reading, not talking and writing. Of course, if they stop and think about it, they realize that we learn from output—talking and writing—but they don't naturally think of learning *as* talking and writing. Notice, for example, how many teachers think of testing as measuring input, not output—as asking, "How well have you learned the ideas of others?" not "What new ideas of your own do you have?"

All this reinforces the problematic banking metaphor of learning or the picture of students as vessels to be filled. In contrast to this, the coalition members emphasized the contrasting metaphor of learning as

the making of meaning, which throws light on what otherwise is paradoxical about learning:

> The more we write and talk, the more we have left to write and say:
> the greater the number of words that come out of us, the greater
> the number of words we find left inside.

> When students feel empty ("I have nothing to say, nothing on my
> mind"), the cause is not insufficient input but insufficient output:
> more talking and writing will put more words in their heads.

> Of course teachers and politicians love to talk: the more people talk,
> the more they want to talk.

If we see learning not as input but as the making of meaning and connections, these phenomena are not paradoxical but natural. If we follow
the pattern of starting with reading and lectures—input—and then writing about them, we reinforce this wrong idea that learning means functioning like a camera or mirror: take it in, get it right. If half the time
we start with speaking and writing—output—we will help reinforce the
idea that the making of meaning is the central event in learning and
thinking and schooling. In the rhetorical tradition it is not uncommon
to start by having students create discourse—speeches or essays—start
by having students figure out what *they* have to say about the topic. These
discourses often become the text for reading and listening and further
speaking and listening. In the poetic tradition, students seldom write
except in response to hallowed texts.

When we assume that reading comes first, not only are we privileging
reading over writing, we are privileging passivity over activity. Yes, I
grant the currently fashionable paradoxes: that reading is really "writing" (actively creating meaning) and writing is really "reading" (passively
finding what culture and history have inscribed in our heads); I guess
I sort of believe this and find it a useful lens. (Indeed, if reading is
"writing" and writing is "reading," then perhaps teachers will assign
"writing" in response to "reading"—that is, ask students to move their
fingers first and then move their eyes in response.) But in the end I
can't help falling back to a Johnsonian stone-kicking stance: writing
simply *is* more active than reading for many reasons:

> Reading asks, "What did they have to say?" while writing asks, "What
> do you have to say?" Thus the ubiquitous human impulse to want
> to know what a speaker was saying to us reinforces the emphasis
> on getting the right answer in reading. And the equally ubiquitous
> human impulse to say what's on our mind reinforces an implicit

invitation in writing for writers to take authority over their own meaning.

Reading tends to imply, "Sit still and pay attention," while writing tends to imply, "Get in there and *do* something."

Reading tends to be a matter of the teacher and author choosing the words; writing tends to be a matter of the student choosing the words.

Reading means consumption, writing means production. Part of the stale passivity of students comes from their being cast always in the role of consumer.

I even point to the crudely physical dimension. It's not just that reading involves less physical movement than writing—though that's important. (Notice how the physical act of reading out loud and even making gestures helps the cognitive dimension of reading.) Try this experiment: on an occasion when a discussion class get soggy, have everyone stop talking and read something; on another occasion have everyone stop and write something. You'll find that students tend to be more awake and involved after they write—even displaying more tonus in their bodies—than after they read.

In short, when we assume that writing is always in response to reading and lectures, we tend to keep students from breaking out of their characteristically passive stance for school and learning. The primacy of reading in the reading-writing dichotomy is an act of locating authority away from the student and keeping it entirely in the teacher or institution or great figure. To enhance good learning, we need to get more authority in the student.

It is probably necessary for me to reiterate here that I am not arguing against input but only against privileging input. I'm not arguing against the importance and special value of reading and listening. Reading and listening are precious for the very reasons why they are different from writing and speaking. Reading and listening ask us to step outside our own preoccupations and hear what others have to say, to think in the language of others, to recognize authority of others without letting it overwhelm us, and above all to relinquish some control. (I hope that my long advocacy of the "believing game" [1973] or "methodological belief" [1987] will show that I don't slight this side of our intellectual life.) Nor am I trying to imply that students are already good at reading and listening. Far from it. Of course learning means getting inside someone else's language and thinking, taking in ideas, indeed, taking in lists of brute facts—and getting them right. But I suspect that part of students' difficulty with reading stems from the ingrained educational pattern I'm pointing to here: It's always "Read first and then write to see if you got it right. What *they* have to say is more important than what *you* have to say." Reading and listening might go better if we sometimes said, "Let's start with what *you* have to say. Try to see if the reading can respond to it and serve it." I find it common for people to be more interested in a subject—more able to listen and explore—after they have gotten involved by working out their thinking about it.

You might argue that participants at the Coalition Conference weren't really "starting the conversation" when we wrote our position papers. That is, some theorists insist that all writing is response to a text or "textuality" (see, e.g., Scholes 65), and so there is no such thing as initiatory writing. But to make this kind of claim is to use language in a problematic way. To do so undermines our ability to notice and talk about a crucial, down-to-earth distinction: the distinction between asking students to write in response to our texts and lectures and asking them to write in response to their own experience (even if their experience is full of texts and voices already inside their heads). Once you undermine this crude distinction between "making it up out of your head" and "writing about texts," you lose one of the most useful ways to teach ourselves and our students about the very ubiquitous textuality that Scholes is talking about. That is, the best way to *see* all the texts that are already jam-packed in our heads is by insisting that we write extensively about something before reading any new texts about it. (However, such writing often shows enormous transformation and integrations of those texts, preventing oversimple statements about what's in our heads. Anytime someone says, "All *x* is *y*" or "There is no such thing as *z*," we know this is an a priori ideological move rather than an empirical claim—a totalizing move to redefine the keys on the keyboard rather than to type in outside information.)

You might also argue that it was appropriate for us at the conference to start with writing because we're teachers and scholars, not mere students. But that simply confirms my point: we're inscribed with the assumption that teaching and scholarship are output—and learning is input. It seems to me that the reason we teachers and scholars learn a lot is that we get a lot of opportunity to be active, to make our own meaning, and to be in charge rather than just passive. We get far more chance to speak and write in school than our students do. Talking and writing and being in charge are the prime enabling conditions for learning, even for learning mere lists of facts.

It would take a genuine shift for us to think metaphorically of learning as output and of the student as primarily a speaker and writer. Anthropologists of schooling like Heath have noticed how real speech—open-ended, back-and-forth, extended dialogue—tends to be discouraged in schools and felt as subversive. Surprisingly, the same goes for writing. Applebee has investigated writing in the secondary schools and found that students spend less than three percent of student class and homework time devoted to writing a paragraph or more—and most of the "writing" time in class consists of writing short-answer exercises. That figure would go down toward zero if we asked how often students are asked to use writing to initiate discourse. I think there is, in fact, a kind of suspicion not only of "the talker" in schools—the troublemaker—but also of "the writer"—someone who goes off on his or her own trains of thought without sufficient attention to input.

My advocacy of writing as initiatory may sound to some like an invitation to romantic solipsism to write wholly out of the private self and thus to reinforce the problem of rampant individualism with students gradually disappearing into cocoons of solipsist isolation. But this fear rests on a misguided model of individual development—a kind of parody of Freud and Piaget that says children start out as monads dominated by selfish desires to stay separate and egocentric and that they cannot become "decentered" or social without a terrible struggle. It's as though our students are each in their own little bathroom, and we must beat on the door and say, "What are you *doing* in there? Why have you been in there so long with the door locked? Come on out and have some wholesome fun with us."

But a very different course of development now seems more believable and generally accepted—a model that derives from thinkers like George Herbert Meade, Mikhail Bakhtin, and Lev Vygotsky: our children *start out* very social and intertwined. Their little selves are not hermetically sealed atoms but are, rather, deeply enmeshed or rooted in the important figures in their lives. (Of course, they have selves and characters too—as any parent of a six-week-old knows). We don't have to struggle to make children want to connect with others—they are naturally already connected. We don't have to bang on the bathroom door to make them listen to, feel part of, and collaborate with the various people and cultural forces around them. They may not want to listen to *us*, but that doesn't make them private and solipsistic. (In fact, it's the more private and solipsistic kids that sometimes listen best to us teachers.) What this picture of human development shows us is that separateness and autonomy are not qualities that children start out with but rather qualities they only gradually achieve—often with struggle and setbacks throughout adolescence and even young adulthood. It can be a slow and difficult process for someone to achieve an autonomous self who can think and do things that are disapproved of by the community he or she feels part of.

To put this in concrete terms, I find that first graders I work with are not very interested in private writing: they tend to want to share everything. But high school students, college students, and adults find private writing precious and empowering. That is, as we get older, we have to work at separating ourselves and sorting out what we choose as our own and where we choose to fit in. It's a life task. The point of my digression into developmental psychology, then, is that even if we invite initiatory writing and let students write out of their private selves (and remember, I'm not proposing that we always start with output—just sometimes), we can nevertheless trust that students come to us with a strong dimension of social connectivity that we couldn't stamp out if we tried.

Participants at the conference had a sense of how easily people misuse a term like "paradigm shift" (see ch. 9; "and I don't give a paradigm shift" from "The English Coalition Blues"). If we really managed to stop privileging reading over writing, if we stopped equating education with input (or recognized that output is input), and if we actually changed our educational practice to reflect the fact that the root learning activity is not just reading or listening to lectures but equally writing and speaking (for example, by occasionally starting our courses with writing rather than reading)—then the term *paradigm shift* might be justified.

But paradigm shifts don't grow on trees. On the one hand, the final report of the college section asserted that "English departments have historically privileged reading over writing" and that therefore "we must strike a new balance by emphasizing the importance of writing in both our curricula and our research programs" (Lloyd-Jones and Lunsford 26). The report enacts that new balance in a new model for a full-year freshman English course, Freshman Writing and Reading, where writing and reading would be completely integrated. This is clearly a good idea, a good course in itself.

But, on the other hand, I wonder whether the proposal doesn't actually push in the opposite direction and further privilege reading over writing. That is, departments are likely to skip the part about it being a full-year course and change their current one-semester freshman writing course (which is all they say they can afford) to a one-semester writing and reading course. Thus the change would probably result in the disappearance of what in many English departments is the only writing course. Even if it were adopted as a full-year course, the new integrated conceptualization of it would tempt departments to staff it by teachers with no training in the teaching of writing—just when we were finally managing to get the freshman course taught by people who do know about the teaching of writing. If so, the course would tend to drift back into the old covert Introduction to Literature course of yore. (Paul Armstrong writes, "It was a poignant moment, I thought, when some of the writing people who had worked conceptually to the wisdom of a reciprocity of reading and writing then stepped back and hesitated and asked if it would be politically wise to give up the emphasis on writing they'd fought for" [response to draft].) In short, here is a proposal to strike a new balance in the department's only major course weighted toward writing—but no proposal for balance in the other ninety-nine percent of the courses that are weighted toward reading.

By beginning the conference by writing and stressing that students be producers of knowledge rather than just consumers, we made an important opening move against the ruling educational assumption that input always precedes output and that reading is more important than writing. But ruling assumptions change slowly.

Writing to Explain or Writing to Render

Near the end of a mixed-level session one afternoon (about how learning should occur in schools), people started telling stories about their own learning. There was a call to stop for a few moments to write—so we could get a story from everyone. We took seven or eight minutes. Everyone agreed to bring in copies of a tiny story to share at tomorrow's meeting. Which we did—and began the session passing them around and reading silently. But gradually in the silence of reading there came to be a nagging dissatisfaction. The silence was wrong; the stories needed to be heard, however inefficient that might seem. Performed, rendered. Presence. Thus an intriguing sequence of emerging moments: "Hey, we need to write these down, not just tell them." Then, "Hey we need to hear these, not just see them on the page."

At the end of another session where there was a lot of storytelling about how people got involved in literature and teaching, people were asked to write about what they found important about that session. (The statements were used as a report on the session.) Here are a few of those comments that pertain to storytelling:

> *The most important thing: the need for stories, narrative. They're shorter and more lasting.*

> *That we shifted from the abstract, from jargon, from generalization to a concern for the human, the anecdote.*

> *The importance of using anecdotes for understanding of more discursive material and the reminder of the importance of valuing our differences.*

> *Insight into the oral-writing split in our culture: anecdotes drop out of documents written later for later discussion.*

> *Change occurs in a context; stories are best for illustrating change.*

We did a lot of writing at the English Coalition Conference. The Wye conference center started out with a couple of sturdy photocopying machines, and they both broke down. Most of it was expository—reports and minutes and manifestos. But a significant proportion (at least for academics) was story, and this is what I want to meditate on here.

All this story writing at the conference undermined another ruling assumption in the profession: that expository writing that explains and argues is more important and more mature than narrative or imaginative writing that renders experience. This proposition sounds absurd on the face of it. How can a discipline so rooted in the study of imaginative literature privilege expository and critical writing over narrative and imaginative writing? But if we look at the educational practice of our discipline, we will see our values in action: students in the early grades are invited to write stories and poems, but once they reach high school and college (sometimes even junior high school), they are seldom invited and often discouraged from doing so in virtually all writing or literature courses we teach. The message is very clear, not just in the shape of the curriculum but often explicitly stated: "Work on serious writing now— expository writing or essay writing. Enough of these juvenile stories or personal experiences."

But it was just this kind of writing that we grown-ups did at the conference (in addition, of course, to masses of expository writing). I include a selection of these stories and renderings as a counterpoint to my chapters.

In describing these stories that people wrote, I spoke of "imaginative writing that renders experience." Perhaps some readers will jump on me as critically naive to stress that language can represent nonlinguistic reality instead of stressing that language is always intertextually pointing to other language or that literature is always a verbal icon pointing only to itself. In emphasizing rendering, my goal is not to leave out the intertextual or self-referential dimension of texts. But I consciously avoid (for the time being, anyway) the larger terms like *poetic* or *imaginative* or *creative* writing to get away from the connotations those terms carry: a baggage of high art, high culture, special talent, high theory, high intellect, and so forth. It is this baggage that may, paradoxically, have played a strong role in getting us into the very jam in the first place— the jam of neglecting imaginative writing in our practice. To write "imaginatively" can lead us to the loftiest and most wonderful art; but my point is that we do better to emphasize the humble, down-to-earth, no-big-deal language practice that virtually everyone engages in unself-consciously—manifested in the little stories we tell every day and the dreams we have every night. I love the term *imagination*—as long as we can purge it of the aura of high art.

Why do we neglect this kind of writing? Why doesn't every high school or university literature class ask students as a matter of course to do an equal amount of rendering or imaginative writing as critical writing? Why don't we normally ask students to write stories when we read Hawthorne, poems when we read Emily Dickinson, a play or some scenes when we read Shakespeare? After all, to respond to a work doesn't

necessarily mean to write critically. It means, perhaps even more help-
fully, to answer—to write back in the same mode or theme. Very few
teachers do it. This kind of response usually exploits and develops more
critical and literary sophistication than just writing criticism. When people make lists of the different modes of responding to literature, however, they tend to omit entirely this most obvious kind.

But there are understandable reasons why this practice is not
common—responses we should listen to if we want to make a change in
practice:

1. One answer is that we value imaginative writing so highly. "I care
   so much about literature that I'm not willing to let amateurs soil
   it: beginners, lousy writers, people with no gift. I reserve imaginative writing for people with genius—or at least talent." Or a
   variation: "I can stand to read lousy essays, but I cannot stand to
   read lousy stories and poems—in fact I refuse." We see here the
   result of putting imaginative writing on a pedestal: cherishing and
   valuing it as high art, magical, sacred. To put something on a
   pedestal is sometimes a cover for fear and dislike; and sometimes
   it leads to fear and dislike. This sacralization of imaginative writing
   is sometimes blamed on the Romantics, but the Romantics had an
   antielite instinct too: a notion of "humble folk" (at least humble
   rural folk) who are all able to create.
2. There is also the opposite answer or excuse: "Stories and renderings of one's own experience are too easy, too thoughtless, too based
   on feeling. They don't require enough critical thinking, analysis,
   self-consciousness, logic. We must get students to move past this
   soft writing to the hard critical thinking required for analysis and
   argument. Stories and rendering is kid stuff—just telling what happened, how you feel."
3. A combination of the previous two: "I mustn't ask students to do
   something I can't do, and I can't write stories or poems or personal
   experience pieces." Insofar as professional academics have sacral-
   ized imaginative writing, they naturally feel, "How can I write even
   a brief scene when we are looking at the great work of Shakespeare?
   I can't reach that high." But as professionals they are also embarrassed by what comes come out when they or their students write
   stories and renderings of experience—weak writing usually rife
   with feelings. Academics are particularly likely to be embarrassed
   by writing about feelings if they are too blurted or not rendered
   with literary sophistication. So the other feeling is just as important:
   "I can't reach that low."
4. Also: "I can grade essays, but I can't grade stories and poems. My

colleagues and I can more or less agree about what is good and bad expository writing [which is of course a myth] but not about stories and poems; sometimes I don't even know what *I* think about the quality of such work; and even when we all agree that something is terrible, how can I give an F to a student on the story of his mother's death?"

5. A few colleagues make a very noble claim: "Yes, we love imaginative writing more than any other kind, but we in English are the only ones who do. Therefore we have a duty to teach the kind of writing that everyone else in the academy wants, namely, expository writing." A variation: "Writing courses have so often tended to be covert literature courses that we should bend over backwards to sever all connections between writing courses and imaginative discourse." (Of course, those covert literature courses were always courses in interpretation of literature, not practice in imaginative writing.)

All these reasons have a kind of logic—or psychologic. One can genuinely sympathize with them. But they all pale before the brute fact of our behavior as a profession: not giving our students after about the fifth grade any practice in the writing of imaginative language and indeed acting as though we want to stop them from doing the kind of writing that leads to literature. Our teaching of literature might have a deeper effect if we didn't continually tell students that imaginative writing is less important and less mature than expository writing (see Hatlen, "Michel Foucault and the Discourse(s) of English" for powerful and cogent thinking on these matters).

Schools and colleges have the job of passing on the great human accomplishment of written language. Discourse that analyzes and explains is of course a crucial part of that accomplishment, but discourse that renders is also important. It is one of the primary tools of humankind. It is the kind of discourse that Susanne Langer tries to keep us from forgetting. Of course we need discursive or explanatory language, but any adequate understanding or effective explanation rests on a foundation of experience or empathy or knowing "what it is like." Thus I've allowed all this to sound very affective: to "render my experience" sounds like it means telling you how I feel—and sometimes it does; I will always fight the assumption that cognition is more appropriate for schooling than affect. But discourse that renders is also thinking. It is nonanalytic, nondiscursive, nonlogical, but it is thinking or cognitive nevertheless—however heavy an affective load it also carries. The importance of narrative thinking was a recurring note at the conference. Jerome Bruner's *Actual Minds, Possible Worlds* is an interesting exploration of how narrative world making is just as important a kind of thinking as discursive or abstract world making (this from someone who made his reputation treating discursive thinking as thinking itself). His was an important book on our reading list and in our library at the conference. We impoverish our students cognitively if we don't also give them practice past the fifth grade in this kind of thinking too. (Also, it's a great pleasure and relief for most teachers to read some stories by students, not just essays.)

Some people feel that our academic duty obliges us to teach students writing that they need for academic work and for their jobs. But, though it's true that students don't know a subject unless they can use the professional discourse of the discipline, we mustn't forget that students also don't know a subject unless they can tell stories about how it concretely affects people's experience. We have all seen students who can explain a principle in technical disciplinary language but who don't really understand it because they haven't really grasped how it affects the world concretely. Virtually every other discipline works on helping students learn to explain and analyze experience and use discursive reasoning. Only we in English (and other literatures) work on helping students learn to render experience and use imaginative and metaphorical reasoning. If we don't do it, no one else will. Besides, school is short and life is long. It's deeply practical to teach students to write discourse that gives others a sense of their experience—or, indeed, that gives them back a sense of their own experience with a little perspective.

If we want students to love literature and connect with it, the best way is for them to write in these imaginative modes. The highest goal is not quality ("Would everyone who is singing off key please stop singing"); the goal is that everyone be able to do it. That is, we can't leave to others the entire job of rendering our experience for us. Yes, Shakespeare and Virginia Woolf can articulate certain things we cannot articulate—yet we can also do what they cannot do, namely, to fish for and find our *own* words for what's happening to us.

Laura

Carol Avery
(elementary school section)

May 8, 1987

WE CELEBRATE Mother's Day in our first-grade classroom this Friday afternoon. The children perform a play for their mothers entitled "The Big Race"—the story of the tortoise and the hare. Laura is the "turtle," who wins the race.

A few minutes later Laura reads aloud the book she has authored about her mother. The group laughs as she reads about learning to count with her cousins when she was three years old. Laura writes: "I was learning six. Then my Mom came in and asked what we were doing. I said, 'I'm learning sex!' " Laura's mother is delighted. The reading continues with a hilarious account of a family squabble between Mom and Dad over a broken plate. Laura concludes the anecdote, "So then I just went in and watched TV." Laura looks at me and smiles as she pauses, waiting for her audience to quiet before she goes on. I wink at her; I know she is thinking, "Wait till they hear the next part. It's the funniest of all." She reads about a llama spitting in Mom's eye on a visit to the zoo. Laura's way with words has brought delight to everyone. I remember a week earlier when Laura and I sat to type her draft and she said, "This is the best part. I put it last so that everyone will feel happy at the end."

May 9, 1987

Saturday night, around 11:45 p.m., a light bulb ignites fabric in a closet outside Laura's bedroom. Laura wakes. She cannot get through the flames, and by the time firefighters reach her it is too late. Laura dies. No one else is injured.

Monday, May 11, 1987

The children and I gather on our sharing rug in the classroom. I have no plans. We start to talk. There are endless interruptions until Michael says,

"Mrs. Avery, can we shut the door so people stop bothering us?" So Michael shuts the door. "Are you going to read us the newspapers?" they ask. "Is that what you'd like?" "Yes," comes the unanimous response. The children huddle close; a dozen knees nuzzle against me. I read aloud the four-paragraph story on the front page of the *Sunday News* that accompanies a picture of our Laura sprawled on the lawn of her home with firefighters working over her. I read the longer story in Monday morning's paper that carries Laura's school picture. We cry. We talk and cry some more. And then we read Laura's books—writing that Laura determined was her best throughout the year and that was "published" to become part of our classroom library. These books are stories of Laura and her family, stories with titles such as *My Dad Had a Birthday* and *When My Grandmother Came to My House*. Laura's voice comes through loud and clear with its sense of humor and enthusiasm. We laugh and enjoy her words. "Laura was a good writer," they say. "She always makes us laugh when we read her stories." Then Dustin says, "You know, it feels like Laura is right here with us, right now. We just can't see her."

A short time later we begin our writing workshop. Every child chooses to write about Laura this day. Some write about the fire, some memories of Laura as a friend. I write with them. After forty-five minutes it is time to go to art, and there are cries of disappointment at having to stop. We will come back to the writing. There will be plenty of time. The last five weeks of school will be filled with memories of Laura as we work through our loss together. The children will decide to leave her desk in its place in the room because "It's not in our way and anyway, this is still Laura's room even if she's not really here anymore." Laura's mother and little brother will come in to see us. On the last day they will bring us garden roses that Laura would have brought. Laura will always be a part of us and none of us will ever be the same.

In the days immediately following Laura's death and in the weeks since then, certain thoughts have been rattling around in my head: I'm so glad that I teach the way I do. I'm so glad I really knew Laura. I know that I can never again teach in a way that is not focused on children. I can never again put a textbook or a "program" between me and the children. I'm glad I knew Laura so well. I'm glad all of us knew her so well. I'm glad the classroom context allowed her to read real books, to write about real events and experiences in her life, to share herself with us and to become part of us and we of her. I'm grateful for a classroom community that nurtured us all throughout the year and especially when Laura was gone. Laura left a legacy. Part of that legacy is the six little published books and the five-inch-thick stack of paper that is her writing from our daily writing workshops. When we read her words, we hear again her voice and her laughter.

Either/Or Distinctions: The Flight from Complexity

Bob Denham

(secondary school section)

*I*N ONE of the A-strand sessions, Janet Emig mentioned in passing the title of an article she was writing, "The Flight from Complexity." The phrase brought into focus an idea that had been slithering around in my mind for the past few days. Its origin was my effort to make some connections between what had been going on in the secondary school discussion group and the talk by Shirley Brice Heath. A great deal of our discussion, as we searched for ways to define goals, seemed to depend on our setting up a series of oppositions. I've come to see this way of defining goals as reductive and as based on false dichotomies. In short, I've come to see a great deal of our talk during the past week as a "flight from complexity." . . .

The source for my first freshman essay was an experience that had been quite painful to me—the death of my father. I suppose what I was trying to express was a feeling of terror and an unmediated sense of loss. What I in fact produced was probably pretty close to the self-pitying moanings of the narrator in Joyce's "Araby"—mutatis mutandis. At the time, I thought that this piece of writing was much more important than the freshman paper I wrote for my Western Civilization class, "The Causes of the Failure of the Triple Entente." In retrospect, however, I'm not so sure. While the freshman essay was student-centered and came directly from my own experience, an experience from which I was trying to construct a meaning, I now recognize the experience of writing that freshman essay as extraordinarily limited and as simply another version of the late Romantic cult of the ego. What I needed in college was not, or at least not just, to bore into my own experience, which, however rich, was nevertheless parochial. What I needed was not self but society. My freshman paper was an example of the ego screaming for attention,

195

but the most valuable thing in my college experience was my introduction to those other times and worlds and ideas—not my introduction to a body of facts about things outside the self but the realization that there was a structure of knowledge that could liberate me from the self. I realized, in short, that my experience as a student needed to be enlarged by secondary-source knowledge.

Now that I've slipped into the confessional mode in these late-night ruminations, I want to remark that the two most important things in my own education have been two teachers. I sat in the classes of one, who happens to be at this conference. The other taught me through his books. If I were forced then to use the metaphor of the center to talk about my own education, I would try to make teachers and books and things other than the self occupy the still point. This geometrical impossibility takes me back to where I began—to the hope that the documents that come out of the Coalition Conference will not slide into those reductive oppositions that misrepresent the rich complexity of English education. When Janet [Emig] asked us to draw our theories of learning the other day, my first impulse was to put a big book in the middle. My experience in the secondary school section prevented my doing this (a testimony to what I have learned during the conference), and I ended up with a drawing that tried to illustrate the interrelationships among teachers, students, structures of knowledge, language, and the experiences we have with others and the natural world.

11 | *The Danger of Softness*

*T*hree excerpts from my notes:

1. One of the first days: Carol Avery describing how she teaches first grade. Lets the kids pick out what they want to read. No drills or basal readers. They continue to love reading all year. Colleagues and parents skeptical at first, but the results gradually come in.

A touchstone for us: With the right spirit, you can trust kids to want to learn and to enjoy reading and writing.

Moments when people describe their actual teaching are rare and valuable.

2. The theme is how people learn in schools—or, as the agenda has it, "knowledge acquisition."

Someone says, "People can't learn without personal, validating support."

I comment to myself: How to make the world safe for the mention of Carl Rogers?

Janet Emig: "We're all here because someone listened to us." I write the name of the teacher who listened to me—and made me want to teach: Bob Fisher.

Jane Christensen: "I learn when someone believes in me. I need so much support."

All this stuff is very suspicious in the world: child-centered; people are smart; support. This was in the Dartmouth report; Dewey; noncompetitive.

How can we make these attitudes not ridiculed and even believed?

Janet Emig: "What are the conditions that all teachers need?" These mentioned: smaller classes, fewer students, more time, support, workshops, leadership. Competitive-male-agonistic is privileged in school . . .

Rosalinda Barrera suggests stories.

A lot of us go on to tell stories. I write on the opposite page: "What's my story?" and list a few phrases that suggest ones that might be central to me.

Janet Emig tells hers: "Why I'm not teaching high school: Tenth house on census. Discovered ninety-hour week. (Census worker asked her for full listing of how she spent the whole week's time.) Decided I had to do whatever was necessary to get out of schoolteaching and teach in college."

At the end of the meeting people write short statements, "bullets," about what they considered important in the session. The photocopied report of the meeting consists mostly of these bullets. I quoted a few of them in the previous chapter. Here are a few more:

- *For me the most important part of our discussion was our emphasis on the affective side of teaching—teacher values, respect for pupils, tolerance for diverse views, etc.*

- *The need for coming up with specifics (list or narratives) based on the dignity of the teacher—especially the need for others' beliefs in the teacher.*

- *What was most important to me today was the thread in our discussion that connected caring about real people—teachers and students—to all the practices and conditions of our classrooms.*

- *That having the power to change the conditions in which we teach may be possible.*

3. Someone remarks, "I don't teach English, I teach students." In reply, a sudden explosion of clench-jawed anger: "Don't give us that old line. It's a fake polarization. Falsely divisive. Sentimental. Anti-intellectual." No one replies in defense of the first speaker. A bit uncomfortable. Someone had been hit over the head once too often by that perhaps sentimental old saying and was prepared to hit back to stamp it out. Agent Orange. Almost succeeded but not quite, for I heard it one more time a week or so later. Here is the passage from my notes about the second occasion:

X tells the story of his teaching: "I teach students"—stressing that who he is and whom he teaches are more important than what he teaches. Y objects, "You can't say 'I teach students.' Students is only an indirect object. What do you teach students?" Nevertheless it's a theme of the conference—with force from elementary group—that we do teach students (and teach ourselves). Teaching as relationship.

Later that evening, using Berthoff's "dialectical notebook" technique, I meditate on the facing page: Passion—with joy. People who are committed to these things are always feeling alienated and writing and speaking in an adversarial mode. Why? Both sides contribute. The larger group is bothered by this "soft" stuff; the minority or fringe group is trigger-happy. Crucial dynamic of the conference.

Betsy Hilbert wrote this in the second or third week:

> *Yesterday I was sitting in my B section, feeling very tired and wishing Paul would let us out of the meeting early. Most of the time those sessions are wonderful, and I love to listen and participate, but that particular day was a trial. There were several things that needed to be done before lunch, and, besides, Janet's mention of "teachers' bladder" had added to my discomfort. The room was cold, too, and other people were wiggling; I thought about suggesting that those who wanted to stay and talk could do so while some of us left, but mentioning the idea seemed rude. That meeting for me dragged inevitably on to its programmed end.*
> *The long, slow tick of my kidneys in the icy air brought home the remembrance of what prisoners of the clock we teachers are. It doesn't matter whether*

a class is jumping with excitement over an interesting topic or everyone's asleep on a rainy Monday after lunch—class will end exactly fifty minutes after it began. We take up a subject when the syllabus says we must and stop a course when the bell rings for semester's end. No matter what psychology has revealed about human beings' intricate and differing patterns and cycles of time, schools must run like railroad stations.

The most passionate moments of reading and writing, of literature, are those that seem to unbind time. We look up from a book, surprised, at the spouse who is yelling down the stairs that it's 3 a.m and were we planning to get any sleep at all that night? We raise our eyes from the computer screen and find with disbelief that writing the greatest paragraph in the world has just taken five hours—or possibly fifteen minutes. We rub our eyes on coming out of the movie, bewildered to discover that while we traveled on the plains of Russia, darkness overtook the world and obscured the place where we parked the car just hours—or was it lifetimes?—ago.

Text is the enemy of time. Schools have yet to notice that phenomenon.

I HAVE TRIED to call attention in these epigraphs to a dimension of the proceedings that was striking to everyone there and that particularly interests me: the personal, storytelling, celebratory, imaginative, metaphorical, relationship-oriented side of things—the connection of the cognitive to the affective, the connection of the professional to the amateur and playful. And let me call attention also to other moments of the conference that illustrate this dimension—many of which I've already mentioned in other parts of the book: all the storytelling and story writing (which I try to represent in the interludes between chapters); the sequence of events where people decided they needed to write stories instead of just hearing a few spoken ones—and then later needed to hear them all uttered instead of just seeing them on the page; and all the diverse performances and renderings at the conference (the role-played class from *I Know Why the Caged Bird Sings*, the drawing and metaphor making we did in Janet Emig's workshop, Bill Teale's rendering of *Three by the Sea*, the sung-and-danced performance of Joe Lostracco's "Coalition Country Blues," the performance of the "Coalition Alphabet Song" and "Mother Goose's Coalition Rhymes").

What I think most people were dreading—three weeks cooped up with academics in a bad climate and an overambitious schedule—turned out finally to be downright jolly. Everyone remarked on it. The conference simply worked better than most academic gatherings. Not because there were better parties and songs (many fewer parties than at the conventions I know—MLA and CCCC) but because people performed cognitively and "professionally" better than usual: a bit more intellectually alive and flexible, more able to work together and hear other points of view. I don't mean to imply that the conference was all play and no work—far from it. What most participants felt was that there was a better integration and acceptance of the personal and playful with the professional and cognitive than they are used to in the academic context.

No doubt many factors contributed to this dimension of the conference, for example that it took place in the summer, that we had much more time with one another than at most conferences, and yet we didn't have to work with each other as permanent colleagues (thus the "shipboard" phenomenon still had a chance to operate). Nevertheless I want to explore the crucial contribution of two groups of participants in helping us achieve this remarkable integration of the affective and the cognitive: the "wholistic" subgroup and the entire elementary section.

The wholistic subgroup. There is an important and complicated story here. It may be minor in the whole scheme of things but it sticks in my mind as much as anything else in the three weeks.

Late in the first week a small splinter group of three people broke away from the college section, objecting to the way goals were being discussed and formulated. They labeled themselves the "Wholistic Group." Here is an interweaving of the accounts by two members of that group (written to me in response to my draft attempt to tell the story):

> The college section was breaking into three parts to produce three reports: one for the freshman-year course, one for general education, and one for the English major. Marie Buncombe, Eleanor Tignor, and I didn't like either the preestablished divisions or the separatenesses they called for, so we decided to go off on our own. Together, in the quiet of one of the lounges, we decided to write a brief, simple statement about the teaching of English, a "wholistic statement." (Betsy Hilbert)
>
> Marie, Betsy, and I just happened to catch each other's glance, and the glance said, "How much more of this theorizing and grandstanding can we stand? It's too hot for all this nonsense. We can't sit through a small group and survive this. Let's form our own group and get down on paper in very direct and simple terms what we think as professionals the goals should be." We got up together and formed our group. (Eleanor Tignor)

Here is part of that first report:

> Goals for the study of English in college should be defined "wholistically"; listening, speaking, reading, and writing should be integrated at all levels of English studies:

Literature is the honest and eloquent re-creation of experience through language.

Literature encompasses the body of linguistic texts of the world, including print and nonprint.

When we teach students to write, that which they write is itself a literary text and an introduction to the literary community. . . .

Whatever the text being studied, the teacher's communication of the joy of literature, of a sense of discovery and freedom in approaching the material, is crucial.

Betsy Hilbert continues:

When we brought our position paper back to the college section, I have a clear memory of general surprise that what we had said wasn't all that radical! People had apparently been expecting fists shaken in the air but discovered that we were saying some eminently rational things. A couple of people commented on how close our position was to theirs, and the college strand decided to endorse the statement.

Then something very interesting happened. Twenty people started to hack away at a position paper that three of us had written. They wanted one thing changed, then another. Somebody objected to the word *joy* as sounding too pollyanna; red pencillers began to play with our wording. Eleanor, Marie, and I took the statement back and rewrote it according to the others' suggestions, then went back to the college section again, where again they tried to revise it by consensus. The three of us met again after that to look at our poor, pitiful little statement, which by that time had had a couple of points flattened and the word *joy* excised, and a quiet thunder of NO! arose in our tiny committee. If it was radical and uncooperative to stand up for saying simply what we wanted to say, to defend our authorship and authority over the text, then radical we would have to be. We went back to our original statement, took it to the college section, and submitted it as a minority report.

A few additions to the story from my notes and memory: The rewriting took place later in the conference as a subcommittee of the college section was adapting the wholistic statement for the preamble to one of the main proposals. (Or maybe there was a second rewriting—to find a way to get some of the minority report into the preamble.) In any event, the rewriting subcommittee was trying to give it "cognitive leverage" rather than just "affective leverage" (subcommittee terms). But one of the wholistic members responds, "This document is no longer so honest and eloquent thanks to the group's help in revising." At one point someone remarks, "Your wheel doesn't touch the ground," and a member of the wholistic group replies, "We're irrelevant." Later that night I meditate on the page facing my notes for the day:

> Tricky case of wholistic group again. Illustrates dilemma. Felt other groups too pragmatic—resenting "instrumental" orientation of the majority and being made a subgroup. Joy, pleasure, honesty always being left out—or added as preamble or afterword. Except in the elementary group, which keeps it alive in the conference. We don't have language and concepts for talking about this business. Or at least the language we do have always makes people uncomfortable: 1960s, emotive, Dewey. It feels unintellectual—as we define intellect. Yet good teachers and scholars know that no one really persists long or does good work without feelings and affect. Still the educational community is scared of it because of the 1960s. Have to get over it and find language. Or dare to use the obvious language.

The wholistic group met intermittently throughout the college section sessions. Their statements sometimes talked about pleasure, joy, honesty, and integrity. They were referred to as "the Joy Group"—though I can't remember whether they used that title or it was only used by others. I sense that they tended to make people feel vaguely uncomfortable, at least for a while: partly because they tended to be seen as standing off and prickly or adversarial and partly, no doubt, because two were black, one Jewish, and all three women. Not that they were a noisy, angry political hit squad. They were more a quiet but stubborn, irritated, ro-mantic, splat squad. They didn't like the language and mode of func-tioning they saw in the college section. They may not have wanted to be a marginal or minority group at the start, but in the end they felt obliged to stick up for what others experienced as marginality. Not fashionable marginality, however. They talked about the importance of "marginal discourse" and they sometimes refused to talk or write "right"—in ac-ceptable "professional" discourses—but they tended to write very well (see Betsy Hilbert's piece in the epigraph above). Their "wholistic" title not only said, "We refuse to analyze"; it also said, "We refuse to use the right word." (People kept whispering to them, "But you've spelled it wrong.") They said, in effect, "This isn't a clever mistake like *différance* and other academic in-jokes, this is simply what you call *wrong*—only we want to spell it this way." It seems to me that they were evoking the anarchist tradition and insisting on practices and language they knew the majority of the college section could not endorse. Marie Buncombe, the third member, disagrees with my judgment here:

> We did not see anything startling or revolutionary about our state-ment. We started out by asking ourselves such questions as, What

made us become English majors in college? Why did we become English teachers? What is it about literature and language that turns us on? How can we best communicate this enthusiasm we have for the subject to our students? How can we get them to recognize the power and experience the joy of well-expressed language in both oral and written form? It was in our attempt to answer such questions as these that we came up with the statement and the name of the "wholistic group." (response to draft)

Perhaps the group sticks in my mind because I also often argue for what others call romantic, corny, old-fashioned—in some ways childish or naive, irrational and affective. Being in that position I am always struggling to say what I have to say in as "grown-up" and "rational" and "professional" a way as possible. What fascinated and attracted me was that (it seemed to me) they refused to do this—insisting on a marginality that often set people's teeth on edge. But I must quickly admit there is a danger that I am projecting my own marginality or "softness" on them. After all, it was one of the wholistic group, Marie Buncombe, who at one point (noted in my epigraph) insisted so fiercely as to scare me: "You can't say 'I teach students.' *Students* is only an indirect object. *What* do you teach students?" And the wholistic participants certainly didn't see themselves as just trying to shake their fists at the majority:

> Our action had nothing to do with marginality or adversarial anything; it had to do with participating in that conference to which we had each made a commitment and participating in a professional and responsible way. Having been a member of the coalition since its inception and having worked toward that conference for five years, I was not about to do anything at that stage but continue to be professional, although it was at that moment difficult. . . . It is my perception that, as a result of the wholistic subgroup's separating itself in part from the larger group (we continued to attend the college section sessions) and particularly because of Marie's insistence upon clear, uncluttered writing, the final draft of the college section document was much more readable than it would have been. . . . In the end, I had no problem endorsing the document. (Eleanor Tignor)

> The important thing—something you may want to emphasize more than you do in your draft, Peter—is that all three of us knew exactly what we were doing, and of course the members of the college section knew what we were doing too. Everyone concerned understood quite consciously that the three of us had chosen a gadfly position out of a conviction that a system that isn't challenged and tested doesn't produce much worth having. All three members of the [wholistic] committee were college professors who could wend our way around academic jargon with the best—all three of us, after

all, are published and respected in our fields—but we wanted to say something about the gifts of simplicity, something about authorship, and something very important about Joy.

Certainly, the college group saw us as cherishing differences (we did), and it seemed that many of the group *wanted* us to be the wild-eyed radicals they would have liked to discount. But the three of us had other things to do. We had something to say that was far more articulate than a shaken fist. (Betsy Hilbert)

The elementary section. Where the story of the wholistic group is complex and slippery, the story that I want to tell about the elementary section is simple (simple to summarize if not to enact). And where the wholistic group was often adversarial in stance, the elementary teachers were not. Though they were straightforward and learned, they nevertheless displayed the highest degree of play, metaphor, imagination, and connection of the cognitive to the affective. They were willing to risk the charge of corniness. They didn't fight or get annoyed, and they weren't particularly pushy. But they were an example, they were good colleagues, and they got through to people. If you were in the elementary section, you wouldn't have had to be adversarial to stick up for this dimension. (Betsy Hilbert, about the wholistic group: "Remember, we were in the college section, speaking *only* to the college section, and there were people in that group who really needed needling.")

I don't know why the members of the elementary section were so good in this respect, but perhaps it's because their job is to work with creatures who so naturally highlight play, metaphor, corniness, imagination, and the connection of the cognitive with the affective and indeed even with the body. Elementary teachers are in more immediate contact with the fact that students cannot learn well unless they have some fun and get some personal support. Because they work with such young students and because they are with them so many hours in a day, they can see a student right before their eyes lose the ability to learn—a young mind shut down for an hour or a day or a week or a month—when that student feels anxious or threatened. And perhaps for that reason we can somehow *hear* better about this dimension of the learning process from elementary teachers than from college teachers. From college teachers it sounds too much like Carl Rogers, and in the world of higher education no one seems to be able to do anything but snicker at the mention of his name.

Thus I was struck by this complex dynamic of the conference: to some outside observers the conference seemed soft, sentimental—too close to the 1960s, to Dewey, to the Dartmouth Conference. Yet we were professional, pragmatic, task-oriented, cognitive, analytic, intellectual, prudent—very "good." Between the low-key but powerful example of the elementary section and the subtle needling of the wholistic group, somehow the whole conference by the end of the three weeks had significantly internalized and integrated these "wholistic" values with more conventional intellectual and professional values. Even in the college section's final report (full version), there appears a remarkable sentence that surely wouldn't have been there except for those two occasions when a participant was willing to evoke a mini-explosion by saying that he teaches students rather than subjects: "Teachers do teach what they are as much as what they know."

But of course this dimension of the conference was cause for concern. We seemed to take turns asking the same question every few days: "How can we avoid terms like *child-centered*?" We were all sensitive to the pervasive assumption that anyone who uses such terms must be against content or discipline or standards. As Paul Armstrong remarks:

> There was indeed a lot of worry that we'd be perceived as simply a throwback to the 1960s. There's a lot about the 1960s I'd want to save (can I confess that reading Carl Rogers and *Summerhill* as a twenty-year-old had still-lasting effects on how and why I teach?), and so I don't quite know how to respond to the charge that we're throwbacks. Dewey found a lot of support and reluctance too. Coming out of the closet for Dewey happened a lot at the conference. (response to draft)

For me, then, the conference ended with an important subtheme—ended by sticking up for a side of the profession that often gets lost in high school and college English departments: play, storytelling, the personal, amateur, imaginative, affective, and informal. I'm not saying that the profession suffers from too much of what is professional, cognitive, analytic, and pragmatic; there can't be too much of those good things —only too little of the other side. Nothing need be lost, but something needs to be gained.

I've been using nice words so far to describe this dimension of the conference that I appreciate so much and that I think most other members appreciated too: "play," "imagination," etc. But it's important to me to bring forward the bad words to highlight the underside of what we appreciated: corny, naive, unprofessional, impolitic, personal, amateur, presence—and, worst of all, soft. We badly need an analysis of the role of two central concepts in our culture, soft and hard, and all they connote.[1] This hard-soft dichotomy with its valorization of hardness and its connection to gender serves as a pervasive piece of cultural infrastructure, a "metaphor we live by" (see Lakoff and Johnson), a lens through which much of our culture is filtered. To see this helps us understand why the profession might be nervous and might tend to avoid what is otherwise so attractive and noble (the imagination and all that). Living as I do in the college side of the profession—and often visiting high schools—I think I see a genuine fear and avoidance in our teaching and scholarship of what is felt as soft and oriented toward presence and the personal.

For example, the cultural hard-soft dichotomy helps explain what I discussed in the previous chapter: why our profession's behavior should be so much at variance with its public values. That is, it seems peculiar that we should organize our curricula as though writing stories were less important than writing analyses and indeed as though writing were less important than reading. But both of these tacit assumptions serve to fend off the danger of softness. Both privilege what seems hard or rigorous: analytic writing rather than imaginative writing and taking in what is authoritative and outside the self rather than seeing and expressing what one has to say.

This hard-soft substratum also helps explain the dynamics of the debate with Hirsch—and shows how it is typical of many debates in our culture. Essentially these debates are games of capture the flag. But there are two flags: one is emblazoned "hard, solid, intellectual, real, meat-and-potatoes" and the other "soft, feelings, no-standards, flaky, dessert." Whoever captures that first flag is always the winner by the very fact of relegating the other team to walk around carrying the second flag. In this game, or cultural grid, there are only two flags and everyone is obliged to take one or the other: choosing both or neither is not permitted. (This fuels the association with gender—where we also have only two possibilities and are not allowed to choose both or neither.)

I think I saw this game being played on two different levels at the conference. On one level we all played it with Hirsch, and, not surprisingly, he beat us to the winning flag and left us labeled soft. The crucial fact that there are only two flags helps explain why the losers often can't seem to stop sniping at the winner, as we (and indeed I too in this book) can't seem to stop talking about Hirsch: the nature of the game means that the losers are labeled with a flag that galls.

But I think I saw another version of this game being played within the college section itself. In this version the wholistic group caught the majority off balance and made a surprise dash for the flags—yet pointedly and even aggressively insisted on grabbing the wrong flag and embracing a taboo word, *joy*. Here, it seems to me, was a move that undermined and indeed violated the structure of the game itself. A refusal to feel gall at having the wrong flag, indeed an insistence on celebrating what is devalued.

And so I think I witnessed an interesting two-part pincer attack on this insidious hard-soft dichotomy. On the one side was this indirect, deconstructive move by the wholistic group. On the other side was the more direct example of the elementary group insisting on violating the cultural norm that says soft is worse and that you must be *either* soft or hard—not both. With these two influences, I think the conference became a place where we could break out of the capture-the-flag game or where we managed to do what is most needed, namely, to integrate what is hard and soft.

The conference participants' interest in teaching played an important role in helping us integrate the soft, personal, playful, storytelling dimension into our professional work: Yes, teaching is about content or scholarship (and coalition members insisted on the necessity of teaching whole texts rather than settling for summaries and information as Hirsch advised). But most participants agreed that teaching is also inherently about personal relationships. Most of us could hear rather than scorn or tune out what was a pervasive subtext from the elementary teachers: that we teach better and students learn better when that relationship is there. The interaction that goes on in teaching is not just between minds and information but also between persons, even in the university setting. If our job is partly teaching, not just research, then we have to care about relationships and persons.[2]

Thus, when participants used a term like *child-centered*, they meant something substantive, concrete, and pragmatic: that learning must connect inward personally and focus outward socially—as opposed to being only organized conceptually. This is what these teachers insist on, but it leads to a certain messiness. If you want students to connect personally with the material, you can't give exactly the same material or task to every student in exactly the same order. And if you want them to connect outward socially with each other about the material, there's got to be some noisiness and even chaos in class as students confer and share thoughts and texts with each other. This emphasis on the personal and social connects with one of the dominant premises at the conference: that students learn in different ways and often benefit from different kinds of teaching and learning activities.

I've gotten interested in looking for places in our culture where people manage to cut through the seemingly inescapable soft-hard dichotomy by doing justice to both (in effect prying it loose from its gender associations). Good parents do it in the same way that good teachers do: they manage to be on the one hand nurturer, ally, and supporter and yet on the other hand someone who is tough, who refuses, and who sets limits or standards. They are good at saying yes and good at saying no (see my "Embracing Contraries").

I've recently seen another example in a group of people who have managed to wrest a term like *learner-centered* away from the disparaging connotations of softness and the free-floating images of loose, privileged radicals of the 1960s. The assistant director of the AFL-CIO Human Resources Development Institute, quoting agreements worked out by the United Steel Workers of America with Bethlehem Steel and by the United Auto Workers with Ford Motors, notes that "worker-centered or learner-centered approaches are best for both the employer and the employee":

> In establishing this program, the United Steelworkers of America and Bethlehem are implementing a shared vision that workers must play a significant role in the design and development of their jobs, their training and education, and their working environment. . . . [W]orker growth and development are stunted when programs are mandated from above but flourish in an atmosphere of voluntary participation in self-designed and self-directed training and education. These shared beliefs shall be the guiding principles of the United Steel Workers–Bethlehem Career Development Program. (United Steelworkers of America)

> Guiding principles of the UAW–Ford Reading Academy, Eastern Michigan University:
>
> 1. Build on what adult learners already know.
> 2. Teachers and learners are equal partners in the learning process.
> 3. Make the learning environment relevant and authentic in the eyes of the learner. (Sarmiento 3)

I suspect that one of the next agenda items for our profession will be to find the best ways to talk about that dimension of experience and practice that academics gingerly step around as soft: how to find language for play, storytelling, the personal, feelings, presence, and the popular that makes these things not seem antithetical to intellectuality and professionalism. Though we made good progress on this front in our practice at the conference, I didn't see any progress in finding better language and thinking for it (in the way we did work out language and thinking that permitted people from all three levels to agree about the importance of looking at ways of making meaning). Our profession has probably gone as far as it needs to go in insisting on what is "hard": critical detachment, analysis, professionalism. Now I sense a slight movement toward play (deconstruction), the personal as political (some feminist work), and a proliferation of "professional" discourses. Yet "imagination" and "creativity" and "poetic" have been tainted with high culture and elitism and used to exclude what is essentially popular or "of the people." We need to figure out how to talk about this business.

In effect I'm talking about the problem of talking about and defining rationality and the intellect in such a way as to integrate the affective and the cognitive, the soft and the hard. Michael Polanyi (*Personal Knowledge*) serves, I think, as a helpful model of a powerful thinker who has made an enormously useful path in this direction with his exploration of how "intellectual passions" and "conviviality" are inherent in knowing. He writes:

> I have tried to demonstrate that into every act of knowing there enters a tacit and passionate contribution of the person knowing what is being known, and that this coefficient is no mere imperfection, but a necessary component of all knowledge. (312)
>
> Tacit assent and intellectual passions, the sharing of an idiom and of a cultural heritage, affiliation to a like-minded community: such are the impulses which shape our vision of the nature of things on which we rely for our mastery of things. No intelligence, however critical or original, can operate outside such a fiduciary framework. (266)

It's helpful that many people in the profession are now interested in the social construction of discourse and thinking. As they explore how cognition is deeply social, they are apt to discover, I think, how it is also deeply *sociable*—and that the first thing that usually happens when humans interact is personal and affective. (Of course, sometimes they are more interested in the social "dimension" as a theoretical concept than in actual bodies working together in a room.) We get students to do some of their work in small groups because we want to highlight how the making of meaning and even knowledge is social, but we cannot fail to notice that they usually don't work out anything that sticks unless they spend a certain amount of time socializing. (For corroboration, see Light's recent study showing that students who study together in groups tend to do better than those who study alone.) This insight should also help academics notice that cognition in the individual is entwined with affect—and indeed that affect *is* cognition.

Perhaps I'm wrong to worry about the neglect of the soft, imaginative, personal, and popular dimension in our practice as a profession. It is probably too powerful to be squashed; it will come back willy-nilly—the return of the repressed and all that. But the lesson I take away from the English Coalition Conference and the exemplary functioning of the wholistic group and the elementary section is that this crucial dimension comes back most fruitfully if invited and accepted and integrated rather than as a disruptive force that must be fought.

Finally, a warning and a request. I am clearly pursuing here my own agenda of trying to explore and undo the cultural devaluation of softness (at least in the academic community). This was *not* an agenda item for others at the conference—not overtly, anyway. Therefore, it would be unfair to let my own preoccupation serve as evidence that people at the conference were guilty of the sin of "softness" (that Dewey is guilty as charged). My position is that we're in trouble till we can stop seeing *soft* as a bad word, but my preoccupation shouldn't be used to tar these teachers and scholars whose defining characteristic was great professionalism.

NOTES

[1]Beneath everything else these concepts reverberate with gender: soft is what men tend to fear in themselves and insist on in women; hard is what men tend to insist on in themselves and fear in women. But I'm reluctant to choose gender as my governing principle or lens or metaphor here. That is, I could write this whole chapter in terms of the repression of the feminine and the need to recover it. It is a tempting analysis, but somehow at this stage I resist it. I want to complicate this matter (or is it simplifying?). I resist signing over softness only to the "feminine." For example, I'm a soft person, but I insist that I am so as a man. I'm not good at being hard in my relationships, my teaching, my scholarship, my writing (perhaps, some readers will say, even in my thinking); I'm very stubborn and persistent, and I often get my way, but I do it as often as not by softness and dithering. Although I see the value of the Jungian perspective, it feels unhelpful to call all that the feminine in me. Surely it's crucial to insist that my softness is wholly masculine. After all, it's perfectly characteristic of many men to be unclear and beat around the bush and of many women to be more direct and plain about what they mean. (Think about Chantecleer and Pertelote in Chaucer's Nun's Priest's Tale.) In short, the damage to our thinking caused by the hard-soft dichotomy may be exacerbated by the linkup to gender.

[2]From Betsy Hilbert (response to draft):

> One thing that constantly amazed and uplifted me at that conference was the overwhelming number of people there who were clearly, obviously, great teachers, teachers who valued and practiced their profession at an incredibly high level. A parent would cheer and praise Heaven to have a child in the classroom of any of those people, elementary through college—you'd sell your house and move into the right school district to get a kid in Carol Avery's class. One key, I think, was that almost everyone there at the conference really *liked* young people. Remember how the young folk who served our meals thought we were the greatest bunch they'd ever had at Wye?

The Death of
a School

Nancy Broz
(secondary school section)

*A*LLEN MIDDLE SCHOOL opened for grades 5–8 in the
fall of 1970. It wasn't quite finished yet. The cafeteria
and gym weren't open; we had to have brown-bag lunches in the resource
center and phys ed in the halls. There were still openings in the building,
so mice came in and ate our lunches as they sat on the shelves. But none
of this mattered. We were a group committed, enthusiastic, and eager
to begin life as a middle school.

Much preparation had come before—preparation for community and
staff. Those of us who eagerly embraced the concept of the middle school
(and that was most of the teachers) had had time not only to meet together
to plan but also to visit the Scarsdale, New York, middle school on which
ours was modeled. The program and population were similar, and both
communities could afford to provide an excellent facility with appropriate
support staff, equipment, and materials. We read books and journals
about what a middle school should be and were committed to providing
a model program.

The building was actually designed with four "houses" (or pods) constructed around the resource center and fine arts rooms, with the gym
and cafeteria attached at the back. Each house contained twelve classrooms, four small conference rooms connected to classrooms (with glass
windows for observation from the classrooms), two science prep rooms,
and a three-room office. In addition, there was an auditorium, a large
group instruction room, and several small conference rooms for the faculty. In other words, we had a flexible facility that would accommodate
a variety of instructional strategies and organizations.

Teachers of math, science, social studies, and language arts were assigned to interdisciplinary teams, and each team of four teachers was assigned a hundred students for a 4½-hour block of time daily. There were no "master schedules," no bells, no defined class periods. Instead, there were four professionals who were given the responsibility for planning, structuring, and monitoring the learning of a hundred students. This team concept guaranteed that the students had a sense of belonging to a group; the teachers, who had 1½ hours of planning time together each day, actually planned each day's schedule to suit the needs of each subject at that time. They knew the students well, met collectively with the parents as they came in for conferences, and often met as a group with a child.

The curriculum itself was developed and continually changed by the team teachers who wrote interdisciplinary units. A central theme or question (Power, Emerging Nations, Science Fiction, Brotherhood, Fact or Fiction) served as the foundation for the units, and the skills of each discipline were built into them. As teachers developed these units (often working nights and weekends at one another's homes without complaining!), a sense of cooperation and collegiality developed, and as teams continued to work together, there was a strong bond and sense of pride between teachers.

Flexibility was the key. On Monday, the language arts teacher may have wanted to show a film, so instead of showing it four times to four classes, it could be scheduled for a single large group viewing with pre- and postviewing activities shared by all four teachers. This then meant that one of the other disciplines could have longer classes or all could. If the science teacher wanted double lab periods, they could be built in. Tests in math could be given at once by all four teachers. There was time for sustained silent reading and writing every day. We could group, regroup, and subgroup for different purposes and often had students in both heterogeneous and homogeneous groups in a single day. Teachers cotaught, learned as they observed one another teach, and learned respect for one another's skills in a setting that is not possible in a typical junior or senior high school, where teachers often never see another teacher teaching.

There was an environment of enthusiasm, sharing, and ownership in the middle school. There was nothing laissez-faire about it; we planned a detailed schedule for the week each Friday, but by midweek we evaluated our progress and made changes if needed. We were able to have frequent guest speakers, field trips, and even our own team concert series because we could schedule it. Most units lasted three to four weeks, and sometimes we would build in a one- or two-week "break" between units for catching up or prepping for a standardized test. At least once a year we planned a unit that would totally eliminate subject divisions, with each teacher doing the same things. The science-fiction unit of my own team was an example. Students spent one intensive week of building four ecosystems. In all classes they read, discussed, researched, planned, and built. The four teachers were simply advisers and resources. Students planned the schedules, set the rules, and determined the evaluative criteria. By the end of the week, the four classrooms had been transformed into four independent habitats for survival.

However, by 1980 the community climate had changed. Back-to-basics had hit Moorestown, and several disgruntled teachers who chose not to work so hard and who wanted the privacy and inflexibility of a fixed, no-team schedule had been making their unhappiness known to school-board members. The principal was promoted from the middle school to central administration, and the death knell was sounded. The interim principal and the new superintendent were very unhappy because they did not understand the principles on which the school was organized. The philosophy sounded too student-oriented, and, worst of all, they could not understand the many schedules turned in on Friday by the twelve teams. Surely, they decided, learning could not be going on in such an unstructured environment. Student scores would definitely rise if we returned to what we had been—a little high school.

And so we did. We are now departmentalized and have eight periods a day; students move around the school for their classes; teachers have little time to know students and no common planning time with other teachers to discuss students, curriculum, parents, or professionalism. Teachers feel no sense of ownership or pride in their program and resent the supervision and structure that are both inflexible and depersonalized. Permanent walls have been erected in the double classrooms, small group rooms have become storage closets, and homogeneous grouping exists in at least half of the school schedule. Instead of having a supportive group of four teachers who work together, who monitor the student's progress together and alert one another to problems and concerns about individual students and brainstorm solutions, the child has four teachers (actually eight, counting the fine and applied arts) who may not even see one another for weeks at a time (there are three lunch periods too).

In other words, all those characteristics that can create a personalized, supportive environment for children and an enthusiastic ownership for teachers have been eliminated. Fifth graders are now treated like high school seniors. We have made it possible for a child to be a "cipher" in the school—to be unknown and unnoticed, a nonperson. That is how many of the teachers who taught in the "real" middle school feel.

We have gone from . . .	*to . . .*
a sense of community	a sense of competition
personalization	depersonalization
flexibility	inflexibility
integrated curriculum	fragmented curriculum
student-centered	subject-centered
teacher involvement	teacher passivity
learning-centered	grade-centered
collegiality	isolation

Susan

Angela Dorenkamp
(college section)

S HE DIDN'T LOOK older than the traditional college student, but I knew that she was. She had the kind of intensity that characterizes students who are paying their own way, though I discovered later that she wasn't, that she was, in fact, the daughter of a well-known physician in the community and that she had dropped out and tuned out for several years. She never talked about it, except obliquely.

From the first day in English Composition, I sensed her divided self: part of her was seduced by learning, part of her believed that she knew more than I could help her learn. But even the part that wanted to know, the part that stayed, was cynical. She liked to ask the "challenging" question and make the patronizing comment, couched, if she could, in the language of Akademic Kool:

"It appears that the thinking in this piece needs to be reexamined in the light of new insights into the psychology of dependency."

When the other members of the class said, in effect, "Whaaaat?" she seemed surprised. Everyone, she implied, knew that. Or ought to. She almost never missed class.

Each student in class was keeping a journal of observations, the kind others could read "for profit." When Susan came in for her first writing conference, she brought her journal for me to look at. I had looked forward to reading it because she had been writing some interesting things in class, although her voice was still more Akademic Kool than it was Susan. I was surprised, then, to find that her journal contained writing that was not only sporadic but empty. The journal had not been a useful activity for her.

We talked about it, and she "put down" the idea of keeping the journal.

"I think we did this assignment in the third or fourth grade." Kool. But by this time, I knew that statements like that were self-defense, not arrogance. I knew, too, that I wanted more than anything to see this student experience the sharp pleasure of insight. If I asked her to keep up her entries, to be patient with herself and the process, she might be even more determined to prove the task worthless.

I decided to set her free and suggested that she stop writing in her journal. Because I thought she would interpret this as a victory, I was unprepared for the passion of her response. She sat up in one movement, then slid to the edge of her chair. She wanted to be sure she had understood me, so I repeated my suggestion, and I was just a little anxious when she enunciated slowly in a sandpaper voice: "YOU . . . SHOULD . . . MAKE . . . ME . . . DO . . . IT!"

Fumbling for words, I tried to explain that we had been making ourselves more aware of how we wrote, what helped us and what got in our way. At this time, the journal was getting in her way, and there was no stone tablet anywhere that said, Thou must keep a journal in order to be a writer.

I didn't think I had done a good job of it. Susan had not given me to understand that she approved or even understood, and I felt the rest of the semester that somehow she held against me what she perceived as my weakness. I never knew whether she ever discovered the joys of her own mind or her own voice. I thought long and hard about the moment in the conference and even accumulated an array of imagined scenarios that would have been the beginning of self-confidence for her rather than the replication of betrayal. But I still cataloged Susan under "failure."

A couple of years later, I happened to be in the Galleria, a shopping center in Worcester, when a young woman came scurrying toward me, calling my name: "Dr. Dorenkamp! Dr. Dorenkamp!" It was Susan. It was as if we were back in that messy office on that fall day. She would be stunned if she knew I had thought so much about her, I thought.

Well, maybe she wouldn't. After the required amenities, the first thing she said to me was: "You know what? I'm keeping a journal—and I love it."

Sometimes—but only sometimes—our failures may not be failures.

Kera

Craig Bowman
(secondary school section)

I DIDN'T THINK I'd ever get through to Kera. She suffered from severe emotional problems. For the first year and a half of her tenure in my class, we fought—and fought and fought.

At least I had a safe, secure job with a large school district that would give me anonymity. And tenure.

Then one day, she started calling me "mama." After that, it was never the same. I was part of the family she never had. I never had it either.

But as a result of that "slip of the tongue," I discovered a teacher named Craig Bowman. And together, we discovered a beauty she didn't think she had.

12 | *Concluding Word: About Teachers and Conditions for Teaching*

*A*n angry moment toward the end of the conference: "What do they mean? All those people in business making one and two hundred thousand dollars a year who criticize education—what nerve! They can't sell cars or computers or TVs abroad to save their ass. They try to hide their incompetence by knocking us, when we produce something that actually sells abroad. Foreign students come to our colleges and universities in droves—and some to our schools. Education is probably the only United States industry that is competitive in a global market" (Betsy Hilbert).

IN THE END the main thing that strikes me about the conference—and I hope it strikes readers too—is that it was a gathering of excellent teachers. By excellent I don't mean better than anyone else—but rather teachers who are representative of what our profession produces when people are simply smart and they care and they work hard at it long enough to become professional. What I love about Tracy Kidder's book about a year in the life of a fifth-grade classroom (*Among Schoolchildren*) is that he shows how Chris Zajac is good, the kind of teacher you would entrust your child to—but her goodness depends not on brilliance or saintliness but on intelligence and caring and remaining open to new learning.

I haven't talked much in my chapters about teaching itself or about all the time spent in sessions and over meals and during walks and late-night talks in discussions about the concrete vicissitudes of the classroom. It's my hope that when a reader reads all the stories, snapshots, and reflections I've interleaved between my chapters, the effect will bring out a tacit subtheme in my chapters: that our thinking about professional and scholarly and theoretical matters is improved when the participants are committed teachers—and particularly teachers from all levels.

The final thought I am left with, then, is that we need to try to persuade society to value its teachers more and treat them better. There is lots of reporting about bad teaching; the media like disaster stories. "Ah ha," people say on discovering that students going into teaching have lower grades than those going into many other fields. Is it any surprise, given the poor conditions and lack of respect for teachers? The question is not whether there is bad teaching: how could there not be lots of it, given the conditions? The question is, What can we do to get rid of terrible teaching? And more important, How can we make most teaching better?

Shirley Brice Heath rightly insisted that we cannot directly change teachers—change their behavior or change their philosophy. All the mania for goals and testing is really an attempt to change teachers' behavior without consulting or involving them; by treating them less professionally rather than more professionally. No wonder it backfires. Has all the testing made our schools better? But we can, Heath pointed out, *bring about change in teachers* by changing the conditions in which they work.

The Conditions for Teaching

The working conditions for most K–12 English teachers and college teachers of writing seem to have been designed to stamp out caring, commitment, and a professional stance—to produce resentment, burnout, cynicism, and, finally, a retreat into doing just the minimum needed to survive. Teachers each month see many of their best colleagues leave teaching or retire early, and we're not getting the replacements we need. In this section I am drawing on what I as a college teacher learned at the conference about the lives of our colleagues in the schools. For us in the colleges, this was one of the powerful experiences of the conference.

Teachers in the schools (and most writing teachers in universities) are seldom treated as professionals. They often have no say in the curriculum they must teach or in the structure and functioning of the school. They are often controlled by administrators who are not teachers and have no sense of teaching. They seldom get to evaluate the administrators who evaluate them. Teachers are often not represented on school boards or boards of trustees. It's as though the goal were to make teachers obey guidelines and follow orders rather than to take initiative and become excited and invested.

Most elementary and secondary teachers who want to go to professional conferences or who hold office in local, state, or national professional organizations find it hard or impossible to get time or financial support to take part in these activities. It is common that teachers can't even take a semester or a year's leave of absence *without pay* without losing their jobs. Because of the way budgets work, many competent and experienced teachers do not have security of employment: year after year they are laid off in the spring and then rehired at the last moment in the fall—and sometimes not rehired. Many teachers do not get a salary commensurate with their professional standing. Teachers who manage to stay invested and excited about their teaching often have to fight a bureaucracy of rules and procedures (and sometimes must buy important supplies out of their own pockets) to do something interesting and innovative that is not part of the routine. Many of our best teachers teach in private schools (often despite much lower salaries) because they are treated there with more respect as professionals.

Perhaps the most important factor for us in our discipline is this: most English teachers in junior and senior high schools have five or more classes a day and 125 to 150 students. We say we want them to assign lots of writing, but every time they assign a paper they get back 125 to 150 of them to read and comment on. We can't ask teachers to provide the kind of one-to-one help that all students need occasionally—to have conferences and to get to know students and think about them as individuals—unless we cut back that load. Because very young children need so much more individual attention, early elementary teachers need to cut back their loads of twenty-five and thirty students to twenty. At a recent meeting of the International Society for the Study of Behavioral Development, Harold Stevenson reported on a comparative study of United States and Asian schools, and a crude fact turned up: Asian teachers of small children "are allowed more time for preparation and individual attention. In Beijing, elementary school teachers teach no more than three hours per day" (Maurer).

On top of all this are a host of other conditions that are spirit-breaking—both nonprofessional and demeaning. Most teachers don't have a place or time in which to meet students or parents in conferences without other students listening in or a time or place to meet with other teachers to plan or discuss particular students—or just to be alone and plan their teaching and read student work. Most teachers don't get a reasonable period in which to stop teaching and eat lunch: often it's only twenty or thirty minutes, during which they also have supervisory duties. Most teachers don't have access to a telephone in a department office or classroom or some other arrangement to ensure immediate and private contact with the out-of-school world. We can't ask for professional behavior if we don't treat people as professionals.

> At the moment, the higher education enterprise in this country is well thought of the world over. Other countries pay to send their best and brightest to American colleges and universities to study and return home to increase the human intellectual capital in those coun-

tries. In many cases those same countries consider the secondary and elementary systems in this country sub-standard compared to their own. What an irony. One of them, a gentleman from Britain, said to me, "Why don't you run elementary and secondary schools the way you run your colleges and universities, giving them a certain amount of control over how they conduct their work?" In fact, we're moving in the opposite direction. (Darling-Hammond 3)

A significant improvement in the conditions for teaching in the schools could occur without new money: simply treating teachers like professionals and giving them more autonomy and control over how they conduct their work. Of course, you can't really treat people like professionals unless you improve material conditions in ways that cost money (for example, cutting the number of students that English teachers teach so that they can actually teach writing). And so it should come as no surprise that the difference between the treatment of school and college teachers is a matter not just of professionalism but of money. It turns out that the United States spends less on elementary and secondary education than almost any other industrial nation does. This is the finding of a recent report ("Shortchanging Education") compiled by the Economic Policy Institute, a nonpartisan research organization:

> The report acknowledged that the United States "spends comparatively more than other countries on higher education." . . . . But when spending on higher education is removed from comparative data, the report said that "the relative position of U.S. spending falls from a three-way tie for second highest in spending to close to the bottom of the group of 16 industrial nations." ("U.S. Is Said")

I worry about a generational competition in this country for scarce goods where children come out on the losing end. The so-called baby-boom population cohort is the largest one in our history. When it was younger, it didn't trust people over thirty; now that it is over thirty, it doesn't seem eager to care about the welfare of children. Children cannot vote, and older citizens show signs of being willing to abandon the interest of children.

Conditions for teaching in high schools. I was surprised, as I think many in the college section were, to discover that the conditions for teaching high school (and the upper junior high grades) seem to be significantly worse than for teaching in the earlier grades. (Did the elementary teachers already know this?)

> High school teachers tend to have the largest student load—often as many as five classes of thirty students. (Teachers of the early grades have the same twenty-five to thirty-five students all day. Late ele-

mentary and early junior high teachers may have more students but often in a team setting where a small group of other teachers all keep track of, say, eighty students.) High school teachers are usually more isolated in their relations with the larger student body.

High school teachers have students who are bigger, harder to handle, more disgruntled about involuntary attendance at school—and at an age where they are more disposed to fight authority. In fact, high school teachers are often subject to significant physical intimidation and violence. Their students use drugs and alcohol. Because they have so many students and such a short time with them, it's hard to develop the personal relationships needed to try to overcome these difficulties. "The higher up in the middle and high school grades one teaches, the more conscious attention should be paid to learning environment. Elementary children actually bring their own climate to school—enthusiasm, motivation, success orientation— whereas secondary students become less interested, more passive, more distant. When we look at most typical secondary schools, we find . . . unmotivated students who are uninvolved, surviving school by doing the minimum" (Nancy Broz, position paper).

High school teachers have much less opportunity to control their environment and to experiment than elementary and college teachers do. Their curriculum is much more likely to be set for them because of pressures from testing and college preparation. As Theodore Sizer points out, there have been and still are many more structural experiments and variations in higher education than in high schools. Elementary teachers, spending all day with their classes, can much more easily experiment with new and different structures. High schools have changed hardly at all over the years and tend to conform to a monolithic model.

Conditions for teaching in colleges and universities, though modest by most middle-class or professional standards, are good when you compare them to the conditions for school teachers. But there is one dismal exception: most teachers of writing in higher education are either part-time or non-tenure-track instructors, graduate students, or faculty members with unreasonable loads. That is, most full-time teachers of writing in two-year colleges teach five or more courses per semester or term. Most part-time and non-tenure-track instructors are paid abysmally (often less than $1,000 a course) and have no fringe benefits, no say in curricular or departmental affairs, no office of their own for conferences (and some not even an office shared with only two or three others). Many graduate instructors have to teach more than one section of writing in a term (while trying to keep up full-time graduate study) and get poor pay, little or no office space for conferences, and no health insurance or other fringe benefits. Worst of all, they have no incentive to care about their teaching—the only incentive being to do their graduate studies. (See the "Wyoming Conference Resolution" about conditions for teachers of writing, which was affirmed by the Coalition Conference and reprinted in the report [Lloyd-Jones and Lunsford 49].)

We discussed the conditions for teaching over a number of mixed-level sessions. The first and most powerful response was to talk about all the difficult and demeaning conditions that teachers must try to work in. There was a certain amount of outrage when the full commonality of the nationwide picture emerged. But as the groups thought about presenting this to the world, people decided to write it up as a set called "Rights and Responsibilities of Students and Teachers" (Lloyd-Jones and Lunsford 45–49). That is, they wanted to make it clear that they weren't just saying, "Treat us better, damn it!" but were saying, rather, "We acknowledge we have these responsibilities too" and "We emphasize that students also have certain important rights."

Some Good Signs

In the last couple of years there have also been some heartening developments. I'm referring to some of the recent moves toward restructuring schools in various parts of the country. Budget problems can make people hopeless and cynical, so it's important to point out that it needn't take any more money to bring teachers into shared decision making with administrators and school boards so as to increase their investment and responsibility for how schools are structured and run. It needn't take any more money to change how time is broken up or how students are grouped or to make other structural changes. Surprisingly enough, it needn't even take more money to reduce radically the number of students that teachers must teach—when schools take the simple restructuring step of giving students more time with fewer teachers. That is, one can give students only three or four teachers for one term and then three or four different teachers for another term—instead of six or eight teachers for both terms. Obviously this is not the same as providing as many teachers as we should, but even if we had twice as many teachers, it would probably be better to use this new structure with smaller classes than stick with the old model of limited contact. This restructuring provides more time for individual attention and mentoring and useful relationships with fewer teachers in a term—instead of giving them more teachers per term in conditions where there is no time for good work together. This approach also helps with discipline problems and with writing. And if teachers with longer time units with students therefore take on subjects outside their discipline, that fosters interdisciplinary integration and the helpful learning climate that results from the teacher's taking on some of the stance of a learner rather than just of an expert. Why must we keep a structure that minimizes the chances for close personal supervision of students by teachers?

Theodore Sizer heads a growing organization, the Coalition of Essential Schools, that coordinates promising work with many high schools around the country. They stress working on fewer subjects, using fewer teachers at any one time, but with more time and attention devoted to essentials and more time with a given teacher.

The 1989 study about middle schools by the Carnegie Council on Adolescent Development recommends giving teachers control over curriculum and holding them responsible for student achievement and creating small school units to replace large impersonal schools. Here is a passage from *Proposals and Plans for Restructured Schools*, a collection of materials and case studies assembled by the American Federation of Teachers (an organization that has helped foster the restructuring process and the negotiating of new contracts involving much greater shared decision making between teachers and administrators):

> Each of the plans collected here shares a similar approach to making fundamental change. First, the plans exhibit an orientation that might be labeled "ecological." That is, they all recognize the interdependence of such elements as scheduling, curriculum, and decision-making, to name only three. . . . Negatively expressed, the plans are not trying to solve problems or improve their schools through the addition of a program, a position, or superimposed process. . . . [M]eaningful change must be holistic and systematic.
>
> Second, the plans propose alternative forms of organization. Do all classes have to be 43 minutes in length, all students grouped in separate "grades," all learning in "school" buildings? Accordingly, some plans alter the time sequences of instruction, others the space in which learning takes place. . . .
>
> Third and most importantly, these plans emanate from a shared vision of student learning, one which differs from the view of learning underlying traditional school structure . . . : The school as a center of inquiry in which active learning is promoted (for student and teacher alike) and in which attention is paid to the accepted notion that students learn in different ways and at different rates. (Center for Restructuring Educational Issues 1)

One example given in the collection involves a handful of teachers getting together and persuading parents, administrators, and the school board to let them start a school within a school based on the principles advanced by people like Howard Gardner that there are multiple forms of intelligence, not just one. Here is some comment about a restructured school in New York City:

> Success is clearly based on small schools, small classes, committed teachers and administrators, and supportive parents. "The schools grew out of teacher-generated ideas and teacher-generated dreams," said deputy district superintendent John Falco. "You have to empower teachers, give them the right to design instruction," he said. "Sometimes teachers work a nine-hour day and weekends. But there have been no complaints and no one has filed a union grievance," he added. (Cohen)

The message that I hope comes across loudest from the English Coalition Conference is that teaching can be an exciting and fulfilling way to spend a life and that teachers can be effective. This might sound like a facile thought to end a book on, unless we look at it against the backdrop of the realities of the profession: teachers are weary and depressed; the profession used to be looked on with great respect, but now it no longer is; people used to be proud to be schoolteachers, but now few are; teachers are looking for ways to get out, and few students are seeking to enter.

The teachers at the conference were passionate—"soft" in a way but hard too. The main thing that strikes one is how much they invest themselves in caring that students learn. Thus they are demanding, insistent; they push students—but they do so in inventive, flexible ways; they individualize; they get a sense of what students need. They've figured out ways to be playful yet pushy. It's encouraging to me that because they have managed to pull this off without any loss of professionalism, they have earned respect in their profession and in their professional organizations and are thus important people in their professional communities: they have made changes and are having an effect.

So I came away from the Coalition Conference encouraged. If the public and the government are willing to support teachers and the schools, they will find a foundation of committed, caring professionals; interesting thinking about the discipline; and exciting models of ways to teach.

Vince

Bob Denham

(secondary school section)

*T*HE DAY AFTER the first meeting of the senior seminar, Vince Singleton, a thin, bearded, twenty-eight-year-old, sauntered self-consciously into my office to discuss his project for the term. I had laid down only one requirement—that the students were to select a topic that deeply interested them. Vince fidgeted. His soft eyes stared at the floor. His first love, he said, was science fiction, but he thought that sci-fi was not a proper subject for his project, not really academic, not highly serious enough for a college course.

Vince, I discovered as we talked, had had little privilege. He was a veteran, married, the father of two young girls. He and his wife worked at a restaurant to support their family and pay his tuition, and he drove sixty miles each day to get back and forth to school. By his account, he had been raised by a hateful grandmother. To escape from her hounding presence, he'd turned to reading comic books. School provided no interest or challenge, though it was, he said, a respite from his grandmother's nagging. To escape from the boredom of his junior high, he'd read his comics in class, hiding them behind an open history or geography book. Comics—and later adventure stories—had hooked Vince into the world of pure romance. Aware of what it took to beat the system, Vince had squeaked through school, received his diploma, and, as one more way to escape from a dreary home life, enlisted in the army. Vince told me his story in his own Appalachian dialect, and I found myself wincing when he'd say "I seen" and "We done."

I asked what science fiction he'd read. "Arthur Clarke, Frank Herbert, Robert Silverberg, Ursula LeGuin." And then he ticked off a long list of writers I didn't know. He was not trying to impress. I'd asked a question about science fiction, and he assumed I knew enough about the subject to recognize his heroes—the authors in that large imaginative world into which he'd moved after leaving comics and macho adventures. He told me about the books he'd read since 1967, about the long reading list he'd compiled, about the extraordinary library he'd been able to amass from garage sales and sci-fi conventions (more than four thousand books altogether), about his correspondence with Robert Silverberg, and about the sci-fi criticism he'd read ("most of it not very good"). He told me about discovering a water-stained copy of *Moby Dick* in a box of used books at a yard sale (he'd never heard of Melville), about how he couldn't put the book down and how he'd read it over and over in the meantime.

Before coming to Emory and Henry, Vince had enrolled in a community college, where in his English survey course he'd discovered a whole new body of literature as compelling as his sci-fi stories. He was puzzled by the differences between the two kinds of writing, yet he felt that there was some common element in the sci-fi stories and the canonical texts that lay behind his appetite for narrative. This, it became clear as we talked, would be an issue that he might spend some time exploring. It was a question he wanted to ask, even though I nudged him a bit to get it to the surface. I suppose I was trying to get him to see that those things he felt deeply about were legitimate areas of inquiry and that he need not repress his love for sci-fi. And Vince did feel deeply about stories. He couldn't understand why other English majors he ran into would grumble about having to read their assignments in Sophocles and Faulkner. These things, he said, were dessert: he couldn't wait until he'd finished his homework in accounting so that he could enter the worlds of Oedipus and Ike McCaslin.

Vince completed his project, which I recommended for "honors." His paper came directly from his own passionate encounter with books. His voice was honest, clear, eloquent. He'd found a topic he wanted to explore. Although his project began with direct experience, he was able to step back disinterestedly from that experience and to make his own meaning out of it. What Vince produced, in short, was the best piece of student writing I'd come upon in eighteen years of teaching.

Mother Goose's Coalition Rhymes

*T*his poem was presented as a giant kindergarten or first-grade reading book. It was at least five feet square, with lovely colored illustrations. The authors read it to the assembled participants on the last day or so, carefully turning the pages and showing us the pictures as if we were seated in a classroom reading circle.

Hey diddle diddle
The kid's in the middle,
Change is now the norm.
And Shirley has said
We should give our support
To language and learning
In new form.

Twinkle, Twinkle, Elementary Strand
We do know we are grand.
Up above in the room so high,
We listened to Pontificating
With a sigh.

Jerry, Jerry, quite contrary
How does your conflict grow?
With metacourse and teacher swap
And theorists all in a row.

Old king Scholes was a merry old soul,
And a merry old soul was he.
No, Despot King was not his goal—
The *best* he wished to be!

Old Mother Hubbard went to the cupboard
To get her poor kid a book.
But when she got there
The cupboard was bare
Except for a basal.
"Look! Look!"

Cultural literacy sat on a wall.
Cultural literacy had a great fall.
All Bennett's horses
And all Bennett's men
Couldn't put the list together again.

There was a young teacher
She *was* fair and true.
She had so many children
She didn't know what to do.

She gave them some basals
Without any meat,
And too many worksheets
Which led to defeat.

AND THAT WAS THAT!

A | *Participants at the Conference*

*A*LL THE PARTICIPANTS were chosen as leaders by the elected officers of one or more of the sponsors, but the organizations tried to sample the variety of a large field. The coalition decided that elementary and secondary school perspectives had to be represented substantially by teachers active in those schools. They also sought from within their large memberships (some 100,000 teachers) people known for work in linguistics, media, speech communication, literary theory, writing, traditional literary criticism, popular culture, textbook and tradebook writing, minority literatures, education, cognitive theory, and other subfields of interest. Finally, they tried to represent social groups of the country—racial, ethnic, geographic, economic—as well as patterns of public and private schooling at all levels. As the conference began, probably not more than a half dozen people, including the conference planners, had even met personally as many as half of the participants, and most people knew only a very few others. The alphabetical list of participants is included below. Each name is identified according to whether the person sat with the elementary (E), secondary (S), or college (C) section.

Name and Strand	*Affiliations*
Gwendolyn Alexander (S)	Calvin Coolidge High School, Washington, DC (NCTE)
Bruce C. Appleby (C)	Southern Illinois University (CEE)
Paul B. Armstrong (C)	University of Oregon (MLA)
Carol Avery (E)	Nathan C. Schaeffer Elementary School, Lancaster, PA (NCTE)

Rosalinda Barrera (E)   New Mexico State University, Las Cruces (NCTE)

Rudine Sims Bishop (E)   Ohio State University (NCTE)

Wayne Booth (S)   University of Chicago (MLA)

John G. Bordie (C)   University of Texas, Austin (MLA)

Craig Bowman (S)   Alameda Junior High School, Lakewood, CO (NCTE)

Nancy Broz (S)   William H. Allen III Middle School, Moorestown, NJ (NCTE)

Marie Buncombe (C)   Brooklyn College (CLA)

Frederick R. Burton (E)   Barrington Elementary School, Columbus, OH (NCTE)

Donna Carrara (E)   Montclair Kimberly Academy, Montclair, NJ (NCTE)

Candy Carter (S)   Tahoe Truckee High School, Truckee, CA (NCTE)

Jane Christensen (S)   Deputy Executive Director (NCTE)

Katherine Cummings (C)   University of Washington (MLA)

Robert Denham (S)   Former Director (ADE)

Angela G. Dorenkamp (C)   Assumption College (CEA)

Richard Dunn (C)   University of Washington (MLA)

Carole Edmonds (C)   Kellogg Community College (ADE)

Peter Elbow (C)   University of Massachusetts, Amherst (MLA)

Janet Emig (S)   Rutgers University (NCTE)

Phyllis Franklin (C)   Executive Director (MLA)

Alice Gasque (C)   University of South Dakota (ADE)

Jeffrey Golub (S)   Shorecrest High School, Seattle, WA (NCTE)

Michael Halloran (C)   Rensselaer Polytechnic Institute (CCCC)

Charles Harris (C)   Illinois State University (ADE)

Joan Hartman (C)   College of Staten Island (ADE)

Betsy S. Hilbert (C)   Miami Dade Community College

Janie Hydrick (E)   MacArthur Elementary School, Mesa, AZ (NCTE)

Julie M. Jensen (E)   University of Texas, Austin (NCTE)

Larry Johannessen (S)   Lyons Township High School, LaGrange, IL (NCTE)

Tom Jones (S)	Wyoming Valley West High School, Plymouth, PA (CSSEDC)
John Joyce (C)	Nazareth College of Rochester (CEA)
Mary M. Kitagawa (E)	Richey Elementary School, Tucson, AZ (NCTE)
Mary Krogness (E)	Shaker Heights Elementary School, Shaker Heights, OH (NCTE)
Richard Lloyd-Jones (S)	University of Iowa (NCTE)
Joe Lostracco (C)	Austin Community College (NCTE)
Andrea Lunsford (C)	Ohio State University (MLA)
John C. Maxwell (E)	Former Executive Director (NCTE)
Kathleen A. McCormick (C)	Carnegie Mellon University (MLA)
Nancy McHugh (S)	Grant High School, Van Nuys, CA (NCTE)
Nellie McKay (C)	University of Wisconsin (MLA)
Vera E. Milz (E)	Way Elementary School, Bloomfield Hills, MI (NCTE)
Diane T. Orchard (E)	Lapeer Community Schools, Lapeer, MI (NCTE)
Jane E. Peterson (C)	Richland Community College (CCCC)
Rosentene B. Purnell (C)	California State University (CCCC)
Robert Scholes (C)	Brown University (MLA)
Faith Schullstrom (E)	Guilderland Central School District, Guilderland, NY (CEE)
George B. Shea (S)	Belleville West High School, Belleville, IL (NCTE)
Susan Stires (E)	Boothbay Region Junior High School, Boothbay Harbor, ME (NCTE)
Peggy Swoger (S)	Mountain Brook Junior High School, Birmingham, AL (NCTE)
William Teale (E)	University of Texas, San Antonio (NCTE)
Eleanor Q. Tignor (C)	LaGuardia Community College (CLA)
Joseph I. Tsujimoto (S)	Punahou School, Honolulu, HI (NCTE)

Gregory L. Ulmer (C)	University of Florida (MLA)
Gary F. Waller (C)	Carnegie Mellon University (MLA)
Jerry W. Ward, Jr. (C)	Tougaloo College (MLA)
Brooke Workman (S)	West High School, Iowa City, IA (NCTE)

Three Teachers

Nancy McHugh

(secondary school section)

MISS PETRIE SMILES and indicates the pile of photocopied short stories on the small table. Each student
who enters the class takes one, sits down to read, and then begins to
write questions. A student new to the class is coached in the process by
a "helper," who is self-appointed. While the students are thus occupied
collectively yet individually, Miss Petrie is quietly calling up students to
her desk singly, in pairs, in triads, depending on the relatedness of the
topics that they have chosen and refined during the preceding two days.
Each student has asked a series of questions about his or her topic. The
first meeting with Miss Petrie is merely to share topics and questions;
students listen to each other and to Miss Petrie. The students return to
their seats after the interview and finish their story questions. Then they
decide on a mode of answering one question that they wish to deal with.
This is the second unit of the year (second series of self-engendered
topics). The next total class activity will be based on the student-
engendered questions on the story and will help the class members to
recall the questioning process, the kinds of questions asked, the varieties
of responses, and the kinds of modes possible for further response. This
discussion will also orient the new student. Options for further response
include film, song, art, and various kinds of writing, among others.

Mr. Thompson has put a poem, a short one, on the overhead projector.
Students enter the class and cluster in circles to read the poem, perhaps
reading it aloud for each other. Mr. Thompson reads the poem aloud for
the whole class. Students write responses in their journals. Students are
invited to share their responses with others in their clusters or anywhere
in the room. Mr. Thompson identifies the poem as one written by a
student the previous year and asks whether that fact would change any
of their responses and why or why not? A lively general discussion follows.
Once again students return to their journals and pose questions engendered by the poem experience (not just the poem itself). Then they write
on their inquiry cards (three-by-five lined cards) ideas engendered by the

experience that they wish to pursue ("research") during the rest of the two-hour time block. Mr. Thompson signs the cards, which constitute passes for students to use if they wish to leave to go to the media center, the library, study carrels, or the VIP center (staffed by parents, volunteers, and occasionally community persons) where students can contact "outside experts" in person or by phone. Students may want to try a poem in response, write their own versions, find other poems on the same subject, locate a poet who writes in this style or on this topic, question others about their responses to the poem, find out more about the poet, or explore other options. Mr. Thompson remains in the room to talk with students who still want to discuss the poem, to counsel students who have problems finding a line of pursuit, or simply to talk with those who wish to talk with him. Tomorrow students will share their probable strategies with Mr. Thompson and each other. The actual project may take several days.

Mrs. Phelps takes attendance while the students copy the week's vocabulary list from the chalkboard. She points out a few peculiarities of the words and asks if there are any questions; then she announces the test for Friday. Students take out their grammar books and look to the chalkboard to see what exercises they are to do for the day. Students work independently and hand in their exercises when finished. Mrs. Phelps will correct them and return them in a day or two. Next the class is assigned a short story to read and the questions at the end to answer. Before the period is over, a few students have finished reading and are passing notes to others. A few have not progressed very far. One student is asleep; one is braiding the cords of the venetian blinds into an intricate macramé design. At the end of the period Mrs. Phelps determines how many students have not completed the assignment and continues it as homework for the next day. The next day the lesson design will be repeated, with spelling words assigned, another grammar lesson, another story with questions to be answered. The questions for today's story will be read, graded, and returned.

The English Coalition National Anthem

A is for the anecdotes we narrate,
B is for the basals they can't read,
C is for the culture of the literate,
D is for the deconstructive deed,
E is for arenas epistemic,
F is for the "F"-word that we prize,
G is for the Graff whom we invited,
H means that we must historicize,
I is for the dominant ideology,
J is for the jargon we refine,
K is for the kiddie lit we cherish,
L is for the lit we can't define,
M is for our marginalization,
N is for the names that we all prize,
O is for the "or" that goes with "either,"
P is for the problems we -atize,
Q is for the dreadful quantifiers,
R is for the readin' and the (w)ri(gh)t(e),
S is how we do our situatin',
T is for the trivia that we fight,
U is for our unrewarded virtue,
V is for our contradictory views,
W is for the discourse that is windy,
X is for the Xerox we abuse,
Y is for the questions that we've got,
Z is for all those Z-words that, when we got to the end,
we found, owing to a great oversight on the part of the
Steering Committee, the NEH, and Chester Finn, not to
forget old Cult Lit Hirsch, we forgot.

B *About Lists: A Proposal*

WHEN CHESTER FINN spoke to the assembled coalition on the first day of the conference, he asked us to come up with a list of the most important or central works of literature. He was interested in common standards and curricula and especially in assessment. He has gone on to head the National Assessment for Educational Progress, a group that administers enormous nationwide tests of children each year. No doubt it seemed to him a perfectly straightforward request. Some disciplines lay out the central things that students should study and know. Why not English literature? In effect, "You people are the authorities in English—you represent the main professional organizations. Since we can't teach students everything, what are the most important works we *should* teach them?" How could we resist a request that sounds so reasonable? But we did. And not because he was trying to get us to produce a bad list. He pretty much said, "I admit that there's a kind of list I'm hoping for, but I also know it's not my job to tell you what kind of list to make. You decide; you're the boss." How could we still refuse a nice fellow like that?

Our grounds had to do with the very notion of a list. A list functions as a fence. Once you have a list, all energy and attention seem to get focused on what's inside the fence and what's outside. What's inside is valued and what's outside devalued, and people get trapped into unending battles to get outside items in and inside ones out. Making a list is fraternity rushing, it's clique building, it's college admissions: it's a process that fuels the common hunger to discriminate what's good from what's bad and that triggers the equally common distress about who's accepted and who's rejected. The effect is always to marginalize what's left out.

So even though Finn said, "You're the boss," there was no way we could create a list that didn't seem to marginalize works from nonmainstream cultures and thus reinforce the feeling among students from those cultures that they are marginal. Even if the canon is greatly enlarged, that process is inevitably experienced as a matter of "additions" and "supplements" and therefore reinforces a sense of what and where the center is. The objection to lists is an objection to the whole notion of a center: an insistence that the very idea of a center is epiphenomenal according to where you sit or what lens you look through—that a center is in itself suspicious. So while Finn was saying, "But you don't have to give me a flawed or narrow list or even a conservative or right-wing list, just give me the list *you* like," the coalition members were saying, "We can't give you *any* list without creating the whole dynamic we are trying to fight."[1]

Nevertheless it's not so easy just to kiss off lists. People at the conference periodically pointed out that the absence of a list invites the very narrowness, lack of diversity, and cultural xenophobia that we are trying to fight by resisting list making—that it invites "center-oriented teaching." If we don't make a list, lists will obviously be made: if not by legislators (and that is increasingly going on) then by school boards, if not by boards then by departments, and if not by departments then by teachers. Many or even most of the syllabi studied by students all around the country will be far more culturally exclusionary than what would have resulted from a list we made.

This was the dilemma. The problem of lists and list making was one of the dominant issues of the three weeks. One morning rather casually at breakfast, Robert Scholes and I came up with the thought that perhaps the dilemma could be finessed if we compiled a list of American works so short that it couldn't pretend to coverage and so diverse that its cultural pluralism was obvious. We suggested a list of no more than ten works that all students should read by the end of high school. Our goal was to promote some sense of commonality and to have works that all teachers could count on and refer back to and also to reinforce some sense of history (which everyone seemed to agree needed more emphasis). Our paradigm example was the Declaration of Independence. Our thought was that if the list were short enough—if most works of merit in anyone's view were left off the list—then being off the list would not be a problem and being on it would not be such a big deal. The list would not try to nail down what's truly best or most important and exclude what's not; it would just point to a few "for examples" that would serve as common boulders in the landscape.

But no one would even nibble at our idea. The idea of any list of any sort seemed doomed. Such, perhaps, was the power of Hirsch's list and

Finn's invitation. They put a hex—or we let them put a hex—on any possibility of leadership in naming important works. (Of course our problem was complicated by the fact that members couldn't work out a position on the role of literature in English or the question of "literature" versus "reading" or "texts.")

I've not been able to stop thinking about this dilemma as I've read over my notes and pondered the conference. I can't help trying to find a way to serve what I see as two vexing goals: on the one hand to give some genuine leadership toward cultural pluralism and on the other hand to avoid having a list with the resulting dynamic of fencing in and out or accepting and rejecting.

Imagine a special committee, say, one member designated by each of the eight coalition organizations, that meets each year to choose three works. (Perhaps two, perhaps four. And of course a "work" might be a handful of poems or essays by one writer.) But this is no permanent list. What they choose are just "works of the year"—works that people agree to pay some special attention to this year. Most important, the committee must follow special guidelines to ensure diversity in this yearly choice. There would be various ways to formulate these guidelines. One crude formulation might be this: at least one piece should be by a woman, one should represent a nonmainstream culture, and one should be a work that is relatively neglected or little known or not felt as part of the canon.

During the year, then, three works would be taught in many classes from elementary school through graduate school. After all, most works of literature can be read by people of widely different age and skill. During the year there would be productions, readings, discussions, and adaptations on radio, TV, and the stage and in libraries. Little-known works would be published in cheap or even pamphlet-sized editions. Third graders would hear older siblings and grown-ups dealing with these works and see discussions on TV. There could be a kind of national conversation about these three works.

Such a conversation would lead to meditation on central works in the canon (for of course some year *The Scarlet Letter* or *Leaves of Grass* will have its turn). But, in addition, every year many people will spend some time with a work or two that they do not know or have never even heard of. The procedure would lead to odd juxtapositions—works coming together that one would not normally speak of in the same breath. Such juxtapositions would throw new light on these texts. There would probably be interesting and fortuitous events to influence which works are chosen: someone's centennial or bicentennial will come up; someone will get a Nobel prize; some national event will throw prominence on a particular work of literature or a particular theme. Different committees would probably function in a different way (for of course membership should rotate fairly briskly, this being no permanent Académie française): one committee might even choose three that have a thematic relation; most would probably not. There would be a certain adventure to the process.

I'm interested in the feel of the thing. Such a nonlist—in effect a moving spotlight—could avoid the problem of reverential anointing and the resulting effect of inoculation against these works: instead of reverence and duty to the same works year after year, there would be one year of celebratory limelight. Instead of eleventh graders reading *The Scarlet Letter* or Chief Seattle's Speech every year, almost all high school and college students would read them in, say, 1994, and younger children would see productions and films. Students who are taking two English courses in one year would probably study these same works with different teachers—an important experience; indeed it's likely that the works would come up in some history, psychology, sociology, or American studies courses. As teachers at all levels, we'd have the fun of putting our attention on two or three new works each year and knowing we'd be able to talk about them with all our colleagues and all our students.

I don't mean to imply oblivion for works after their year in the sun. Of course students will go on to read *The Scarlet Letter* and Chief Seattle again in certain literature courses, but when it happens, they'll probably do so in a better spirit than if they all did it as an eleventh-grade ritual of obligatory coverage. For an additional value would accrue through the years: we'd have a gradually evolving but collecting pool of works that students and citizens would come to know more than trivially. Students in senior high school and college would find works in their literature courses that they remember coming up when they were in third grade. The dream, of course, is that a process like this could lead to a gradual deepening and complicating of the culture.

The important thing is that this wouldn't be a permanent list with boundaries and the swirl of psychological energy around the question of which works are in and which out. The goal is not to decide what is permanently great as opposed to only of the second water, for it would be obligatory to choose works that are *not* great but rather unknown and merely interesting. (Sometimes the attention given to such works will lead them to become "great"—often not.) Rather the goal is to decide on works that would repay special attention for a given year: not a static body of texts—a list that one guards and protects—but an activity or practice—an ongoing process that is never final or closed, always open, continually remaking itself. (Michael Halloran [response to draft] points out how this arrangement would break the old pattern of college teachers handing down marching orders to schoolteachers: the yearly choices would be made by a committee in which both groups are equally represented.)

I hope this proposal might also serve to untangle the different goals that often lie tacitly confused behind the championing of lists and canons. It's really a matter of different hungers. First, there is the hunger to discriminate—to decide what's first-rate and what's second-rate, who's in and who's out, the hunger to rank. Second, there is the hunger to enforce a common culture—to get us all to be alike. Third, there is the hunger to get us, with all our differences, nevertheless to work together now and then on the same thing and thereby have some community and shared experience. It's crucial to realize that these are separable goals.

I think that the need to build a fence around what is first-rate and try to wall out what is inferior is an unhelpful obsession. Perhaps I resent it most because it tends to undermine the chances for people to work together in a spirit of mutuality. For people don't seem to be able to decide what's first- or second-rate quietly and for themselves as a private pleasure: they somehow need to beat others over the head in an attempt to make everyone agree with their judgments. If we skip the question of whether something is first- or second-rate, we have a better chance of agreeing that it's important or interesting and of talking together in productive collaboration across our differences.

I hope it is clear that I am also not arguing for the second goal of getting us all to be alike. It is the third goal that I wish to salvage—and keep it from being polluted by the first two. In fact what I emphasize about that third goal is difference: the goal is communication across cultures or across differences. *Community* may be a dangerous word, but community doesn't depend on us all being the same or having the same culture. The community most worth having is a community of people who are very different. By looking at a couple of works together each year in our schools and colleges, we might manage to spend some time learning about one another's languages, cultures, and values. The goal is to promote diversity by the variety of these works yet also to promote community or shared culture through the shared experience of works that are extremely diverse.

NOTES

[1]On top of all this, we are heirs to a bad history of "important conferences" working out lists of "important works of literature." Applebee tells the story of how college professors got together at the end of the nineteenth century to decide what works should be taught in the schools (49–51). (Why is it always in one direction? Why are college teachers

always telling schoolteachers what they all must teach, lockstep, but retaining individual choice for themselves to teach whatever they want? Surely the opposite argument makes just as much sense: that students in their early schooling should have free choice and diversity, that they should read what they enjoy to learn to love reading and literature—to *be* readers—but that college is a time for seriousness and discipline, and so it's our duty as college teachers to create some coherence and common experience.)

It was this turn-of-the-century list making that gave us "*Silas Marner*" and "*Julius Caesar*" and "*Ethan Frome*"—that peculiar phenomenon whereby perfectly fine works of literature end up in both italics and quotation marks—encased in an invisible plastic bubble, transformed into obligatory *items* on a universal syllabus. Their status somehow serves to inoculate students and teachers against them; we get SilasMarnerJuliusCaesarEthanFrome antibodies that fend off any attack by the actual works themselves. The same thing happens when perfectly wonderful essays are put into "readers" or other anthologies: somehow it's harder to experience them as discourse from real writers who write for real readers; somehow they lose their roots in a genuine transaction between actual writers and readers and become instead mere hurdles in a school transaction of requirements. Wayne Booth comments:

> I've thought often, since the conference, of the ways in which various lists were useful to me as a seventeen-year-old out there in small-town Utah, as I tried to educate myself by reading. Yet they did implant a lot of crazy notions about the fixity of true culture.... You might want to add, when you mention *Silas Marner*, that you know one English professor who was turned away from George Eliot for decades by the force-feeding of *Silas* in the ninth grade. (response to draft)

A Change in Teaching

Andrea Lunsford

(college section)

I CAN SAY without qualification that last year was the most stressful, painful, hurtful, debilitating year of my life. Many of my days were wrapped in blackness. One day—this day I am remembering—I was unable to create a face to "meet the faces that we meet," and I called the office and asked someone to post a note in my class, saying that I could not attend class that day but would be there the next day. It was the only day I had missed that year, and I spent a bit of time feeling guilty for leaving my class in the lurch.

How little I had learned about how I—and my class—had changed.

When I arrived the next day, I walked toward the classroom, concentrating on what I would say about my absence. I should have known better. The day before, the students had arrived, had *not* found the secretary's note, had waited a few minutes, and then held class. "Gee," they said, "you missed a great class yesterday, but we assigned Erin to take notes for you—and Gary taped the last thirty minutes. Hey—where were you, anyway?"

Ten years ago, my class would have waited ten or fifteen minutes and then left. What has changed? Me, my classroom, and my course organization. My theory of learning. *The locus of control.* And that, as Frost says, has made all the difference.

Karen

Nancy McHugh

(secondary school section)

K AREN WAS VERY nervous and shy, almost to the point
of paranoia. She kept begging the teacher not to call
on her. She appeared to have few friends and made none in the first few
weeks of class. She had come from a private school to our school and
had been in average-level tracked classes. In those classes she evidently
did her work and seldom if ever had any exchange with other students
in the class. Her level of aspiration was very low. She wanted to get out
of school and be a cosmetologist. She had trouble reading, mostly because she became so nervous that she could not retain what she had
read. She ended up in an elective class of English literature because she
needed an elective and didn't even want a say in what she took.

At first she was overwhelmed by the class and the literature, but slowly
she began to share ideas, participate in group discussions, and even make
friends. I used to see her reading and discussing in the quad during lunch
and after school. She remained a fairly average student, but she lost much
of her defensiveness. She became interested in going to college and finally
was able to enter a small liberal arts college.

Under a tracked and restrictive system she would probably never have
taken such a course, never have been challenged as much, and never
have raised her sights.

APPENDIX

C | *Evaluation, Grading, and the Hunger to Rank People: A Proposal*

*I*N MY NINTH chapter I described how the coalition participants worked their way through some conflict and ambivalence to what I would call a sensible position about goals and testing. But I'm not willing to let go of the issue of evaluation without some further struggle—and, finally, some kibitzing about grading.

I start with a simple question. What if we applied to our evaluation practices what we said about theory at the English Coalition Conference? In particular, what if we said that interpretation is always open, never settled, always dependent on the interpreter? Consider any grade or comment on a paper, any score on a test, any grade for a course: these are all interpretations of texts or claims to knowledge. In our scholarly thinking we seem to acknowledge the fragility of such interpretations and claims. We realize that if I think a text means x and you think it means y or if I think the text is great and you think it is second-rate— it is often impossible to settle our disagreement. Even if we happen to work out an agreement by intelligent and charitable discussion (or you badger me into agreement through authority or win me over through superior rhetoric), we know that neither literary theory nor philosophical theory gives us any agreed-upon rules for figuring out if either of us was right or if there is a better answer. Of course many good thinkers propose intelligent guidelines for working out validity of interpretation, but neither our profession nor the profession of philosophy can agree on any of them.

It's odd that in our scholarly work, where the stakes are mostly low and questions are "academic," we freely admit that we lack grounds for valid interpretations or evaluations. But when it comes to scores and grades, where the stakes are often high—who gets into college, who gets a scholarship, who gets into graduate school, who gets a job, who gets put into the dead-end dummy tracks of schools—*we pretend we have trustworthy knowledge.* How can people say with assurance or even glee, "There's no such thing as validity in interpretation," and then turn around and quickly, single-handedly give paper and course grades that have high stakes and carry with them institutional sanctions? Perhaps some colleagues will reply, "Oh come off it, everyone knows that my grades and your grades are just the opinions of single observers—partial and partisan opinions, not truth." But if that's true then they should put their grades up for discussion in some way, to be debated or contested by interested parties—whereas, of course, few faculty members treat their grades that way. We give grades knowing that they are recorded in such a way as to carry clear connotations of being final or definitive —almost impossible to quarrel with or change. If we don't apply our theories about reading and interpretation to our practices in grading, we throw doubt on our seriousness about those theories.

Am I arguing against judging or evaluating? No. Obviously we need to find ways to choose some students and reject others, whether we are acting as employers or as admissions committees for colleges, graduate schools, or professional schools. Society needs ways to test the competence of people like doctors, pilots, and day-care workers—not to mention teachers! Obviously such evaluations must be claims to knowledge based on interpretations of texts. What I'm arguing is that interpretations and evaluation can be . . . well, *more* trustworthy. That is, even though nothing can remove the deep epistemological fragility that surrounds any interpretation or claim to knowledge, nevertheless we can have an evaluation that, though not sure, is at least something we need not be ashamed of. There are some obvious practices that lead to more trustworthy evaluation. Let me list the major ones that come to mind:

1. The use of multiple observers. Flipping a coin five times may not yield a better verdict than flipping it once, but most of us will agree that using five observers genuinely reduces the likelihood of extreme idiosyncrasy or unfairness. Many evaluators use a procedure that gives a big boost in trustworthiness with a relatively small cost: they use just one additional reader—and bring in a third only where the first two diverge by a significant amount.

2. Observation of work done on multiple occasions. Students perform very differently on different days for any number of obvious reasons.

3. Observation of different kinds of work or modes of activity or genres. The new policy by the California mathematics board that I mentioned in "Goals and Testing" was obviously based on this principle.

They had the simple good sense to say, "We can't trust our knowledge about students' skills in mathematics if we just look at whether they got the right answers on tests. For when we look at how students go about solving problems, how they explain in words the relevant mathematical concepts, and how they go about doing their homework, we see that some students with the right test answers don't understand the mathematics—and some with the wrong answers do understand quite well. (These second and third practices—multiple occasions and modes—show why many people in testing are interested in the use of portfolios.)

4. The use of multiple criteria or scales. Perhaps the main enemy of trustworthiness in evaluation is the urge to reduce the diversity of evaluative evidence or perception to a single number along a one-dimensional continuum such as 1 through 100 or A through F. We see this problem most graphically in intelligence tests that rank everyone along just one sequence or scale of numbers: by doing so, they imply that there is only one kind of intelligence. That is, even though skill with words may not correlate to skill with numbers—or to skill with pictures or to skill with people—the standard IQ test gives everyone one number that ranks his or her "intelligence" with a precise degree of superiority or inferiority to every other person.

We see the same ranking problem in most standardized tests. We even see it in the holistic scoring of student writing, where all the pieces of writing are ranked along a single continuum (usually from 1 to 6)—as though there were just one kind of "good writing" or "good essay" or even "good persuasive essay." How do we find the proper number along one scale, when one persuasive essay has a powerful argument but is rhetorically obtuse or syntactically unclear—and others have the opposite qualities? Diederich has shown how agreement among readers is significantly increased when they rate the features of a piece of writing as opposed to the piece as a whole. This is not surprising, since people obviously differ as to how much weight or value they give to, say, logical power versus rhetorical sophistication versus syntactic clarity when they are assessing the merit of whole texts. We see the same principle in literary evaluation when we try to decide which literary figures or works are better than others along some single continuum of excellence: which is better, Emily Dickinson or Henry Fielding? Evaluation is a bit less problematic if we refrain from squashing all our evaluative perceptions into one numerical scale and ask instead, "excellence with respect to which criterion?"[1]

It follows, then, that the key move in planning evaluation is a balancing of factors: How high are the stakes? How trustworthy does the evaluation need to be or how much untrustworthiness can we tolerate? How much do we really need this evaluation? If the stakes are high enough, we'd better find the money and time to increase the trustworthiness; if we can't find the money or time, we'd better lower the stakes or even skip the evaluation. Let's look at a few examples of evaluation where the stakes are high and we already naturally employ these key aids to trustworthiness.

When we make tenure and promotion decisions in colleges and universities, we use multiple observers and evaluators to look at different modes of activity and a portfolio of work (usually in different modes)—all done over a long period of time. That is, we avoid reliance on a single observer, mode, number, or occasion. (We sometimes distrust tenure decisions, but shouldn't that give us reason for even more skepticism about the conventional grading decisions that we all make much more hurriedly and single-handedly on narrower grounds?)

When we award doctoral degrees, we use multiple occasions and modes of activity (dissertation, exams, course work) and multiple observers of the dissertation and usually of the exam. And we don't usually grade or rank dissertations or doctorates, reducing a judgment of quality to a single number along a one-dimensional continuum; we give a crude yes or no (sometimes honors)—recognizing that for finer discriminations we need more discursive information in the form of letters of recommendation from faculty members who worked with the students, especially from teachers who worked with them on the dissertation.

When most departments award bachelor degrees with honors, they use another mode in addition to course grades, namely, a dissertation, and it must be evaluated by more than one reader.

For a final, interesting example of a procedure based on the assumption that when the stakes are high the mode of evaluation needs to be as careful as possible, look at the currently developing national teacher certification procedure sponsored originally by the Carnegie Foundation. A carefully chosen group of teachers, administrators, and politicians has been working out a way to identify and license strong teachers. I don't know the exact evaluation activities involved, but all the elements I pointed to above are being used: multiple observers, multiple occasions, and multiple modes or activities (a portfolio of work by teachers and of evidence about them; observations of teachers in action and in simulations). Finally, and most important, the procedure does not reduce the results to a single number along a one-dimensional continuum. The evaluators recognize the hubris of trying to rank teachers since that would mean pretending to measure all of them. They are just trying to identify strong, competent ones. They are acknowledging that the best they can do is arrive at a rough, crude but multidimensional, considered judgment.

Representing Course Grades Differently: A Proposal

After looking at these examples of high-stakes evaluations—single judgments that speak to a person's whole career—mere course grades may seem like small potatoes. When a freshman protests, "That C − you gave me will keep me from getting into medical school!" we are tempted to laugh. But the ludicrousness of some students' grade grubbing makes it too easy for us to laugh. Course grades are often far from trivial in their consequences for students—especially grades in their upperclass or major courses. Just one or two important grades can determine whether someone gets a scholarship or gets into a certain college or graduate program. But, if we look at the principles I've been exploring about trustworthiness, stakes, and costs of evaluation, it turns out that we can see a low-cost way to make course grades much more trustworthy and clear in meaning and at the same time reduce the mystery and the stakes.

The problem with course grades is not evaluation itself but how we represent our evaluations. That is, the teacher's evaluative process in most courses has a great deal to recommend it. Though teachers are only single observers, they can usually base their evaluation on multiple observations over a long period of time of students doing multiple kinds of activity: not just performance under test conditions on a single day. Richard Lloyd-Jones was the original author of this perceptive passage in the coalition report on testing:

> Lest we fall into thinking that assessment always necessitates the use of large, formal instruments, we should remember that the most trustworthy assessment is usually conducted by the individual teacher in his or her own classroom as an integral part of the teaching process. After all, a reliable and valid test is more likely to be possible when the activities or materials to be covered are discrete and sharply defined, as in a classroom. Sometimes one can test performance quite directly; in fact, most classroom activities test student skills and knowledge as part of the continuing efforts to improve. When any single measure is ineffective or insufficient at showing what the student really knows or can do, the ongoing teaching situation demands and inevitably brings forth a more successful measure in another mode. (Lloyd-Jones and Lunsford 43)

But notice what this passage is describing: the various observations and evaluations made by teachers—not the representation of them into a single letter or number grade. All those valuable perceptions and data are rendered less trustworthy and less useful when they are reduced to a single number. That is, the conventional grading system traps teachers into the key mistake of mass testing: producing a single letter grade that tells us nothing about what the student knows or doesn't know, can or can't do—and, in doing so, heightening bias by keeping hidden or tacit the value system that has permitted all those data to be reduced to a single number. (And if the teacher grades with any degree of "curve," it creates that artificial and needlessly "scarce good" that Astin spoke of in chapter 9.)

Most teachers in school and college know a great deal about their students' learning and ability, but the single letter or number grade doesn't permit them to communicate that knowledge to readers. Students get preoccupied and sometimes even obsessed with grades not only because they are sometimes very important but also because their meaning is so mysterious. No one quite knows what that B− or D really means, and people get more hypnotized or cathected to what seems ambiguous, mysterious, or magical.

But most students and teachers take conventional grading so much for granted that they feel hopeless that evaluation could ever be more accurate and less vexed—as it is with those report cards given by early elementary teachers, where students get English grades on particular criteria such as comprehension, word recognition skills, oral expression, and written expression. Indeed the main argument for "regular grades" in upper elementary school is usually something like this: "Everything would be better if we didn't have to, but the kids have got to get used to regular grading to be ready for high school." But in fact the typical report card for early elementary grades provides the key to a simple and major improvement. If teachers simply graded by means of a grid of multiple criteria, they would provide much more accurate, trust-worthy, and useful information to other teachers and to colleges, em-ployers, and graduate and professional schools. What I am suggesting, then, is not a different process or amount of evaluation but a different means of representing evaluation.

There are various ways this general principle might be fleshed out. Course grades in high school and college could consist of teacher ratings on a short, simple list of criteria such as memory of important infor-mation, understanding (or the ability to apply central ideas), effectiveness of writing, and effort (or conscientiousness). Teachers might check off the student's level of accomplishment from three or four or even five boxes for each criterion, using mere numbers or else words (such as weak/satisfactory/strong or poor/fair/good/excellent).[2]

I am not arguing for the particular criteria I use above as illustrations. Teachers would have to work out which skills or areas of knowledge are most important and discriminable, given the nature of their course. Other criteria that come to mind, also by way of illustration: critical thinking, creative thinking, effectiveness in speaking, or improvement over the semester. Literature teachers might use more specifically literary criteria, for example, close literal interpretation, imaginative or creative interpretation, or understanding of theoretical and critical issues. Writing teachers might use criteria more specifically geared to composition, for example, clarity of language, rhetorical sophistication, skill at exploratory writing, skill at revising, and skill at giving feedback to others. Even in huge lecture courses where evaluation is accomplished wholly by machine-graded exams, such exams could easily be designed and graded to yield scores on at least two or three criteria (for example, skill criteria like memory, interpretive skill, and problem-solving skill or content criteria like understanding of poetry and of prose). Some teachers would scorn criteria like effort or conscientiousness or improvement, but others would value the chance to use them since they point to things that readers of grades often want to know about. At first glance, this approach might seem much more difficult than regular grading, but it wouldn't take much more time for teachers to check off three to six boxes than to figure out a grade, and many would find it psychologically easier.[3]

The crucial principle I insist on here is that the system for representing evaluations must be flexible enough to fit the data—as opposed to the conventional approach, where the system of representation is inflexible and the data must be distorted to fit it (and all for the sake, it seems, of being able to distinguish between someone with a 3.15 and 3.16 grade point average). Interesting consequences follow from this decision to give priority to the evaluative data rather than to the system of representation. That is, there is no necessity that a teacher use all of his or her criteria on every student. A teacher might not be in a position to evaluate one student's speaking skill or effort, but that is no reason to hold back the crucial information that another student was very strong on both counts. Similarly, there is no necessity that all teachers use the same criteria: different teachers, because of what they teach and how they teach it, will have different evaluative information that they need to communicate. The simple fact is that it can be communicated without much trouble.

The logistics of this approach would not be difficult, especially in the age of computers. (Certain experimental colleges such as Hampshire College and the Evergreen State College produce much more unwieldy evaluations—transcripts of many pages of narrative evaluative prose—

yet their students are accepted at the full range of graduate and professional schools, and they get all kinds of jobs.) No doubt many registrars might lobby against the idea or might prefer to have a whole department or school agree on a master list of a dozen or a score of criteria—and of course that would be possible and perhaps even desirable. But the reason for evaluation systems is to serve learning and the communication of accurate evaluative information—not the other way around. A high school or college transcript of little grids would be bulkier than at present, but it would still fit on just a few pages. The added bulk would be gratefully received by students, parents, colleges, and employers because the transcript would communicate much more useful information: a record of different teachers' assessments of a student on particular abilities or skills. This system would decrease the need for letters of recommendation—a nontrivial burden on high school teachers who often have to write more than fifty or seventy-five a year. The need for letters of recommendation comes from the widespread and justifiable distrust of grades because of how little they say and how easily they are inflated. When colleges, employers, or graduate and professional schools see a B, they don't know whether it means that the student who got it was a dutiful striver or erratically brilliant. Even if the grade is an A, readers have no way of knowing whether the student was a truly good thinker or a conscientious memorizer—a good writer or a poor one.

If we communicated our evaluation of students in this more accurate way, students couldn't sum up their high school or college performance in a single misleading number (grade point average or rank in class). This would vastly improve the climate of learning since students would have to think about specific strengths and weaknesses in their learning process—instead of just about the misleading question of where they fall on a scale or ranking. It tends to feel as though life couldn't go on without a GPA, but my nine years at Evergreen showed me that we all continued to live and breathe—and better.

Of course one department cannot unilaterally change the official system for recording and communicating course grades. (On second thought, what if an English department decided to refuse on professional grounds to give conventional uninformative grades and insisted on providing a superior but bulkier set of evaluative information? I don't see what the rest of the institution could do but accept and transmit this more accurate evaluative information—and perhaps learn from it.) But, granting for the moment that we are stuck for a while with regular grades, it would be a vast improvement if we in English provided to students and colleagues the kind of criterion-based grids or reports I am talking about in addition to regular grades. This would show other departments how much is gained and how little lost by the new procedure. High school teachers could save these evaluative grids for each student and provide them to colleges in addition to or in lieu of recommendation letters. College English departments could save them for each student major and provide them to graduate and professional schools and even employers.

These criterion-based course evaluations would still be based on only single observers and thus would be less trustworthy than if based on two or more observers, but that is no cause for concern because of one very important consequence of the system: by replacing a single quantitative grade with multiple ratings or judgments about abilities, we would in one stroke lower the stakes. That is, these new course evaluations could no longer be used to rank students with fine gradations along a single dimension—except in the most general way. If one student has lots of "strongs" and another has lots of "weaks," it will be obvious to anyone that the first one has a better transcript—and that's as it should be. But for many or most students—those with many mixed or middling verdicts—comparative holistic ranking among them would be almost impossible. If one student has strong marks in memory and weak ones in understanding and creative thinking and another student has the opposite verdicts, which has a "better" report card? Colleges, employers, and parents will often disagree among themselves about which criteria are most important and correctly so: their judgments would depend on what qualities they are looking for. And students would have to be more thoughtful in trying to assess how they are doing. It is true that people might have a lamentable impulse to count "strongs" or compute averages, but the results would clearly have little value since different students would have ratings on different criteria, and different students would have different numbers of ratings—sometimes even in the same course.

But of course the stakes cannot always remain low. Sometimes we need to make a more definitive and global verdict about quality—for example, as to whether someone is doing genuinely unsatisfactory work and should not get credit for a course or should even be flunked out of school. We don't have unlimited space in our classes or colleges, so we need to make these judgments. As for excellence, we may not have such a pressing pragmatic need to identify it, but learning and teaching probably benefit from designating excellent work as an illustration and an incentive. Thus we might have two global or holistic boxes on an evaluation grid to check, *fail* and *honors*. (The system would help to restrain grade inflation. Teachers would be less likely to overuse "honors" if they had a way to say that someone was terrific at certain particular abilities.)

These global verdicts of *fail* and *honors* would be given by single observers and thus would be less trustworthy than we could wish, but they would still be far more clear, communicative, and helpful than the F's and A's we now give, since the accompanying grids would communicate the grounds for the verdicts—as our present grades do not. In so doing, the grids would also communicate the teacher's values or priorities, which also remain hidden with our present grades. For example, suppose one teacher fails a student who is poor in memory of important information but good on all other criteria, and another teacher doesn't call the same situation a failure. This might seem like a problem with the system: a discrepancy in standards. But of course this is exactly what happens all the time with conventional grading, only the discrepancy is disguised: one teacher gives a failing grade and another gives a passing grade, and the reader has no idea that these two contrasting verdicts represent exactly the same student performance!

The Hunger to Rank

I hope it's clear that none of what I've been saying in this chapter is an argument against evaluation itself.[4] I'm only arguing against doing any more high-stakes, single-number-ranking evaluation than we absolutely need to do because it is that kind of verdict that is most likely to be untrustworthy and most likely to undermine a good learning climate. In a sense, the problem with conventional course grades is that they represent *too little* evaluation: just one crude holistic leap in the dark.

The problem, then, is not the hunger to evaluate but the hunger to rank: the hunger to evaluate in such a way that we end up with people strung along a single continuum, with every student located at a precisely quantifiable distance above or below every other student: every student should know his or her place—precisely. This is really a hunger to simplify the data, to come up with one answer, one scale, to have a horse race, to see who wins—to reduce evaluation to a question of "who's better?" rather than "who's better with respect to what?" It's the temptation to forget that there are different criteria, different kinds of writing or literature, different skills that go into doing physics. It seems to me that in our recent thinking about theory and reading and interpretation, we've begun to wean ourselves from that hunger for simple answers. It's time for us to wean ourselves from it also in the realm of grading and evaluation. We don't much distort careful evaluation if we give people single numbers to represent their ability at spelling or at finding interesting interpretations of a text or at building arguments for a claim. The distortion comes from giving people single numbers to represent their ability at "English" or "literature" or "writing." None of these entities represents one skill or ability.

In short, the mindless hunger to rank subverts the responsible desire to evaluate—that is, to see clearly and carefully. When we engage in careful examination, we can't help noticing that certain *parts* of a performance are stronger than others and thus that performances cannot be crudely ranked along a single scale. The Coalition Conference showed that our profession is at a historical moment where many teachers and scholars from all levels—not just a few literary theorists—seem to be interested in being more critically reflective about our practices in making claims about reading, interpretation, and knowledge. But if members of the profession refuse to train that critical reflectivity on the part of our professional behavior that makes the most concrete difference in our students' lives—grading—I believe they will show that they weren't really serious in the first place about critical awareness.

NOTES

[1] I probably offend psychometricians by omitting from my list of key aids to trustworthiness the hallowed practice of *norming*: measuring how a performance compares across a population of others. But norming is problematic. On the one hand, I already imply a bit of norming in my list: teacher evaluations usually reflect how a student does in comparison to the others in the class—even in comparison to the larger population of students the teacher has taught. If we bring in more than one observer, we have wider norming, and if we have a committee with geographical diversity, the norming is wider still. "But how do students stack up nationally?" People seem to have a hunger to know. Formalized national norming is probably the biggest argument in favor of mass testing.

On the other hand, the price we pay for formalized national norming is very high. We are obliged to reduce performance to a single number (with the price that I speak of here and that Astin spoke of in chapter 9); we are virtually obliged to lose multiple modes of demonstration and multiple occasions; we are virtually obliged to use machine-graded, multiple-choice questions—which means emphasizing learning as the finding of correct answers from a set list of four alternatives. Thus, the advantages of formalized national norming are very small compared with the prices, especially in the light of the genuine norming we get with the key elements I've named above. Look at a jury trial in our legal system: the stakes are enormously high—sometimes human life itself—but we are content to settle for an emphasis on multiple observers and the informal norming entailed there rather than on more formal mechanisms for norming (example from Brown).

[2] Here, by way of illustration, is the kind of grid I am talking about:

Name: _____	Course: _____		Honors ☐ Fail ☐

Strong		Weak	
☐	☐	☐	Memory of important information
☐	☐	☐	Understanding or ability to apply central ideas
☐	☐	☐	Writing
☐	☐	☐	Ability to work well with others
☐	☐	☐	Effort or conscientiousness

[3]Many teachers have found that students get more invested in their learning if they are invited to become involved in the evaluative process—instead of being defined as wholly passive receivers of evaluation. This is especially useful when students have no choice about being in school or about being in a given course. Many of us have found that it is difficult (though not impossible) to get students to evaluate their performance responsibly when they are asked to come up with just one grade: the process always boils down the vexed question of, "Do I *deserve* a D?"—with all sorts of moral overtones. Students tend to evaluate themselves much more accurately and responsibly when they are asked to rate themselves on explicit criteria. For example, I've found that students in a writing course find it relatively easy to give themselves an accurate rating like this one at the end of the semester: "I still have trouble at organization, copyediting, and making a strong logical argument, but I've gotten good at thinking of things to say when I sit down to write, I tried very hard, and I have made improvement."

[4]In truth I confess I do yearn for less of it. Do we really need all these evaluations we make? Do they really do much good? I've become interested in all the useful things we can say about a text or a performance without talking about how good or bad it is (see the section on evaluation in *Writing With Power*). As C. S. Lewis remarks, "most people are obviously far more anxious to express their approval and disapproval of things than to describe them" (7). In this essay, however, I restrain my impulse to ask for restraint. I'm arguing for just as much evaluation—but more careful evaluation.

Karen and Evaluation

Brooke Workman
(secondary school section)

KAREN TAUGHT ME about evaluation—and it was painful for both of us.

Karen was in my first eighth-grade class. She had difficulty with what I assumed was a good test; certainly my tests looked very much like those of my older colleagues in the junior high school. I heavily weighted the mastery of information—authors, names, titles, lines from works to identify and then develop in various questioning modes—true and false, matching, multiple choice, short answer. And I always had a required essay that I thought would reveal what some educators today call "higher-level thinking skills."

And so she always failed, sometimes dramatically. I felt badly about it, especially because she was always so eager to talk in class, always cooperative, always delighted with literature. But when test time came, I could see her tremendous anxiety; when the tests were returned, she was always in tears.

Then one evening after I had given back one of my unit tests, I received one of the more traumatic telephone calls of my life. It was from a local physician. "Do you know what you have been doing to Karen?" he asked. Then he told me that Karen was an epileptic, that she had been having seizures when she returned home with her tests. And that evening she and her mother—also an epileptic—had both had seizures.

Of course, I was angry that someone at the school hadn't told me about Karen's background. We had no school nurse then, no reporting of students' health problems. And while I could lay the blame on my inexperience and puzzle over her hesitancy to tell me herself, I realized that I had to do something—fast.

And so I did. I began to rethink what really is important in my teaching. I began to realize her problem may have been anxiety. Or maybe it was just that I had placed too much emphasis on memory—which I now know is a low-level cognitive skill. So I designed my tests to probe many levels of learning. While I included some memory questions, I also developed tests where students applied their knowledge to a new story or a new poem. I offered more balance with more emphasis on alternate essays, take-home essays, chances to develop a story beyond what the students had read (for example, what the central character would be doing after the story ended).

Karen had no trouble with my class after that. She felt better and so did I. I now know that learning is more than memorizing lists, that individual teachers must tailor their assessments to their students and to modern learning theory.

D | *Situating Me*

I've been so situated
    That I'm constipated
—Jose Lostracco
"The Coalition Country Blues"
(to the tune of "Faded Love")

THINKING ABOUT how "situatedness" was a theme at the conference, I suddenly had the notion that perhaps I should somewhat formalize in an appendix the act of trying to acknowledge and explore my class, gender, and so forth. I do that here. But no one can pretend to believe in the importance of situatedness without also talking openly about what critical theorists sometimes pass over—feelings. I've never felt I could trust someone's interpretation of a text or thinking about an issue unless I got a sense of his or her feelings about that text or issue. To situate myself as a commentator requires, it seems to me then, the somewhat personal tone I take throughout this book. It's interesting to me that a personal tone and talk about feelings are still felt as unprofessional by people who deny the possibility of nonpartisan objectivity.

When I was invited to take part in the conference, I was initially pleased. Here was a chance to take part in what one hoped would be a consequential meeting. I remembered reading about the Dartmouth Conference soon after it occurred and being jealous of the participants. But in fact I almost said no to this one: three weeks away from home with no chance to visit my family or have any of them visit me; no compensation; in a summer when I and my family were moving from

Long Island to Amherst. And though I care about the issues, I was also leery of three weeks of nonstop academic talk and committee-functioning with sixty colleagues.

But I was won over when the MLA Executive Council invited me to write a book about the conference. Foolish perhaps; this book has taken much more of me than I expected or hoped. But I was flattered and hoped it would give me a chance to stick an oar into the conversation that makes up the profession of English. My subjectivity is no doubt all too evident throughout, but I will try an exercise in greater explicitness here.

I am a white male who went to traditional schools and who has what you might call a conventional PhD, which led to a book about Chaucer. Nothing if not privileged—but somehow I experienced it as struggle. When I went from Williams to Oxford and then Harvard, I wanted to grow up to be a cultured, tweedy, pipe-smoking professor just like the teachers I admired. But I couldn't seem to pull it off. I gradually found myself having a harder and harder time writing at Oxford—in fact finding myself unable to produce my papers at all for about five months. Then at Harvard I found myself completely unable to study and write, and I had to quit. I felt this as complete failure; I assumed I would never come back or be an academic. I looked for nonacademic work and only fell by accident back into a teaching job after a year. Thus I write very much as an academic, having almost always either studied or taught; yet also with a deep sense of detachment, perhaps even alienation, having failed and quit.

I have taught at a wide range of places: MIT, Franconia College, the Evergreen State College, Wesleyan University, SUNY–Stony Brook, Breadloaf School of English, and now the University of Massachusetts at Amherst. I used to think of myself as being on the fringes of the profession. I taught at a lot of alternative institutions and was long seen as a radical young whippersnapper for my *Writing without Teachers*. I've spent most of my twenty-seven years of full-time teaching without tenure: seven at MIT, two at Franconia, nine at Evergreen. (Franconia and Evergreen don't give tenure.) This perspective gives me a sense of how much tenure muddies personal and collegial relationships.

In the last seven or eight years I've consciously tried to work in the mainstream of the profession and do what I can to keep my approach from being seen as peripheral or "alternative." I was for four years a member of the MLA Executive Council. People ask me to write letters of support for job applications and tenure decisions, and chairs ask me to read for tenure cases. In fact I've recently found my work not infrequently characterized as "old-fashioned" (or, worse yet, "Romantic" because of my interest in voice).

I write as someone committed to teaching. It was this interest that got me back into the academy in a teaching job after I'd quit graduate school and then finally back into graduate school five years later. But I find teaching difficult and often anxious-making, and I love to write. So I am grateful but sheepish about now having a teaching load that is lighter than that of most college teachers (and enormously light compared to that of teachers in community colleges and schools). But for nine years at Evergreen State College and two at Franconia my teaching load was fifteen or more hours a week.

I write as someone who has come to define his field as writing and who has a strong sense of writing as the downtrodden side of the English profession. My experience with English departments has made me feel somewhat embattled on that score—feeling a need to correct some blindness and injustice in how people in literature see writing. Nevertheless I also consider myself a literature person and believe that writing and literature belong together—for both their sakes (for my sake?). With my roots in both fields, I hope I can help them work together better.

I write as one of many who started out in New Jersey—in my case in an upper-middle-class home with a businessman father and artist mother. I would now have to call myself a kind of straight, square bourgeois with wife and two early adolescent children; someone who cares about corny virtues and defines himself as in some sense religious; a conscientious objector; and someone who thinks the world can be made better not only by people banding together but also by the efforts of individuals.

About my writing process in working on this book: I took notes like mad during the conference and went over them in the evening, using dialectical notebooks with right pages for things said and done and left pages for reflections on what I see on the right (see Berthoff, "A Curious Triangle").

I'd hoped I could do a lot of writing during the conference but did none. Starting somewhere in the second week, however, I began to sense certain themes as important and started separate pages for notes on these themes. When I came home from the conference I took months reading through all my notes again and the position papers and the extensive final papers and stories and other documents (also moving, working on a house, and trying to finish another book). I spent much of the rest of the fall and winter in that awful process of taking notes on notes and worrying whether the whole thing would somehow disappear—and ended up feeling I'd never write a book because the conference was too far away.

I produced a rough but shareable draft of about three-quarters of the book by the end of the following summer. I sent that to some coalition members and friends for comments. It took me till the end of the following summer to finish a draft of the rest. That too I got comment on from a number of readers. I revised the whole thing the winter after that (1989–90).

Walking down the Road toward Learning

Tom Jones
(secondary school section)

*E*ACH DAY SINCE we arrived at Wye, a group of us walk each morning before breakfast. The group numbering between six and nine conference members gathers outside the front portico at 6:25. The camaraderie of those present is quite evident in the exchanged greetings. "How are you this morning?" "Headache gone?" "Did you finish your reading?" "Sleep okay?" After we finish our polite conversation and stretching, the walk begins.

Although we start together as a large group, invariably smaller groups of twos and threes form as we wind over the roads and paths of Wye. One member has dubbed them the accelerated walkers, the developmental walkers, and the remedial walkers. These groups are not that static, however. We feel free moving from group to group based on our physical, cultural, social, and informational needs. The groups also vary in number because we are joined occasionally by some tennis player, swimmer, or runner who wants a different form of exercise that particular day.

During the course of the walk there is lively, animated conversation. We talk interactively and question what sometimes seem like tentative statements. Gestures figure heavily in our discussions. As we walk to Wye Island, nature abounds in the mooing of cows, the golden yellow of the sunflowers, and the boat and animal life on the river. Daily we pass another of our colleagues who has chosen jogging as her form of exercise. She cheerfully exchanges greetings with each of the groups as she meets them on her return from her daily routine.

While the ultimate goal has been to reach a particular point across the bridge, only the faster walkers achieve it. Those middle and slower groups simply turn around at whatever point they reach and retrace their steps to the manor house. As we return, again in our separate groups, we part company, wishing each other success in the conference and vowing to return tomorrow.

It seems to me that this cadre of walkers holds significance for us in the light of our discussions. First, learning, like any form of exercise, involves some sort of pacing. The runner we meet daily obviously is ready to exercise at a different pace than we are. Even in the group, not all persons walk at the same pace. Some stride, some meander, some stroll. We are motivated by differing abilities, interests, and goals. On any given day the goal may change, and those who are slow one time may be accelerated the next.

There is something more here though. The common spirit keeps people coming back. There is a certain joy that has developed that no one can quite explain. In one week this particular group will disband, but we will take a little part of this experience with us. This seems to be what we want for our students too.

Thank-Yous

Diane Orchard
(elementary school section)

WHEN BRUCE MENTIONED his file of thank-you letters (I keep one too!) and his need to reread them on occasion, I was reminded of the power of language and the *extended* power of *written* language.

One of the things I like to encourage my students to do is to write real thank-you notes to real people, preferably someone they have never thanked before, for something they might not normally say thank you for.

I often use as my introductory illustration the true story of a university professor whose office had just been relocated. She wrote a thank-you note to the custodian who had removed the door and made it fit over the new carpeting. On seeing the professor in the hall, the custodian thanked her for the special note and then remarked that he had only received one other thank-you note in his career, and that one had been six years ago, but he still had it pinned to his bulletin board. After a moment's more contemplation, he declared in astonishment that he was sure that one had also been written by this professor. Sure enough, it had, and its benefits had been continually renewed every time the custodian had glanced at his bulletin board.

Works Cited

Allen, Kathleen. "A Non-Linear Model of Student Development: Implications for Assessment." Fourth National Conference on Assessment in Higher Education. Atlanta, June 1989.

Angelou, Maya. *I Know Why the Caged Bird Sings*. New York: Random, 1969.

Anrig, Greg. "Testing and Student Performance: Now and in the Future." Fourth National Conference on Assessment in Higher Education. Atlanta, June 1989.

Applebee, A. N. *Writing in the Secondary School: English and the Content Areas*. Research Report 21. Urbana: NCTE, 1981.

Arac, Jonathan, Christian Messenger, and Gerald Sorensen. "The Place of Literary Theory in the Freshman Literature Course." *ADE Bulletin 82* (Winter 1985): 22–26.

Archbald, Doug A., and Fred M. Newmann. *Beyond Standardized Testing: Assessing Authentic Academic Achievement in the Secondary School*. Reston: National Assn. of Secondary School Principals, 1988.

Armstrong, Paul. "The Conflict of Interpretations and the Limits of Pluralism." *PMLA* 98 (1983): 341–52.

Association of American Colleges. *Report on the Study of the Major*. Washington: Assn. of American Colleges, 1990.

Astin, Alexander. "Assessment and Human Values: Confessions of a Reformed Number Cruncher." AAHE Assessment Forum. June 1988. Washington: American Assn. of Higher Education, 1988.

Atwell, Nancie. *In the Middle*. Portsmouth: Boynton, 1987.

Avery, Carol. "From the First: Teaching to Diversity." Jensen 37–56.

Belanoff, Pat, and Marcia Dickson, eds. *Portfolio Grading: Process and Product*. Portsmouth: Boynton, forthcoming.

Belenky, Mary Field, et al. *Women's Ways of Knowing: The Development of Self, Voice, and Mind*. New York: Basic, 1986.

Berlin, James. *Writing Instruction in Nineteenth-Century American Colleges*. Carbondale: Southern Illinois UP, 1984.

Berthoff, Anne. "A Curious Triangle and the Double-Entry Notebook: Or, How Theory Can Help Us Teach Reading and Writing." Berthoff, *Making of Meaning* 41–47.

———. *Forming/Thinking/Writing: The Composing Imagination*. Rochelle Park: Hayden, 1978.

————. *The Making of Meaning: Metaphors, Models, and Maxims for Writing Teachers*. Montclair: Boynton, 1981.

Blumenstyk, Goldie. "Twenty-Four States Found to Require Programs to Assess What College Students Learn." *Chronicle of Higher Education* 10 Aug. 1988: A19+.

Booth, Wayne. "Arts and Scandals, 1982." Presidential address. *PMLA* 98 (1983): 312–22.

————. *Modern Dogma and the Rhetoric of Assent*. U of Chicago P, 1974.

Brown, Rexford. "You Can't Get There from Here." AAHE Assessment Forum. June 1989. Washington: American Assn. of Higher Education, 1989.

Bruner, Jerome. *Actual Minds, Possible Worlds*. Cambridge: Harvard UP, 1986.

————. *The Process of Education*. New York: Random, 1960.

Bruner, Jerome S., Jacqueline Goodnow, and G. A. Austin. *A Study of Thinking*. New York: Wiley, 1956.

Carnegie Council on Adolescent Development. *Turning Points: Preparing American Youth for the Twenty-First Century*. Washington: Carnegie Council on Adolescent Development, 1989.

Center for Restructuring Educational Issues. Introduction. *Proposals and Plans for Restructured Schools*. Washington: American Federation of Teachers, 1989.

Cohen, Muriel. "In East Harlem, a School of Choice." *Boston Globe* 10 Mar. 1989: 2.

Commission on Reading. *Becoming a Nation of Readers: The Report of the Commission on Reading*. Washington: US National Institute of Education, 1984.

Culler, Jonathan. "Beyond Interpretation: The Prospects of Contemporary Criticism." *Comparative Literature* 28 (1976): 244–65.

————. "Paul de Man's Contribution to Literary Criticism and Theory." *The Future of Literary Theory*. Ed. Ralph Cohen. New York: Routlege, 1989. 268–79.

Daniel, Beth. "Pedagogue in Process." *Correspondences* 10 (Winter 1988): n. pag.

Daniels, Harvey. *Famous Last Words*. Carbondale: Southern Illinois UP, 1983.

Darling-Hammond, Linda. "Assessment and Incentives: The Medium Is the Message." AAHE Assessment Forum. June 1988. Washington: American Assn. of Higher Education, 1988.

Diederich, Paul. *Measuring Growth in English*. Urbana: NCTE, 1974.

Dixon, John. *Growth through English: A Report Based on the Dartmouth Seminar 1966*. Reading, Eng.: National Assn. for the Teaching of English, 1967.

Eagleton, Terry. *Literary Theory: An Introduction*. Minneapolis: U of Minnesota P, 1983.

Elbow, Peter. *Embracing Contraries*. New York: Oxford UP, 1987.

————. "Embracing Contraries in the Teaching Process." Elbow, *Embracing Contraries* 142–59.

————. "Methodological Doubting and Believing: Contraries in Inquiry." Elbow, *Embracing Contraries* 253–300.

————. *Oppositions in Chaucer*. Middletown: Wesleyan UP, 1975.

————. "Poetry as No Big Deal." Elbow, *Writing with Power* 101–19.

————. "Trying to Teach While Thinking about the End." Elbow, *Embracing Contraries* 99–140.

————. *Writing with Power*. New York: Oxford UP, 1981.

Elbow, Peter, and Pat Belanoff. "State University of New York: Portfolio-Based Evaluation Program." *New Methods in College Writing Programs: Theory into Practice*. Ed. Paul Connolly and Teresa Vilardi. New York: MLA, 1986. 95–105.

————. "Using Portfolios to Increase Collaboration and Community in a Writing Program." *WPA: Journal of Writing Program Administration* 9.3 (1986): 27–40.

El-Khawas, Elaine. *Campus Trends, 1989*. Washington: American Council on Higher Education, 1989.

Farr, Marcia, and Harvey Daniel. *Language Diversity and Writing Instruction*. Urbana: ERIC Clearinghouse on Reading and Communication Skills, NCTE, 1986.

Fiske, Edward B. "Lessons." *New York Times* 3 Jan. 1990: B6.

Fontaine, Sheryl. "The Unfinished Story of the Interpretive Community." *Rhetoric Review* 7.1 (1988): 86–96.

Franklin, Phyllis. Letter to James Morris, program director, Andrew W. Mellon Foundation. 16 Aug. 1989.

Freedman, Samuel G. "New York's Schools: A National Test." *New York Times* 23 Oct. 1989: A23.

Freire, Paolo. *Pedagogy of the Oppressed*. Trans. Myra Bergman Ramos. New York: Seabury, 1968.

Frye, Northrop. *Anatomy of Criticism: Four Essays*. New York: Atheneum, 1967.

Gardner, Howard. *Frames of Mind: The Theory of Multiple Intelligences*. New York: Basic, 1983.

Gilligan, Carol. *In a Different Voice: Psychological Theory and Women's Development*. Cambridge: Harvard UP, 1982.

Goodlad, John I. *A Place Called School: Prospects for the Future*. New York: McGraw, 1984.

Goodman, Kenneth. *What's Whole in Whole Language?* Portsmouth: Heinemann, 1986.

Graff, Gerald. *Professing Literature: An Institutional History*. Chicago: U of Chicago P, 1987.

Grant, Gerald, and Wendy Kohli. "Contributing to Learning by Assessing Student Performance." *On Competence: A Critical Analysis of Competence-Based Reforms in Higher Education*. San Francisco: Jossey-Bass, 1979.

Graves, Donald. *Writing: Teachers and Children at Work*. Portsmouth: Heinemann, 1983.

Hairston, Maxine. "Breaking Our Bonds and Reaffirming Our Connections." *College Composition and Communication* 36 (1985): 272–82.

Hartwell, Patrick. "Grammar, Grammars, and the Teaching of Grammar." *College English* 47 (1985): 105–27.

Hatlen, Burton. "Michel Foucault and the Discipline(s) of English." *College English* 50 (1988): 786–801.

Heath, Shirley Brice. *Ways with Words: Language, Life and Work in Communities and Classrooms*. Cambridge UP, 1984.

Hillocks, George, Jr. "Mode and Focus of Instruction: Teaching Procedural and Declarative Knowledge for Writing." Unpublished study, 1987.

———. *Research on Written Composition: New Directions for Teaching*. Urbana: ERIC, 1986.

———. "What Works in Teaching Composition: A Meta-Analysis of Experimental Treatment Studies." *American Journal of Education* 93 (1984): 133–70.

Hillocks, George, Jr., E. A. Kahn, and Larry R. Johannessen. "Teaching Defining Strategies as a Mode of Inquiry: Some Effects on Students' Writing." *Research in the Teaching of English* 17 (1983): 275–84.

Hirsch, E. D., Jr. *Cultural Literacy: What Every American Needs to Know*. Boston: Houghton, 1987.

———. *The Philosophy of Composition*. Chicago: U of Chicago P, 1977.

Huey, Edmund Burke. *The Psychology and Pedagogy of Reading*. Cambridge: MIT P, 1908.

Jacobs, Leland B. *Using Literature with Young Children*. New York: Teachers Coll. P, 1965.

Jensen, Julie M., ed. *Stories to Grow On: Demonstrations of Language Learning in K–8 Classrooms*. Portsmouth: Heinemann, 1989.

Johannessen, Larry R., E. A. Kahn, and C. C. Walter. *Designing and Sequencing Prewriting Activities*. Urbana: ERIC/NCTE, 1982.

Kidder, Tracy. *Among Schoolchildren*. Boston: Houghton, 1989.

Lakoff, George, and Mark Johnson. *Metaphors We Live By*. U of Chicago P, 1980.

Langer, Judith, and Arthur Applebee. *How Writing Shapes Thinking: A Study of Teaching and Learning.* Urbana: NCTE, 1987.

Langer, Susanne. *Philosophy in a New Key.* 3rd ed. Cambridge: Harvard UP, 1957.

Lee, Doris, and R. V. Allen. *Learning to Read through Experience.* 2nd ed. New York: Appleton, 1963.

Lewis, C. S. *Studies in Words.* 2nd ed. Cambridge UP, 1967.

Light, Richard J. *Harvard Assessment Seminar: Explorations with Student and Faculty about Teaching and Learning and Student Life.* Cambridge: Harvard Graduate School of Education, 1990.

Lloyd-Jones, Richard, and Andrea A. Lunsford, eds. *The English Coalition Conference: Democracy through Language.* Urbana: NCTE, 1989.

Lunsford, Andrea, Helene Moglen, and James Slevin. *The Future of Doctoral Studies in English.* New York: MLA, 1989.

Marshall, Edward. *Three by the Sea.* New York: Dial, 1981.

Maurer, Charles. "Study: US Pupils Learn Less than Asians in Grade School." *Boston Globe* 18 Sept. 1989: B1.

McCormick, Kathleen, Gary F. Waller, and Linda Flower. *Reading Texts.* Lexington: Heath, 1987.

Miller, Jean Baker. *Toward a New Psychology of Women.* Boston: Beacon, 1976.

Milz, Vera E. "A 'Whole Language Approach' Writing Program." *Perspectives on Writing in Grades 1–8.* Ed. Shirley Haley-James. Urbana: NCTE, 1981.

Moran, Charles. "Teaching Writing/Teaching Literature." *College Composition and Communication* 32 (1981): 21–30. Rev. and rpt. as "Reading like a Writer." *Vital Signs.* Ed. James L. Collins. Portsmouth: Boynton, 1989. 60–69.

Muller, Herbert. *The Uses of English: Guidelines for the Teaching of English from the Anglo-American Conference at Dartmouth College.* New York: Holt, 1967.

"National Snapshot: Racial and Ethnic Enrollments and Degrees." *Chronicle of Higher Education* 1 Sept. 1988: 81.

Nelson, Cary. "Against English: Theory and the Limits of the Discipline." *ADE Bulletin* 85 (Winter 1986): 1–6.

North, Stephen. *The Making of Knowledge in Composition: Portrait of an Emerging Field.* Upper Montclair: Boynton, 1987.

Peck, Jeffrey M. "Advanced Literary Study as Cultural Study: A Redefinition of the Discipline." *Profession 85* (1985): 49–54.

Polanyi, Michael. *Personal Knowledge: Toward a Post-critical Philosophy.* New York: Harper, 1958.

"Popular Education." Rev. of *Practical Observations upon the Educating of the People,* by Henry Brougham. *North American Review* 23.52 (ns 14.27) (July 1826): 52–56.

Quine, W. V. O., and J. S. Ullian. *The Web of Belief.* New York: Random, 1970.

Riesman, David. *On Higher Education: The Academic Enterprise in an Era of Rising Student Consumerism.* San Francisco: Jossey-Bass, 1981.

Rodriguez, Richard. *Hunger of Memory.* Boston: Godine, 1981.

Rosenthal, Robert, and Lenore Jacobson. *Pygmalion in the Classroom: Teacher Expectation and Pupils' Intellectual Development.* New York: Holt, 1968.

Sarmiento, Tony. "The Climate for Broadening Workplace Literacy Efforts." North American Regional Forum, Education for All. Boston, 6–7 Nov. 1989.

Scholes, Robert. *Textual Power: Literary Theory and the Teaching of English.* New Haven: Yale UP, 1985.

Scott, Fred Newton. "The Report on College Entrance Requirements in English." *Educational Review* 20 (1900): 289–94.

Shanker, Albert. "Students Flunk Again: NAEP on Reading and Writing." *New York Times* 14 Jan 1990: E7.

Sizer, Theodore. *Horace's Compromise: The Dilemma of the American High School.* Boston: Houghton, 1984.

Slevin, James. "Depoliticizing and Politicizing Rhetoric and Composition." *The Politics of Writing Instruction.* Ed. Richard Bullock. Portsmouth: Heinemann, forthcoming.

Smith, Frank. *Reading without Nonsense.* New York: Teachers Coll. P, 1979.

Stewart, Donald C. "What Is an English Major, and What Should It Be?" *College Composition and Communication* 40 (1989): 188–202.

Teachers Networking: The Whole Language Newletter. Apr. 1987.

United Steelworkers of America. *Summary: Proposed Agreement between United Steelworkers of America and Bethlehem Steel Corporation.* Pittsburgh: USWA, 1989.

"U.S. Is Said to Lag in School Spending." *New York Times* 16 Jan. 1990: A23.

Veatch, Jeannette. *How to Teach Reading with Children's Books.* 2nd ed. New York: Owen, 1968.

Watson, Dorothy. "1987 Report on Trends and Issues: NCTE Commission on Reading." *Council-Grams.* Urbana: NCTE, 1987. 1–11.